MIGRANT LABOR IN THE PERSIAN GULF

MEHRAN KAMRAVA AND ZAHRA BABAR

Editors

Migrant Labor
in the Persian Gulf

CIRS
CENTER FOR
INTERNATIONAL
AND REGIONAL
STUDIES

GEORGETOWN UNIVERSITY
SCHOOL OF FOREIGN SERVICE IN QATAR

Published in Collaboration with
Georgetown University's
Center for International and Regional Studies,
School of Foreign Service in Qatar

HURST & COMPANY, LONDON

Published in Collaboration with
Georgetown University's
Center for International and Regional Studies,
School of Foreign Service in Qatar

First published in the United Kingdom in 2012 by
C. Hurst & Co. (Publishers) Ltd.,
41 Great Russell Street, London, WC1B 3PL
© Mehran Kamrava, Zahra Babar and the Contributors, 2012
All rights reserved.
Printed in the United Kingdom

The right of Mehran Kamrava, Zahra Babar and the Contributors
to be identified as the authors of this publication is asserted by them
in accordance with the Copyright, Designs and Patents Act, 1988.

A Cataloguing-in-Publication data record for this book
is available from the British Library.

ISBN: 978-1-84904-210-9 *paperback*

This book is printed using paper from registered sustainable
and managed sources.

www.hurstpub.co.uk

Contents

Acknowledgments

The chapters in this volume grew out of three Working Group meetings under the auspices of the Center for International and Regional Studies of Georgetown University's School of Foreign Service in Qatar. Grateful acknowledgment goes to all the participants at the Working Groups for their individual and collective intellectual contributions to the project that eventually resulted in this book. We are especially grateful to Mahmood Monshipouri, Kasim Randeree, and Helene Theollet for helping shape our discussions along the way. Invaluable assistance also came from the capable staff of the Center for International and Regional Studies, namely John Crist, Suzi Mirgani, Kasia Rada, Naila Sherman, Nadia Talpur, and Maha Uraidi. We gratefully acknowledge their multiple and varied contributions to the Working Groups and to this volume.

About the Contributors

Attiya Ahmad is Assistant Professor of Religion and Feminism, Gender and Sexuality Studies at Wesleyan University. In 2009–10, she was a Post-doctoral Fellow at the Center for International and Regional Studies at Georgetown University in Qatar. Her work focuses on the interrelation between Islamic piety and reform movements and transnational migration in the Gulf. She is currently revising her book manuscript focusing on Islamic *da'wa*, domestic work, and migrant women in Kuwait.

Zahra Babar is Project Manager at the Center for International and Regional Studies (CIRS), Georgetown University School of Foreign Service in Qatar. Babar has held positions with United Nations Development Program as well as the International Labor Organization. Her prime areas of research interest have been gender and development, micro-finance, employment promotion, and women in the economy.

Mary Breeding is a Consultant in the Independent Evaluation Group at the World Bank. Her work and research interests include evaluation, governance/ politics of developing countries, South Asia, and international migration. Prior to starting at the World Bank, Breeding was a Post-doctoral Research Associate in the Institute for the Study of International Migration at Georgetown University and a Warren E. Miller Fellow at the American Political Science Association.

Jane Bristol-Rhys is Associate Professor of Anthropology at Zayed University, where she has taught Social Anthropology, Emirati History and Heritage, and Studies in Transnational Migration since 2001. Her publications include articles on Emirati historical narratives, identity issues in the UAE, and Abu Dhabi's heritage initiatives. She is the author of *Emirati Women: Generations of Change*, and the forthcoming *Future Perfect: Societies in the Emirates*, an examination of migrants and their hosts in Abu Dhabi.

Andrew M. Gardner is Assistant Professor of Anthropology at the University of Puget Sound in Tacoma, Washington. Between 2008 and 2010 he also taught at Qatar University. His publications include *City of Strangers: Gulf Migration and the Indian Community in Bahrain* as well as articles in *City and Society* (2008), *The Journal of Arabian Studies*, and *Human Organization*.

Dirgha J. Ghimire is a Social Demographer, Associate Research Scientist; Associate Director at the Population Studies Center (PSC) at the University of Michigan and Director of the Institute for Social and Environmental Research Nepal. Ghimire studies social change, family and demography, migration, population health and population and environment dynamics.

Mehran Kamrava is Professor and Director of the Center for International and Regional Studies at Georgetown University's School of Foreign Service in Qatar. His most recent publications include *Iran's Intellectual Revolution*, *The Modern Middle East: A Political History since the First World War* and the edited volumes *International Politics of the Persian Gulf* and *Innovation in Islam: Traditions and Contributions*.

Pardis Mahdavi is "Associate Professor of Anthropology at Pomona College. Her research interests include sexuality, human rights, youth culture, transnational feminism and public health in the context of changing global and political structures. In addition to a number of journal articles, her publications include *Passionate Uprisings: Iran's Sexual Revolution* and *Gridlock: Labor, Migration, and Human Trafficking in Dubai*.

Susan F. Martin holds the Donald G. Herzberg Chair in International Migration and serves as the Director of the Institute for the Study of International Migration in the School of Foreign Service at Georgetown University. Her recent publications include *A Nation of Immigrants*; *Women, Migration and Conflict: Breaking a Deadly Cycle; Managing Migration: The Promise of Cooperation*; and the edited volume *Mexico-U.S. Migration Management: A Binational Approach*.

David Mednicoff is Assistant Professor of Public Policy and Associate Director of the Social Thought and Political Economy Program at the University of

Massachusetts-Amherst. His areas of expertise include Middle Eastern law and politics, international law, human rights, globalization and comparative public policy. His publications and ongoing research deal broadly with interdisciplinary connections between legal and political ideas and institutions at the national and transnational levels, particularly as these relate to current policy issues in the Middle East. He is currently completing two book manuscripts, the first on the endurance of ruling monarchies in contemporary politics, and the second on the politics of the rule of law, democratization and US foreign policy in five Arab societies.

Mansoor Moaddel is Professor of Sociology at Eastern Michigan University and Research Affiliate at Population Studies Center, Institute for Social Research, the University of Michigan. Moaddel studies religion, culture, ideology, political conflict, revolution and social change. His work currently focuses on the causes and consequences of values and attitudes of the Middle Eastern and Islamic publics. Moaddel is the author of a number of books, including *Islamic Modernism, Nationalism, and Fundamentalism: Episode and Discourse* and *Class, Politics, and Ideology in the Iranian Revolution*, as well as edited volumes such as *Values and Perceptions of the Islamic and Middle Eastern Publics*.

Caroline Osella is Reader in Anthropology at the School of Oriental African Studies in London, has worked since 1989 in Kerala, south India and with Malayali migrants in the Persian Gulf states. Her broadest research interest is the way projects of identity crafting are brought back to the body, while socially constructed bodies are differentiated to reflect class, ethnic and gender differences and to forge social hierarchies. Her recent work has explored Kerala as an Indian Ocean region, questioning the nation bias, and has been interested in the ways in which Kerala and Gulf are entangled. In current research, she is following interests in Self/Other encounters and (especially non-verbal) modes of self-making, inter-relating and experiencing the immediate environment.

Filippo Osella is Reader in Social Anthropology at the University of Sussex. For the last twenty years he has conducted research in Kerala in south India, and lately in a number of West Asian Gulf countries. His current research focuses on the emergence of Islamic reformist movements and the rise of a new Muslim middle class in Kerala in the context of intensified economic, cultural, and religious links between south India and the Gulf region.

ABOUT THE CONTRIBUTORS

Arland Thornton is Professor of Sociology at the University of Michigan-Ann Arbor, where he is also Research Associate, Center for Middle Eastern and North African Studies and Research Professor at the Population Studies Center and Survey Research Center. For much of his career Thornton has focused on the study of family and demographic issues, with a particular emphasis on marriage, divorce, childbearing, and gender roles. He is the author of *Reading History Sideways: the Fallacy and Enduring Impact of the Developmental Paradigm on Family Life* (University of Chicago Press, 2005).

Nathalie E. Williams is a Post-doctoral Scholar at the Carolina Population Center of the University of North Carolina at Chapel Hill. She is a social demographer who specializes in migration and studies of armed conflict. Her research focuses on South and Southeast Asia, with particular emphasis on Nepal where she has studied the relationship of migration to education, gender, employment, political instability, and violence. Williams has published articles in *Social Science Research, International Migration, Research on Aging*, and *AIDS Care*. Before joining academia, she worked for the United Nations Population Fund in Cambodia.

Linda C. Young-DeMarco is a Lead Social/Behavioral Research Area Specialist in the Family and Demography Program at the Institute for Social Research, University of Michigan-Ann Arbor. She has co-authored numerous substantive papers, book chapters, and appendices concerning attitudes, values and beliefs. Young-DeMarco currently serves as project director for several federally funded projects including "The Impact of Ideational Influences on Marriage and Fertility Behaviors in Nepal" (Arland Thornton, Principal Investigator) and "Cross-National Analysis of Values and Values Change in the Middle East" (Mansoor Moaddel, Principal Investigator).

1

Situating Labor Migration in the Persian Gulf

Mehran Kamrava and Zahra Babar

For a number of decades, scholars from a whole variety of disciplines tended to ignore the domestic politics of the small sheikhdoms that line the southern coast of the Persian Gulf, assuming that the relatively small states that dotted the Arabian Peninsula were too insignificant in themselves or too inconsequential to regional and global politics to merit in-depth study and examination. Insofar as the Middle East was concerned, the region's centers of gravity, in terms of both policy attention and academic study, were such larger and historically older countries such as Egypt and those in the rest of North Africa, the Levant, Iran and Iraq, and to a lesser extent Saudi Arabia. What study of the Persian Gulf did take place often saw the region through the lenses of its two giants, Iran and Saudi Arabia.

The last couple of decades are beginning to see major shifts in both the political and economic powers of the Persian Gulf's once neglected smaller states, and, not surprisingly, the scholarly attention being paid to them. These policy and scholarly shifts are fueled by these states' efforts at positioning themselves as major global entrepots, as regional hubs of education and innovation, and as advanced economies and globalizing pioneers. Sustained by immense wealth derived from hydrocarbon resources, in one form or another each of the sheikhdoms has engaged in economic and infrastructural development at breakneck speed, thus profoundly changing the geographic and physical landscape of the Persian Gulf and the Arabian Peninsula forever.

But also forever changed in the process is the region's human landscape. Historically, the Persian Gulf region has always been at the crossroads of civilizations, a place whose inhospitable interior belied a rich mosaic of peoples and interests along the coastline in search of pearls, trading opportunities, and later, in the twentieth century, oil. Migration to the Persian Gulf is not a new or recent phenomenon. What is new, in fact unprecedented, is its scale and magnitude. As the twentieth century began to draw to a close, and as the pace and magnitude of infrastructural development in the region increasingly picked up speed and intensity, the demographic balance between the nationals and the laborers they imported began to shift. Today, in such ostensibly global cities as Doha, Abu Dhabi, and Dubai the national populations are dwarfed by the populations of imported foreigners tasked with engineering and implementing the manifold development projects that literally build cities into the sea and in the sky.

Despite the ubiquity of migrant labor across the Persian Gulf, there are few comprehensive studies to date that examine the phenomenon of labor migration in the region. Credit needs to go to anthropologists for being among the first group of scholars to pay detailed attention to the subject, and, to this day, as the contributions to this volume attest, most studies of the topic continue to be conducted by anthropologists. Our goal here is to present a comprehensive analysis of the migration cycle from inception to completion through the multi-disciplinary prisms of anthropology, sociology, and political science. The central questions guiding this project, by their very nature, span across all three disciplines and do not lend themselves to disciplinary silos and boundaries. What is labor migration and who is a migrant worker? Why and how does labor migration perpetuate itself? What is the range of experiences - spatial, economic, cultural, legal and political - that migrant laborers go through in their host countries? And, how have host governments and international legal regimes responded to the ever-growing numbers of migrant workers all across the Gulf Cooperation Council (GCC)? Answers to these and other similar questions form the central premise of the chapters that follow.

In this introductory chapter, we begin by tracing some of the more prevalent theoretical perspectives on labor migration over the last few decades. We then situate these studies in relation to Persian Gulf states and examine the broader context of labor migration to the region. We end by highlighting how the arguments of each of the chapters in this volume contribute to the larger theoretical debates or empirical knowledge about the topic of labor migration in general and in relation to the Persian Gulf in particular.

Studying labor migration

A broad scan of the literature on migration reveals a rich diversity of theoretical perspectives on the topic.[1] For a number of decades, migration has been a topic of interest across disparate academic disciplines and conceptual frameworks, leading to the splintering of migration studies into various pockets of scholarship.[2] By its very nature, migration is of interest to sociologists, anthropologists, geographers, demographers, political scientists, and economists. Disciplinary partitions and diverging methodological approaches, especially between socio-anthropological and economic studies of migration, have at times proven to be quite resilient.[3]

For some time now, much of labor migration theory has been embedded in the primacy of economic rationality. Migration is rooted in the inequities and economic imbalances of our world, and the underlying assumption is that given the opportunity, those from underprivileged areas will move to where the money is. Both classical and neoclassical theories of migration posit that rural-urban and cross-border movements of people are based simply on the supply and demand of labor. Within the neoclassical school, over the years a variety of scholars have developed and refined concepts and tools for understanding various dimensions of labor migration.[4] Wage differentials are said to act as the equilibrating mechanism in the neoclassical macro-model, deter-

---

[1] For further detail, see Massey *et al.*, "Theories of International Migration: A Review and Appraisal," *Population and Development Review*, 19, 3 (September 1993), pp. 431–66.

[2] Ibid.

[3] Hein De Haas, "Migration and Development: A Theoretical Perspective." Working Paper, IMI (University of Oxford, 2008), p. 46.

[4] See Larry A. Sjaastad, "The Costs and Returns of Human Migration," *The Journal of Political Economy*, 70, 5 (1962), pp. 82–3; Everett S. Lee, "A Theory of Migration," *Demography*, 3, 1 (1966), pp. 47–57; and Michael P. Todaro, "A Model of Labor Migration and Urban Unemployment in Less Developed Countries," *The American Economic Review*, 59, 1 (1969), pp. 138–48.

mining the flow of labor within both domestic and global labor markets.[5] People will migrate from lower-wage, labor-surplus regions to capital-rich, labor-scarce regions. Human beings function primarily as *homo economicus*, are conscious of their economic lives as individuals, judge their value in the transnational free market, and choose to migrate on the basis of a cost-benefit calculation, to seek financial betterment and assist their own and their families' economic development.[6] An individual's decision to migrate is based on a calculated assessment of the opportunities and limitations at home versus potential opportunities elsewhere, combined with an assessment of the possible costs that migration would entail. Neoclassical economics presumes that people in a particular geographical area and labor market are aware of employment opportunities and wage levels available at other—and possibly distant— labor markets.[7] The process, then, is seen as mutually beneficial to both the states and the societies that send and receive migrants. Sending countries benefit from lowered levels of unemployment, and from potential earnings and the skills acquired when migrants return home. Receiving countries benefit as their labor scarcity is addressed and as their capital is put to use to further economic growth and productivity.[8]

For their part, historical-structural approaches point to the overall structure of the global system, and its inherent inequities, as the primary force behind domestic and international migration.[9] It is not human agency but rather entrenched structural inequalities in the global economy that propel streams of people to search for opportunities outside their home countries. Demanding competitive sources of labor, industrialized economies consistently lure lower-wage workers from the less developed countries on the periphery of the capitalist system.[10] The imbalanced and inequitable structures that abound both domestically and internationally contribute directly to the perpetual flow of labor migrants, robbing the developing world of both skilled and unskilled labor. Migration, most historical-structuralists argue, only perpetuates divergent development paths and disparities in income between poor and rich countries.

---

[5] Sjaastad, "The Costs and Returns of Human Migration," pp. 82–3.
[6] Lee, "A Theory of Migration," p. 51.
[7] Sjaastad, "The Costs and Returns of Human Migration," p. 84.
[8] De Haas, "Migration and Development," p. 14.
[9] See Stephen Castles and Godulla Kosack, "The Function of Labour Immigration in Western European Capitalism," *New Left Review*, 73, (May-June 1972), pp. 3–21.
[10] Ibid., pp. 5–6.

While neoclassical and historical-structuralist theories may differ in how they interpret various dimensions of the global political economy, in essence they still continue to view migration and migrants through the same lens, an economic one. By reducing complex processes of migration down to their economic logic, these theoretical frameworks at times overlook the equally important social, political, or cultural determinants of labor migration. While socio-economic conditions, and in certain circumstances population pressures, often act as catalysts for migration, there are many additional factors that contribute to migrants' decision making. People may migrate from one destination to another because they assume that they will enjoy a better quality of life, greater political and social freedoms, better opportunities for education and skill development, enhanced safety and security, improved social services and health care, and more access to recreational activities. Migration may also be based on ambiguous personal ambitions and motivations. Moreover, the capacity to migrate will also depend on particular individual skills, abilities, and capacities.

In the late 1980s, theories on the "new economics of labor migration" introduced fresh dimensions to the discussion by drawing attention to the role of households and families in migrants' decision making.[11] These theories move beyond the narrow neo-classical interpretation of the individual as an autonomous economic actor. They look instead at mediations between agency and structure and focus on human agency as it interacts within the larger social context.[12] Rural-urban and international migration is based on an individual household's assessment of risks and the desire to diversify sources of income. For the sake of improving the financial health of the whole unit, a *family* makes the decision to send its ablest and most skilled to work in an urban or international location.[13] Thus new economics of labor migration introduces the concept that a potential migrant does not make an autonomous decision to leave home based on his or her individual income-generating capacity. Instead, the decision to migrate is the outcome of a joint decision made by the entire family.[14]

---

[11] De Haas, "Migration and Development," p. 35.

[12] Alexandre Abreu, "The New Economics of Labor Migration: Beware of Neoclassicals Bearing Gifts," *Forum for Social Economics* (2010), http://dx.doi.org/10.1007/s12143–010–9077–2, p. 8.

[13] De Haas, "Migration and Development," pp. 35–6.

[14] Abreu, "The New Economics of Labor Migration," p. 9.

New economics of labor migration also provides a more robust explanation for the phenomenon of remittances. Most neoclassical interpretations have difficulty explaining remittances, as a migrant's behavior is assumed to be motivated by economic self-interest for the individual's own financial betterment.[15] The new economics of labor migration framework attempts to integrate elements of earlier "livelihood" concepts developed by anthropologists and sociologists. Livelihoods approaches posit that labor migration is a phenomenon that moves beyond the limitation of economic perspectives and meaning, and is embedded within the broader socio-cultural context. These approaches frequently emphasize the need to conceptually ground people and their economic decision making within their social settings, their communities, and, most important, their families.[16]

While scholars such as De Haas promote the value of the new economics of labor migration as a useful analytical tool in the study of labor migration, the approach has not been without its critics. Some researchers suggest that the approach is merely a reconstruction and reworking of neo-classical theories of migration.[17] Alexandre Abreu has asserted that while NELM (the New Economics of Labor Migration) takes into account the previously ignored role of the household in the decision-making process as well as the asymmetry of information in the market, he suggests that the overarching theoretical counterpoint remains within the boundaries of neo-classical rational choice theories.[18] The only difference that NELM offers is that the "agent" may be a household unit rather than the sole individual, whose choices and motivations are merely shaped by the "information field." Abreu contends that NELM's inherent theoretical weakness is its total disregard for the dynamics of social relations both within the home and globally, and thus NELM fails to shed light on current patterns and processes that can influence migration systems on a structural level. By neglecting the critical analysis of transformative social processes such as international proletarianization and capital accumulation, Abreu concludes that NELM theory fails to reconcile agency and structure in any innovative way.[19]

---

[15] Ibid.

[16] Jeevan Sharma, "Labor Migration, Pathology and Livelihoods: The Case of Migration from Nepal to India" (Rotterdam: Erasmus University Institute of Social Studies, 2007), p. 6.

[17] Abreu, "The New Economics of Labor Migration," pp. 1–17.

[18] Ibid., p. 11.

[19] Ibid.

Subsequent migration systems theory and network theory have focused on other forces that cause, shape and perpetuate patterns of migration.[20] They provide a framework for analyzing the ways in which migration flows tend to be geographically clustered, and how their development over time cannot be explained merely by factors related to employment, unemployment, individual cost-benefit decision making, or particular structural or environmental factors. A central hypothesis of migration systems theory is that migration changes the social, cultural, economic and institutional conditions in *both* the sending and the receiving countries. Migration systems theory places particular attention on how these processes of migration shape the originating and destination societies, and stresses the importance of social remittances alongside financial ones.[21] Network theory is built around an examination of the interpersonal relationships of migrants, and how they use their social capital to assist them through the various phases of the process. Migrant networks bring countries of origin and destination together through a series of connections and associations. These associations are often forged between migrants and non-migrants through various social and familial networks. Often the result is the emergence of high-density pockets of migrants originating from the same area over time, and once begun, a particular migration chain may gather a momentum of its own. Given the transformative nature of the phenomenon, only through attention to both the sending and the receiving communities can a thorough picture of migration process be acquired.

The Persian Gulf context

The discovery of petroleum wealth in the middle of the last century had a wholly transformative impact on the social, political and economic configuration of the Persian Gulf.[22] In a short few decades, the flush of oil earnings changed especially the region's smaller sheikhdoms into modern nation-states, boasting some of the most dynamic and globalized cities of the Arab world. Hindered by small local population size and low levels of labor force participation, the six states of the GCC had to seek alternative sources of labor. In

[20] De Haas, "Migration and Development," pp. 21–2.

[21] Ibid., p. 19.

[22] Andrzej Kapiszewski, "Arab Versus Asian Migrant Workers In The GCC Countries," Conference Paper, United Nations Expert Group Meeting On International Migration and Development in The Arab Region (2006), pp. 1–3.

order to meet the burgeoning labor demands of their ongoing development projects, the GCC imported armies of foreign workers, in the first place primarily from neighboring Arab states and Palestine, but, especially after the Iraqi invasion of Kuwait in 1990, increasingly from South and Southeast Asia.[23] Andrzej Kapiszewski credits what he calls the "Asianization" of migrant labor across the Persian Gulf to several additional considerations. Asian immigrants appear to pose less of an ideological threat to the host states, generally tolerate lower wages, tend to migrate without their families and are easier to segregate, are easier to lay off, and are considered to be more efficient and easier to manage as compared to Arab workers.[24]

Recent estimates indicate that there are about 15 million migrant workers present in the Arabian Peninsula. As indicated in table 1.1, across the region about 40 percent of the population is made up of non-nationals, and in most of the six GCC countries the majority population is foreign. According to the United Nations, all six of the GCC countries are listed amongst the top twenty nations in the world boasting the highest proportion of migrants to nationals.[25]

Table 1.1: National and Non-National Population in the GCC, 2008.

	Total Population	Expatriate Population	% Expats to Total Population
Bahrain	1,100,000	572,567*	52
Iran	73,300,000	1,300,000	2
Iraq	30,100,000	N/A	N/A
Kuwait	3,400,000	2,310,000	68
Oman	2,870,000	900,000	31
Qatar	1,600,000	1,376,000	86
Saudi Arabia	24,800,000	7,110,000*	29
UAE	5,600,000	4,730,000*	84

* figures based on data from the end of 2007
Source: The Economist Intelligence Unit, "Country Profiles" (2008 and 2009) and "Country Reports" (April and May 2010).

[23] Laurie Brand, *Citizens Abroad: Emigration and the State in the Middle East and North Africa* (Cambridge University Press, 2008), pp. 208–209.
[24] Andrzej Kapiszewski, "De-Arabization in the Gulf: Foreign Labor and the Struggle for Local Culture," *Georgetown Journal of International Affairs*, 8, 2 (2007), p. 83.
[25] Barry Mirkin, "Population Levels, Trends and Policies in the Arab Region: Chal-

With vast hydrocarbon resources at their disposal, these six states have seen extraordinary growth in per capita incomes in recent years. However, the improved standard of living for citizens has come at a price, as the rentier political economies of the region also boast very low levels of nationals performing in the regional labor market. Approximately 70 percent of the regional labor market is composed of non-nationals.[26] Highly skilled foreign workers dominate private sector technical jobs, while less skilled workers permeate positions lower down the employment ladder and across many sectors, including construction and domestic work. Nationals are employed primarily by the bloated public sector, which has become another mechanism through which GCC governments transfer a portion of rents to their people. To address the pitfalls of over reliance on imported skilled labor, each state has undertaken concerted efforts aimed at building up the educational and technical capacity of its nationals, including especially highly publicized campaigns to "nationalize" the regional labor force. Training and educational programs have been supplemented by policies to restrict visa entries for foreign workers, enforcement of compulsory quota systems for hiring in the public and private sectors, and a variety of efforts designed to make private sector employment more attractive to nationals. So far, the impact of these efforts have been negligible in actually reducing dependency on foreign workers, and for the foreseeable future the GCC states will continue to rely on an imported workforce.[27]

---

lenges and Opportunities," *Arab Human Development Report Research Paper Series*, UNDP (2010), pp. 16, 37.

[26] Ibid., p. 4.

[27] One of the areas in which the GCC states have indeed devised coherent policies regarding labor—if inconsistent and inconsistently applied—is in nationalization efforts. There have been a number of policy efforts across the GCC aimed at increasing employment levels of nationals in both the public and private sectors. These policies are often motivated by political pressures stemming from high levels of unemployment among nationals and the potential political risks that are likely to follow as a result. Ultimately, by themselves political pressures are unlikely to solve the problem of over-reliance on expatriate laborers, particularly highly skilled workers, so long as longer-term structural exigencies are not addressed. Some of these shortcomings include inadequate educational facilities and opportunities that are ill-equipped to prepare national citizens for the highly globalized economies of the region; insufficient efforts at encouraging local citizens to enter the more competitive private sector; and the prevalence of cultural and at times structural barriers to women's entry into and participation within the labor force.

Local authorities across the GCC states prefer to view foreign workers as being strictly temporary in nature, even if reality belies the truth of this. GCC countries do not consider themselves to be destinations of choice for permanent settlement or immigration. The presence of foreign workers in each state is tied to the provision of their labor within a particular sector for a defined duration of time. There is no policy in place that allows migrants to work toward a permanent citizenship status, nor are there any state-driven attempts to encourage social integration.[28]

Recent scholarship on transnationalism questions the validity of the earlier assumptions that integration and settlement are preferred and sought-after solutions. Given technological advances that have greatly impacted on the efficiency of inter-state communications, travel, and financial management, it is becoming more and more possible for migrants to live in a transnational world, where they are bound to their original communities through a series of social and financial transactions and relationships, yet also have meaningful lives within their host countries. As De Haas states:

This de facto transnationalisation of migrants' lives has also challenged assimilationist models of migrant integration, as well as the modernist political construct of the nation-state and citizenship. The implication is that clear-cut dichotomies of 'origin' or 'destination' and categories such as 'permanent', 'temporary', and 'return' migration are increasingly difficult to sustain in a world in which the lives of migrants are increasingly characterized by circulation and simultaneous commitment to two or more societies. This has fundamental implication for the study of migration and development, because this implies that integration in receiving societies and commitment to origin societies are not necessarily substitutes, but can be complements.[29]

Importing non-national workers to meet domestic labor needs brings with it benefits as well as costs. Non-nationals can be brought in quickly—and in most cases cheaply—to meet labor needs as and when required on a project-by-project basis. They can also be easily released and sent back to their countries of origin when no longer needed. There is, however, considerable discussion amongst both state actors and local citizens about the potential costs of hosting such large numbers of non-nationals for long periods of time.[30] These costs are not merely economic, but potentially social and cultural as well. Especially among the more conservative strata of Gulf societies, the massive influx of foreigners from all over the world is often seen as a threat

---

[28] Mirkin, "Population Levels, Trends and Policies in the Arab Region," p. 26.

[29] De Haas, "Migration and Development: A Theoretical Perspective," p. 38.

[30] Kapiszewski, "Arab versus Asian Migrant Workers in the GCC Countries," p. 11.

to national heritage and cultural values, and even a latent threat to political stability.[31] This unease over the existence of an outsized, culturally disparate workforce is not something unique to the Persian Gulf. Safeguarding the "national identity" against the influence of migrants continues to be a matter for public debate in many regions of the world, and even in states that are politically less sensitive to the preservation of cultural homogeneity.[32] In addition, the phenomenon of high unemployment amongst nationals, juxtaposed with the presence of large swathes of a foreign workforce, often causes grave concern to policymakers across the Arabian Peninsula.

Within the Persian Gulf, over the past decades governments have played a limited role in administering the migrant labor population. Managing labor needs has largely been left to private sector interests, with the "*kafala*," or worker-sponsorship system, being the dominant configuration for how the process has developed. This region-wide sponsorship system has been increasingly criticized for its limited ability to protect migrant workers' rights and its vast potential for abuse, and several states in the region have at least signaled that they are considering its reform.[33] Abolishing or reforming worker-sponsorship laws, along with other targeted regional policy initiatives, largely ignores the root causes and consequences of regional labor migration, and focuses instead on advancing strategic improvements for its effective management by the host countries. Labor migration is thus accepted as a practical necessity of the development demands of the region's political economies, a positive contributor to the development needs of the labor sending states, as well as a natural element of the global economic structure.

Policy attention within the GCC is too often focused on the costs of migration, financial and other, especially for those who migrate and those who host them. The systematic exploitation of potential migrants during the migration

---

[31] Ibid.

[32] Ibid., p. 12.

[33] "Bahrain commended for sponsorship reforms," *Gulf Daily News* (Bahrain, April 30, 2010); "Bahrain introduces job switch visa rules," *The National* (United Arab Emirates, August 1, 2009); "Bahrain scraps foreign labour sponsorship scheme," www.arabianbusiness.com (May 5, 2009); "Kuwait new labour law to abolish sponsorship system," *Gulf News* (United Arab Emirates, October 7, 2009); "Kuwait plans to abolish sponsorship system for foreign workers," *Xinhua News Agency* (September 10, 2009); "Other Gulf states may also scrap sponsorship system," *Gulf News* (United Arab Emirates, May 7, 2009); "Saudi Arabia may do away with sponsorship system," *PTI—The Press Trust of India Ltd* (February 12, 2008).

process itself, the abuse of workers' rights in their countries of destination, and the frequently inhumane working and living conditions that many experience have all turned into the pivot points for much of the discussion on migrant labor in the Persian Gulf. For large numbers of labor migrants to the Gulf, our understanding is that they experience lives fraught with restrictions and limitations, at times even broken promises and exploitation. At the very least, many do not enjoy the sort of liberties and social service benefits available to nationals of host countries.

But there is much more to the process and experience of migration. Through the thick ethnographic descriptions that the chapters in this volume contain, the authors demonstrate that migrants' lives and their experiences before, during, and after migration are much more nuanced and complex, multi-layered and conditioned by networks of local communities in both the sending and the receiving countries. The very notion of who is a migrant and why people migrate is itself open to debate (Ahmad). When they do migrate, migrants often find themselves socially and spatially segregated (Bristol-Rhys), and at times even in the gray world of informal economies (Mahdavi). But many still choose to return to their migrant lives after returning home (Gardner). Embedded connectivity with their home communities and the networks they establish while abroad continue to bind them with the communities they left behind (Osella and Osella), even if part of those of communities comprises corrupt recruiting agencies that skirt legal regulations aimed at curbing their efforts (Breeding). Undeniably, migration profoundly changes the migrants' lives, in terms of both the legal structures and predicaments within which they find themselves and the ways that recipient states react (Mednicoff and Martin), as well as the values they adopt, the ways they behave, and the goals to which they aspire (Williams *et al.*). All of these multiple aspects of the labor migration process are covered in the chapters to come.

This volume

In this volume we move beyond the development discourses that either problematize or promote labor migration, as well as the neo-classical, historical-structuralist, and neo-liberal perspectives that rely solely on economic analytical models for migration.[34] Shifting away from these over-arching and

---

[34] De Haas, "Migration and Development," p. 12.

deterministic discourses, our goal is to present a more comprehensive and nuanced picture of labor migration in the Persian Gulf. The following chapters demonstrate, for example, that the driving causes of labor migration can and often do go far beyond considerations based solely on economics. Gardner and Williams *et al.* posit that economic decision making may be tempered by the conditions that migrants face in their home countries when deciding to migrate to the Persian Gulf. Migration offers a mitigating response not only to the risks proposed by the imperfect labor markets in sending countries, but also to certain chronic conditions of political strife and armed conflict. As Gardner argues, structural violence in a labor-sending country can be the added impetus propelling streams of migrants to opt to return to the destination countries in the Gulf. Gardner's chapter is based empirically on his ethnographic research tracing the lives of a dozen South Asian workers over the course of a year in Qatar. Combining regular interviews with the migrants while in their host state with a series of targeted fieldtrips to their countries and communities of origin, Gardner's work adds to recent scholarship on migration that stresses the importance of the transnational dimensions of the process.

Without trying to negate the potentially abusive aspects of labor migration systems in the region, it is important to examine the nature of the process and lived experiences of migrants through a broader lens. A number of chapters in this volume offer socio-cultural assessments of the conditions for migrant labor in the Persian Gulf. Attiya Ahmad, Andrew Gardner and Jane Bristol-Rhys all address aspects of the daily life experiences of migrants in the region.

The original contributions in this volume all add more depth, perspective and empirical data to the existing scholarship on the topic. The chapters are all premised on the assumption that labor migration is a complex process with its own internal logic, and that it exists as a transformative process for individual migrants and their host societies, as well as their families, communities, and countries of origin. Not limited to a review of the economic causes and consequences of labor migration to the Persian Gulf, this volume examines the broader socio-cultural contexts of the phenomenon and the transnational nature of the process. To do so, the chapters sweep across a broad range of disciplinary and theoretical frameworks, providing, inasmuch as space limitations allow, as comprehensive a picture of labor migration in the Persian Gulf as possible.

Ahmad starts off the discussion by examining how the scholarship on migration to the region has developed over the last few decades, and draws on her own ethnographic fieldwork in Kuwait to highlight those elements of migrants' experiences that have been sidelined by most existing scholarly works. In the process, she questions the "hegemonic discourses" on labor migration that often "obfuscate" and "reduce their presence in the Gulf to their labor." Ahmad points out that the lives of migrants in the region are crafted as more than mere labor identities. They are, instead, full of nuanced experiences and exposures. She asserts that despite the lack of opportunities available to migrants to benefit from citizenship or even social integration, within the Persian Gulf labor migrants often have a strong sense of socio-political belonging and connectedness to their host societies. Ahmad situates her study within the broader historical and geographic interrelations that for centuries have bound South Asia and the Persian Gulf into a larger Indian Ocean community. According to Ahmad, these historical connections still inform relations between migrants and their hosts in the contemporary Persian Gulf.

Clearly, low-skill migrants have to cope with considerable difficulties during their stay in the host country. Even if the reports sent back home paint a rosy picture of life as a migrant laborer, the potential perils of labor migration are seldom unknown to both migrants and the families they leave behind. Andrew Gardner poses a deceptively simple question: why, despite knowledge of the risks and difficulties involved, does labor migration perpetuate itself? The answer, he posits, rests largely in the lucrative nature of the labor migration industry.

Gardner's ethnographic exploration of a small group of labor migrants in Qatar is premised on the notion that many low-skill migrants to the Persian Gulf have to cope with considerable difficulties during their stay in the host country. As Gardner points out, this premise arises from decades of ethnographic research that highlights the range of abusive and exploitative practices faced by migrants. Gardner's chapter provides an opportunity for some understanding of the reasons why migrant workers keep returning despite the widely known reality that life may be harsh and unpleasant in their host countries and may not even offer them economic advantages of higher income levels. Gardner posits that in addition to economic imperatives, it is existing "structural violence" in the sending countries—the push factors of social unrest and conflict—that drives waves of migrants to the region. Gardner demonstrates that economic rationale alone does not account for migration and other social factors are equally important to migrants' decision making.

One of the realities of life that migrant workers in the Persian Gulf have to contend with is isolation within the host countries in which they find themselves—spatial, cultural, social and otherwise. Jane Bristol-Rhys examines Abu Dhabi's hierarchical social structure and the ways in which migrant workers are socially marginalized and spatially segregated from the rest of society. The different mechanisms of spatial segregation ensure that there is little room for interaction amongst different national, ethnic and social groups. According to Bristol-Rhys, foreign workers on the lowest rung of the migration ladder suffer the greatest forms of social and spatial exclusion. Many reside in labor camps in remote locations, and by and large they remain invisible to most residents in these golden cities.[35] In Abu Dhabi, the focus of Bristol-Rhys's chapter, there are few spaces that are commonly shared by locals and expatriates or migrants to Abu Dhabi, and migrants respond to these realms of exclusion in mediated ways, developing their own sense of belonging as members of an excluded social group.

The development of a unique sense of belonging once again highlights the need for nuanced and contextualized analysis. As Ahmad points out in her chapter, migrants in the Persian Gulf lead complex existences that move well beyond their simple identification as "migrant workers," and yet the term persists in ways that limit and curtail a holistic understanding of a self-identified migration experience. Pardis Mahdavi makes a similar argument in relation to human trafficking in the Persian Gulf. She points to the need to re-examine prevailing conceptions of human trafficking and to broaden them beyond the existing gendered concepts revolving around transnational sex work. Both Ahmad and Mahdavi highlight the elemental problem of designating migrants into simplified and static categories of "labor migrant," "refugees," and "trafficked persons." Such categories are state-derived and created largely for legalistic and practical reasons, obscuring the complex nature of migrants' lives both in the Persian Gulf and elsewhere.

Mahdavi's chapter focuses specifically on the presence of illegal workers in Dubai, and the thriving informal economy that they inhabit. She asserts that the presence of this active informal sector is partially due to systemic failures to provide adequate safety and security to migrant workers in general, and female migrants in particular. Mahdavi's ethnographic fieldwork in Dubai's illicit economy demonstrates how the structures of the locally existing worker-sponsorship system, in conjunction with international legal mechanisms for

---

[35] Jim Ward, *City of Gold: Dubai and the Dream of Capitalism*, (New York: St. Martin's, 2009); Syed Ali. *Dubai: Gilded Cage* (New Haven, CT: Yale University Press, 2010).

managing human trafficking, actually come together to drive migrants into the informal economy. The migratory system that conveys misinformation to migrants, and often traps them in cycles of abuse and fraud, may indeed propel them into the status of illegal migrants, as many arrive in the region only to find that their expectations for employment and living standards are not met. The worker sponsorship program that makes legal migration to the Gulf so difficult leads would-be migrants to seek alternative, insecure, and illegal means of obtaining work in the region. Those who enter the country legally may end up entering the illicit economy after facing harsh work and living conditions. Potential abuse by employers over their sponsored employees may well cause legal migrants to flee their sponsors for entry into the illegal job market. Mahdavi draws attention to the gray areas that exist between the informal and formal economy that are traversed by many migrants, and how both the licit and illicit economies are rife with exploitative situations for migrants.

Insofar as public policy is concerned, current migration levels to the Persian Gulf present states and international institutions with yet another challenging outcome of globalization. Clearly, existing patterns of migration to the region have created tensions within Gulf societies and have also placed pressures on the relationships between the receiving states (GCC) and those sending migrants. National, regional, and international systems of governance have struggled to create an acceptable policy regime that responds to the needs of individual migrants while also addressing the interests of the states from which and to which they migrate. Our volume would be incomplete without some assessment of existing policy developments concerning migration of labor to the region. The chapters by Breeding, Mednicoff, and Martin examine the existing regulatory environment, and review the impact of some of the relevant policy regimes.

Mahdavi's arguments about inadequate or misleading information about working conditions are further reinforced by data presented by Mary Breeding in her chapter on the role of recruiting agencies in both India and the GCC. Breeding demonstrates that systems of misinformation, lack of regulatory compliance, and weakness in state regulatory capacity all lead to systemic failings to create healthy, functional, and safe migration opportunities for Indian workers in labor markets across the Persian Gulf. Breeding argues that unregulated processes of recruitment allow for greater potential abuse and exploitation of migrant workers; that information asymmetries in the recruitment process lead to migrants having insufficient knowledge of their destinations or potential jobs; and that increasingly, as dissatisfied workers return to India from the Gulf with their harrowing stories of poor living and working conditions, recruiters for the Gulf labor market are forced to go "fishing" for new labor sources in more and more remote parts of the country to attract workers.

Breeding's attention to the role of recruitment agencies points to a much larger patchwork of formal and informal networks that connect migrant workers in the communities they forge in host countries with those they left behind back home. These connectivities are the focus of the chapter by Filippo Osella and Caroline Osella. Drawing on the stories of their interlocutors from the Indian state of Kerala, historically a region that has sent large streams of people to work in the Gulf, Osella and Osella assert that it is social as well as financial and human capital that facilitates successful migrations. Similar to Breeding, through scrutinizing social networking practices in Kerala the Osellas help us to better understand how Indian migrants use their social capital to avail of opportunities for migration to the Persian Gulf, and the challenges and obstacles that exist within the system.

Whereas Breeding and Gardner point out the negative impact of those who oil the wheels of the migration chains from South Asia, Osella and Osella maintain that at least as far as Kerala is concerned, the role of brokers and middlemen cannot easily and sharply be defined as negative and illicit. They point out that these middlemen may indeed engage as social hustlers and exploiters for profit, but they may also genuinely be assisting migrants in obtaining necessary documentation and even a job in the Gulf. Osella and Osella maintain that even those seen as engaging in illegal and illicit profiteering may actually be simultaneously playing a beneficial and crucial role. Understanding the degree of ambivalence and removing normative judgments may be essential when proclaiming certain policy solutions.

Much of the existing migration literature on the Persian Gulf has been either on the causes and processes of migration or else on the importance and impact of migrants' remittances. Adding texture and depth to this scholarship has been the small body of work undertaken principally by anthropologists. What has remained largely absent from the scholarship is substantial datasets necessary to develop quantitative analytical frameworks for examining migrants' lives in the GCC. Nathalie Williams and her co-researchers address this absence by collecting data from Nepalese migrants working in and residing in the Gulf. Based on extensive interviews conducted with a representative sample group of Nepalese workers in the six countries of the GCC, their chapter provides us with rare insight into Gulf migrants' characteristics, behaviors, and experiences. Contrary to popular perceptions, we learn from Williams *et al.* that most (Nepalese) migrants actually earn enough money both to save and to send home a portion of their wages. Many, in fact, plan not to return home upon the completion of their contracts but instead to migrate to another GCC country in search of additional employment opportunities.

In some ways, the very predicament of migrant workers across the GCC states highlights the profound tensions and contradictions that mark Persian Gulf societies at multiple levels—architecturally and in terms of infrastructure; culturally in terms of values, customs and preferences; linguistically with Arabic and English competing for pervasiveness; politically in managing change while maintaining political systems steeped in static notions of rule and governance; etc. Insofar as migrant workers are concerned, perhaps nowhere are these contradictions more apparent than in the states' attempts at devising legal frameworks for dealing with them. David Mednicoff examines such attempts in Qatar and the UAE in his chapter. Mednicoff argues that instead of devising comprehensive legal infrastructures in relation to migrant workers, these states—and the cities of Doha and Dubai in particular—prefer to resort to *ad hoc* accommodation and informal regulations that are inherently flexible and fall outside of international regulatory regimes. This preference, he maintains, stems directly from two considerations. First, it is a product of the tensions between what he calls the two different "development narratives" that inform the separate lives of foreign residents and the national population. The narrative of globalization, and the attendant need to develop rapidly and thus to import labor, come into conflict with the need to provide employment opportunities for nationals and to encourage their upward economic mobility. Second, given that there is a multiplicity of national and transnational actors involved in any potential attempts at regulating the throngs of foreign residents, informality and *ad hoc* accommodation are the preferred alternatives to shedding the spotlight on a less savory aspect of development.

Whereas Mednicoff looks at efforts to craft regulatory frameworks for labor migration within the GCC states, Susan Martin examines the efficacy and success of transnational efforts at doing so in general and protecting migrant workers' rights in particular. More specifically, Martin examines some of the multilateral regional and international frameworks of cooperation on migration, and how these have devolved down to the administrative and legislative level in the Gulf countries. Important to the regional context is the Abu Dhabi Dialogue, a process that began in 2008 and brings together eleven countries of origin and destination in order to build collaborative partnerships to address some of the outstanding issues regarding labor migration to the GCC. The Abu Dhabi Dialogue requires its signatories to cooperate in determining and resolving problems that exist at different stages of the migration process, from pre-deployment in the country of origin, through the period of contractual employment in a destination country (in the GCC), to the return/repatriation phase. One of the main contributions of the Abu Dhabi Dialogue is that it has brought the question of migrants' rights to the forefront of discussions around regional labor migration. Martin's chapter also discusses the role that the GCC countries have played in another international mechanism for migrant labor governance, which is the Global Forum on Migration and Development. Martin examines the agendas that have been set by both these multilateral processes, and discusses the tangible ways in which these platforms are assisting GCC states and sending countries in developing effective strategies for managing regional migration.

Together, the chapters in this volume represent the first comprehensive, multi-disciplinary study of migrant labor in the Persian Gulf. Our goal here has been to provide a thorough picture of a phenomenon that is all too often little understood and is seldom comprehensively studied despite its pervasiveness and significance. There is, of course, still much room for further research. Three particular aspects of labor migration in the Persian Gulf merit further study. They include analyses of skilled and semi-skilled migrant laborers as well as second-generation migrants. Much of our focus here has been on unskilled, low-wage migrants, many of whom come from South and Southeast Asia and other Arab and Middle Eastern countries. Equally important, and often equally omnipresent, are skilled, highly paid migrants, who come mostly from Western and especially European countries. Future research also needs to consider the experiences of semi-skilled migrants who serve as shopkeepers, clerks, cashiers, and other middle-rank functionaries. Finally, many of these skilled and semi-skilled migrants end up as long-term residents, and future research also needs to examine the lives and experiences of their offspring as second-generation migrant laborers.

Whatever direction future research on the topic may take, as the chapters in this volume amply demonstrate, one-dimensional analyses of the phenomenon of migrant labor, whether in the Persian Gulf or elsewhere, seldom capture the subtleties and the broad range of dynamics that combine to form complex and multilayered narratives. Labor migration is by no means a recent historical development. In fact, since time immemorial, long before nation-states emerged and separated themselves from one another through national and geographic boundaries, groups of individuals moved long distances in search of better ways of making a living. Today, advances in transportation technology have made such movements easier and more coordinated; the speed and nature of economic development have magnified and multiplied them in scale; and the spread of communication technology has made their causes and consequences more evident to observers far and near alike. Studying the manifold facets of labor migration—in our case in the Persian Gulf, where the region's phenomenal economic and infrastructural growth would not have occurred had it not been for migrant labor—is a necessary and critical starting point.

2

Beyond Labor
Foreign Residents in the Persian Gulf States

Attiya Ahmad

Inspired by the life story of Mariam, one of my research interlocutors in Kuwait, as well as by Hannah Arendt's discussion of *vita activa*,[1] this chapter points to how labor is necessary to, yet also limits our analyses of foreign residents' experiences in the Persian Gulf states.[2] Non-citizens are a significant part of the Gulf states' population—ranging from 25 percent in Saudi Arabia to 66 percent in Kuwait, to over 90 percent in the United Arab Emirates (UAE) and Qatar. Unlike transnational migrants and diasporic groups in other parts of the world, in the Gulf they are unlikely to ever become naturalized citizens. Research on this diverse and dynamic population has expanded in recent years. Today there exists a relatively small yet robust set of studies documenting foreign residents' experiences. By far, "labor" is the predominant theme and analytical category through which policy-makers, human rights workers, and scholars examine this population's status and situation. They conceive of foreign residents as "temporary labor migrants" or "guest workers,"

---

[1] Hannah Arendt, *The Human Condition*, 2nd ed. (University of Chicago Press, 1998).
[2] Henceforth referred to as "the Gulf."

and the working conditions of this population are seen to be determinant of their experiences in the Gulf.

This emphasis is not accidental. With the booming of the Gulf states' petrodollar-driven economies from the early 1970s onwards, a vast and consolidated assemblage[3] of government policies, social and political institutions, and public discourse developed to manage and police the region's foreign resident population. Anchored by the *kafala* or sponsorship and guarantorship system, this assemblage both constructs and disciplines[4] foreign residents[5] into "temporary labor migrants." While it is important to account for these processes, in this chapter I argue that they should not delimit our analyses of foreign residents in the Gulf. Doing so not only runs the risk of naturalizing foreign residents' disciplining as "temporary labor migrants," it unwittingly reinscribes the assemblage that produces them as such. It also elides two other dimensions of foreign residents' experiences in the Gulf, namely the historical interregional relations and contemporary forms of socio-political belonging that connect many to the region, as well as other activities they undertake in

---

[3] "Assemblage" is a term I borrow from the work of Gilles Deleuse and Felix Guattari that refers to a collection of heterogeneous structures, consisting of both human as well as non-human elements. Deleuze and Guattari use "assemblage" as a verb-noun, a process of becoming as much as a state of being, to denote dynamism, and to steer readers away from construing actor-networks as fixed entities, instead conveying a sense of them as dynamic entities. For further discussions about this issue, consult the following works: Gilles Deleuze and Felix Guattari, *A Thousand Plateaus. Capitalism and Schizophrenia* (Minneapolis: University of Minneapolis Press, 1987); and Manuel DeLanda, *A New Philosophy of Society: Assemblage Theory and Social Complexity* (London: Continuum Press, 2006).

[4] By "disciplining" I am referring to Michel Foucault's use of the term, which he uses to refer to processes whereby individual selves are shaped and become subject to broader systems of discourse and power. See, Michel Foucault, *Discipline and Punish: The Birth of the Prison,* 2nd ed. (New York: Vintage Books, 1995).

[5] In this article, following Nagy, I use the term "foreign residents" to refer to the Gulf's non-citizen population. This term points to the way this population, although it has contributed and continues to contribute to the development of the Gulf, and population has remained and remains long-standing residents of the region, they are deemed "foreign" by Gulf states and citizens. For further discussion about this matter, consult: Sharon Nagy, "'This Time I Think I'll Try a Filipina': Global and Local Influences on Relations between Foreign Household Workers and Their Employers in Doha, Qatar," in *City and Society* Annual Review (1998), pp. 83–103; Sharon Nagy, "The Search for Miss Philippines Bahrain—Possibilities for Representation in Expatriate Communities," in *City and Society* 20, 1 (June 2008) pp. 79–104.

the region, such as social reproduction and remunerated domestic work, that do not fit—or fit awkwardly—under the rubric of labor.

In pointing to the limitation of "labor," my discussion draws on the work of Hannah Arendt. In *The Human Condition* Arendt examines at length three forms of activity which she argues are fundamental to the human condition.[6] These activities or *vita activa* are *labor*, "which corresponds to the biological process of the human body," a realm more conventionally referred to as "social reproduction"; *work*, which "provides an 'artificial' world of things, distinctly different from all natural surroundings, a realm more conventionally referred to as "labor"; and *action*, "the only activity that goes on directly between men without the intermediary of things or matter," a realm more conventionally referred to as political activity.[7] Arendt argues that through processes of modernity, labor has come to subsume all other forms of activity, a historical phenomenon her analysis seeks to problematize. Arendt's examination of how "the theoretical glorification of labor" and the "transformation of the whole of society into a laboring society" is a defining feature of the modern age underscores the historical processes—rather than historical inevitability—by which labor has come to assume such importance in our contemporary world.[8] Arendt's discussion is invaluable to examining foreign residents' experiences in the Gulf. Her work opens up analytical space to not only scrutinize the historical circumstances by which "labor" has gained ascendency in defining foreign residents' experiences of the Gulf. It also pushes us to consider other activities that they undertake in the Persian Gulf—activities often obfuscated by hegemonic discourses that reduce their presence in the Gulf to their labor.

The production and disciplining of temporary labor migrants

On a brisk March day in 1968, Mariam boarded a boat in Bombay's harbor. After a ten day voyage she described as intensely disorienting—her physical and social footing less certain after several days of swelling waves and listening to the unfamiliar sounds of her fellow travelers speaking the Indian subcontinent's many languages and dialects—she arrived in Kuwait. Once past the immigration desk, where the officials questioned her in an Arabic laced with

---

[6] Arendt, *The Human Condition*, p. 7.
[7] Ibid.
[8] Ibid., p. 4.

Hindi, Mariam found an elderly couple waiting for her. The man, a tall bearded fellow, insisted she call him "Baba Abu Ibrahim." The woman, enveloped in a black *abaya*, held up a small picture of Mariam, proof she was indeed Mariam's *kafeel* (sponsor/guarantor), and then ushered Mariam to a waiting car. The couple took her to their home, where Mariam began—and would continue—to work within their household over the next forty years.

Mariam arrived in Kuwait on the cusp of a profound set of changes reshaping the Gulf and its surrounding regions. Although predating this period, the scale of migration to the Gulf increased dramatically during this time, an increase attributed to a number of broad-stroke political-economic factors. In the early 1970s spikes in the price of oil resulted in the burgeoning oil wealth of the Gulf states, and their governments' plans for rapid state and infrastructural development. Increases in oil prices also resulted in the Third World's ballooning trade deficits, bankrupted state budgets, and nascent structural adjustment and liberalization programs. A concatenation of these factors, massive waves of people from throughout South and Southeast Asia, the Arab world, Iran, East Africa, and to a lesser extent Europe and North America, began migrating to the Arab Gulf states.

These vast movements of people changed the social and spatial topography of the Gulf. Travel to the region increased tremendously. Boat trips, like the one taken by Mariam, bus routes and air flight to and from the region proliferated, as did enterprises facilitating these movements. Typist and translation services, travel agents, professional embassy mediators (so-called "fixers") and labor recruitment or "manpower" agencies developed apace. A play of presences and absences developed between the Gulf and its surrounding regions. The emergence of shops, housing complexes, and large gatherings of foreign residents in public squares and parks in Gulf cities both correlated and contrasted with the shuffled households, missing cohorts of young and skilled workers, and eventually, the spread of luxury household goods and newly built houses in foreign residents' countries of origin. For instance, Mariam's decades-long presence in Kuwait—her work in Abu and Umm Ibrahim's home, her regular attendance at the Catholic Church on Sundays, her periodic visits to her uncle's home—all marked long stretches of time when she was absent in India. Her periodic visits to her family mitigated her absence, as did her assiduously collected earnings, which enabled her to underwrite her sister's dowry and to build her parents a modest home on the outskirts of Mumbai.

By the mid-1960s, just before Mariam's initial journey to Kuwait, foreign residents' status in the Gulf was also changing dramatically. Never permissive but porous, the process by which Gulf states conferred citizenship became more restrictive during this period. The governments of the Gulf applied their country's nationality codes in a loose manner until the 1960s; thereafter, they not only implemented existing codes, but also passed a series of further amendments.[9] Principles of *jus sanguinis* rather than *jus solis* increasingly defined citizenship, rendering naturalization impossible for foreign residents. Gulf states only granted citizenship to the children of male citizens, a gendered process based on the patrilineal understanding that the father channels national belonging and citizenship.[10] Gulf citizens began conceiving of national belonging in increasingly racialized terms: being a Khaliji (term that means "of the Gulf") became synonymous with being Arab, as illustrated by Kuwait's national constitution, which proclaims the country to be "an Arab state, independent and fully sovereign...the people of Kuwait are part of the Arab nation."[11] Gulf states and citizens elided their region's interregional pasts and emphasized their Arab genealogies.[12] This process was an integral means through which many Gulf ruling families, descendants of migrants from the Najd region of Saudi Arabia, entwined their family mythos with those of the city-states and nations they had come to rule.[13]

Gulf states and citizens increasingly considered and treated foreign residents as though they were "builders of the nation," rather than fellow "nation builders." They conceived of foreign residents' work as being contracted by—rather than contributing to—the nation. Foreign residents' changing status was reflected in the terms by which they came to be referred, including

[9] Anh Nga Longva, *Walls Built on Sand* (Boulder: Westview Press, 1997); Jill Crystal, *Oil and Politics in the Gulf: Rulers and Merchants in Kuwait and Qatar* (Cambridge University Press, 1990); Jill Crystal, *Kuwait: The Transformation of an Oil State* (Boulder, CO: Westview Press, 1992).

[10] Paul Dresch, "Debates on Marriage and Nationality in the United Arab Emirates," in Paul Dresch and James Piscatori (eds), *Monarchies and Nations: Globalisation and Identity in the Arab States of the Gulf* (New York: I.B. Tauris, 2005).

[11] James Onley, "Transnational Merchants in the Nineteenth-Century Gulf: The Case of the Safar Family," in Madawi Al-Rasheed (ed.), *Transnational Connections and the Arab Gulf* (New York: Routledge, 2005), p. 62.

[12] Madawi Al-Rasheed, "Introduction: Localizing the Transnational and Transnationalizing the Local," in Madawi Al-Rasheed (ed.), *Transnational Connections and the Arab Gulf* (New York: Routledge, 2005), p. 8; Onley, "Transnational Merchants in the Nineteenth-Century Gulf," p. 62.

[13] Crystal, *Kuwait*, p. 52.

migrant laborers, guest workers, and expatriates. An assemblage of laws, policies and institutions (henceforth referred to as "labor assemblage")—comprising migration and residency laws in both the Gulf and migrant-sending countries, labor recruitment agencies, embassies and consulates, and state institutions including the police, border patrols and ministries of the Interior, Foreign Affairs, and Social Affairs—developed that disciplined foreign residents into "temporary labor migrants."[14] The *kafala* system anchored this labor assemblage. In order to work and reside in the Gulf, foreign residents required a residency permit, which they could only obtain by entering into a *kafala* arrangement with someone who had the right to act as their *kafeel*, or sponsor and guarantor. Gulf states conferred this right upon citizens in good civic and legal standing, and to a far more limited extent, upon well-heeled foreign residents.

A citizen-devolved system of governance, the *kafala* system became the primary means of managing and policing the Gulf's burgeoning population of foreign residents.[15] Focused as they were on maintaining the political and economic status quo, and on redistributing their countries' oil wealth to their citizens in the form of services and subsidies, the governments of the Gulf states saw foreign residents as unimportant to, or falling outside the ambit of their activities.[16] Whether it developed out of the Gulf states' concerted strategies or limited capacities, the *kafala* system constitutes a set of relationships and agreements that fundamentally shape foreign residents' experiences in the Gulf. No matter how long they reside in the Gulf, or whether they are born in the Gulf, and regardless of the role they play in these countries' development and prosperity, foreign residents are only allowed to reside in the Gulf on a temporary basis. Their presence remains contingent upon, and policed by, citizens. Foreign residents are allowed to stay in the Gulf for periods of time delimited by the labor contracts they enter into with individual citizens and institutions—their *kafeel*. Emerging in tandem and parallel to the Gulf countries' state infrastructure, the *kafala* system plays an integral role in bolstering

---

[14] Anh Nga Longva, *Walls Built on Sand* (Boulder: Westview Press, 1997); Crystal, *Oil and Politics in the Gulf*.

[15] Anh Nga Longva, "Neither Autocracy nor Democracy but Ethnocracy: Citizens, Expatriates and the Socio-Political Systems in Kuwait," in Nils A. Butenschøn *et al.* (eds), *Citizenship and State in the Middle East: Approaches and Applications* (Syracuse University Press, 2000).

[16] Crystal, *Kuwait*.

the existing division of power between citizens and foreign residents, and in ensuring the impermanence of the region's non-citizens.[17]

Mariam was integrated into this labor assemblage well before she stepped foot on Kuwaiti soil. Months before, through mail correspondence, she had entered into a *kafala* arrangement with Abu and Umm Ibrahim. She also registered with the Ministry of Foreign Affairs in India and went through a series of complicated bureaucratic procedures at the Kuwaiti Embassy in order to receive permission to travel to the region. Mariam required a *kafeel* in order to obtain a visa, and she had to sign a series of legal documents attesting that she would only reside in Kuwait so long as she was gainfully employed and had a *kafeel*. These procedures were part and parcel of the processes disciplining her into becoming, and regarding herself as, a person whose purpose and presence in the Gulf hinged upon her labor. Over the course of forty years of living and working with Abu and Umm Ibrahim's family, however, Mariam's understanding of herself and her presence in Kuwait changed. She came to think of herself as, and Abu and Umm Ibrahim's household considered her to be, a vital part of their household and family. Despite her deep, intimate ties with the family, the fact she was effectively retired, and the total length of time she had resided in Kuwait, Mariam remained subject to the country's *kafala* system. In order for her to remain in Kuwait, every two years Abu and Umm Ibrahim had to undertake the necessary bureaucratic procedures to renew her residency permit.

Early academic accounts of foreign residents in the Persian Gulf

Mirroring hegemonic understandings and practices, the earliest academic accounts of foreign residents in the Gulf depict them as temporary labor migrants. The first line of scholarly inquiry that developed, one written in the late 1970s and early 1980s, sought to ascertain the scope of migration to the Gulf. Scholars, often linked to policy-making projects and institutions, undertook research to determine how many foreign residents were present in the region, and from where they had migrated. A large body of statistical accounts began to develop, one that continues to play a significant role in the field

[17] Anh Nga Longva, "Keeping Migrant Workers in Check: The Kafala System in the Gulf," *Middle East Report*, 211 (1999), pp. 20–22; Longva, "Neither Autocracy nor Democracy but Ethnocracy," pp. 114–35; Andrew Gardner, *City of Strangers* (Ithaca, NY: Cornell University Press, 2010).

today.[18] From this initial focus, scholars began to branch out into other realms of inquiry, including examination of the structural reasons and individual motivations for migration; the remittance patterns and relations that developed between foreign residents and their communities of origin; the broader socio-economic impacts of migration on both host and sending countries, most notably with respect to economic development; and questions of security or rights linked to migrants' status as non-citizens in the region.[19]

Cumulatively, these works contribute greatly to our understanding of the economic and political dimensions of foreign residents' presence in the Gulf. Assuming rather than analyzing the processes by which labor assemblages discipline foreign residents into temporary labor migrants, these studies document the effects of this disciplining. In so doing, they treat foreign residents as a largely undifferentiated population. Whether from the Philippines, India or Egypt, foreign residents are posited as having similar motivations and decision-making patterns—ones based on the model of *Homo Economicus*. These studies assume foreign residents to be, or heuristically treat them as, rational, calculative actors who make decisions to maximize their individual self-interest. They do not account for other understandings and socio-cultural elaborations of selfhood and agency. Anthropologists have sought to redress this lacuna by examining how kinship relations, understandings of the self predicated on mutualism rather than individualism, and other forms of economic distribution, most notably gift exchange and prestige economies, also underpin and structure foreign residents experiences in the Gulf.[20]

---

[18] A notable example of which is: Andrzej Kapiszewski, *Nationals and Expatriates: Population and Labour Dilemmas of the Gulf Cooperation Council States* (Dryden, NY: Ithaca Press, 2001).

[19] Rashid Amjad, *To the Gulf and Back: Studies on the Economic Impact of Asian Labour Migration* (New Delhi: ILO Asian Employment Programme, 1989); J.S. Birks and C.A. Sinclair, *International Migration and Development in the Arab Region* (Geneva: International Labour Organization, 1980); N.S.A. Mohammed, *Population and Development of the Arab Gulf States: The Case of Bahrain, Oman and Kuwait* (Burlington, VT: Ashgate Publishing, 2003); Fred Arnold and Nasra M. Shah, *Asian Labour Migration: Pipeline to the Middle East* (Boulder, CO: Westview Press, 1986); F. Eelens, T. Schampers and J.D. Speckmann, *Labour Migration to the Middle East: From Sri Lanka to the Gulf* (London: Kegal Paul, 1992); Ali Kouaouci, "Labour Migration in the Gulf System," in Douglas S. Massey, Joaquin Arango, Graeme Hugo, Ali Kouaouchi, Adela Pellegrino, J. Edward Taylor, *Worlds in Motion: Understanding International Migration at the End of the Millennium* (Oxford University Press, 2005).

[20] Akbar S. Ahmed, "The Arab Connection: Emergent Models of Social Structure

Works focusing on relations of oppression in the Gulf constitute another area of study examining the effects of foreign residents' disciplining as temporary labor migrants. From anecdotal accounts of incidents of violence to analyses of structural violence, these works analyze foreign residents' experiences of hierarchical, racialized, and exploitative labor relations in the Gulf. Many provide persuasive arguments about how these asymmetrical relations stem from the *kafala* system.[21] While drawing much needed attention to the ethically and politically problematic treatment that a number of foreign residents encounter in the Gulf—treatment that underscores the more damaging aspects of the labor assemblage all foreign residents are subject to—we should not make the analytical (or political) leap and assume that foreign residents and migrants will necessarily articulate their identifications and socio-political consciousness in relation to these processes.[22] This phenomenon may be attributed to the systematic efforts of Gulf governments, and politically influential classes of merchant elites, to discourage the development of solidarity amongst foreign residents, whether by recruiting migrants of different ethno-national and linguistic background, or discouraging the multiple renewals of contract cycles, or actively repressing and stopping any forms of organizing that develop.[23] Foreign residents' internal differentiation along occupational

---

among Pakistan Tribesmen," *Asian Affairs* 12:2 (1981), pp. 167–72; Akbar S. Ahmed, "Dubai Chalo: Problems in Ethnic Encounters Between Middle Eastern and South Asian Muslim Societies," *Asian Affairs* 15:3 (1984), pp. 262–76; Sulayman Khalaf, "Gulf Societies and the Image of Unlimited Good," *Dialectical Anthropology* 17 (1992), pp. 53–84; Sulayman Khalaf and Saad Alkobaisi, "Migrants' Strategies of Coping and Patterns of Accommodation in the Oil-Rich Gulf Societies: Evidence from the UAE," *British Journal of Middle Eastern Studies* 26:2 (1999), pp. 271–98; Karen Leonard, "South Asian Workers in the Gulf: Jockeying for Places," in Richard Perry and William Maurer (eds), *Globalization Under Construction: Governmentality, Law and Identity* (Minneapolis: University of Minnesota Press, 2003), pp. 129–70; Filippo Osella and Caroline Osella, "Migration, Money and Masculinity in Kerala," *Journal of the Royal Anthropological Institute* 6:1 (2000), pp. 117–33.

[21] Anh Nga Longva, "Keeping Migrant Workers in Check: The Kafala System in the Gulf," *Middle East Report 211* (1999), pp. 20–22; Anh Nga Longva, "Neither Autocracy nor Democracy but Ethnocracy," pp. 114–35; and, Gardner, *City of Strangers*.

[22] Although from the standpoint of rights-based political systems predicated on individual self-interest, and Marxist-socialist analyses, it may appear so.

[23] John Chalcraft, *Monarchy, Migration and Hegemony in the Arabian Peninsula* (London School of Economics, 2010).

and class lines may also explain this phenomenon. Research conducted in recent years points to how middle or upper-middle class foreign residents may perpetuate hierarchical and exploitative labor relations by acting as intermediaries and implementers, for example managers and supervisors of these systems.[24]

Cosmopolitan and interregional pasts

Recent scholarship on transnationalism and diaspora in the Gulf suggests another explanation for why foreign residents do not develop identities and socio-political forms of belonging reducible to their laboring status.[25] Although foreign residents may not be citizens of the Gulf, they are from communities and places with longstanding and extensive connections to the Gulf. Histories, imaginaries and relations undergird these connections, and forge other forms of identifications and belongings in the Gulf.[26] Mariam's stories both instantiate and illustrate this issue.

---

[24] Andrew Gardner, "Strategic Transnationalism: The Indian Diasporic Elite in Contemporary Bahrain," *City and Society* 20:1 (2008), pp. 54–78; Neha Vora, "Producing Diasporas and Globalization: Indian Middle-Class Migrants in Dubai," *Anthropological Quarterly* 81:2 (2008), pp. 377–406.

[25] Janet Abu-Lughod, *Before European Hegemony: The World System AD 1250–1350* (New York: Oxford University Press, 1989); Sugata Bose, *A Hundred Horizons: The Indian Ocean in the Age of Global Empire* (Cambridge, MA: Harvard University Press, 2006); Amitav Ghosh, *In an Antique Land* (New York: Granta Books, 1992); Engseng Ho, *The Graves of Tarim: Genealogy and Mobility Across the Indian Ocean* (Berkeley: University of California Press, 2006); James Onley, *The Arabian Frontier of the British Raj* (New York: Oxford University Press, 2007); Filippo Osella and Caroline Osella, "'I am Gulf': The Production of Cosmopolitanism in Kozhikode, Kerala, India," in Edward Simpson and Kai Kress (eds), *Struggling with History: Islam and Cosmopolitanism in the Western Indian Ocean* (New York: Columbia University Press, 2008), pp. 323–55; Rasheed Al-Madawi, *Transnational Connections and the Arab Gulf* (New York: Routledge, 2005); Edward Simpson and Kai Kresse, *Struggling with History: Islam and Cosmopolitanism in the Western Indian Ocean* (New York: Columbia University Press, 2008); Paul Dresch and James Piscatori, *Monarchies and Nations: Globalisation and Identity in the Arab States of the Gulf* (New York: I.B. Tauris, 2005); Fred Anscombe, *The Ottoman Gulf: The Creation of Kuwait, Saudi Arabia and Qatar* (New York: Columbia University Press, 1997).

[26] Ibid.

Young, impoverished, with few options, and determined, Mariam began work as a housemaid in her early teens. When she was a child, her father suffered a debilitating accident, making it impossible for him to continue his work as a mason. Mariam's mother sought to support her family through odd jobs—sometimes working as a laundress, sometimes taking on tailoring work, sometimes selling vegetables in the market; however, a chronic respiratory illness limited the amount of work she could take on. Through church-based contacts, Mariam's parents found her a position with a wealthy Bombay household, where she was trained with and worked alongside the household's other domestic workers. In a villa down the road from where she lived, Mariam learned of a family popularly referred to as the "Bombay-Kuwaiti wallahs"—Arab merchants from Kuwait City who had married into and lived in India for generations. It was to this family that Mariam turned for advice when she began hearing of lucrative job opportunities for domestic workers in the Gulf. The "Bombay-Kuwaiti wallahs" put her in touch with a small Kuwaiti merchant family with whom they traded, assuring her that the family was both respectable and kindly, and they continued to act as Mariam's intermediary until she entered into a *kafala* arrangement with the family. When she arrived in Kuwait, Mariam discovered, much to her surprise and delight, that in Abu and Umm Ibrahim's neighborhood there lived a few Kuwaiti families of mixed Indian-Arab parentage "whose talk, food and manners were like ours...just like in India."

Mariam's narrative is indexical of the Gulf's cosmopolitan past. A number of recent ethno-historical accounts amply demonstrate that interregional interconnections between the Gulf and other parts of the world, most notably Iran, Iraq, the former Ottoman Empire, and peoples and places throughout the Indian Ocean, are longstanding ones predating the recent oil boom.[27] These interconnections may not be historically unprecedented, but the forms in which they are articulated have changed. In the past, the pearling industry, kinship relations, trade and commerce, religion, and legal and financial systems knitted together interregional connections. In the present day, trade, finance capital, and especially migration hold sway. Although they have changed, these historical relations remain important. The presence of the "Bombay-Kuwaiti wallah" in Bombay and the Arab-Indian families in Kuwait, for instance, belies Gulf nationalist myths that depict the region as intrinsically and exclusively Arab. They highlight how peoples from throughout the Arab world, Asia and

[27] Ibid.

Africa were not always assumed to be non-Khaliji, inherently foreign, or a temporary part of the region—as foreign residents are today.

These historical interconnections continue to shape contemporary relations. Mariam's connection with the "Bombay-Kuwaiti wallahs" facilitated her migration to Kuwait—an example of how previous interregional connections influenced and enabled the formation of labor assemblages that foreign residents are subject to today. The research I conducted in the Gulf on the transnational domestic work sector in 2006–7, 2008, and 2010, for example, indicated that labor recruitment or "manpower" agencies, travel routes, and the *kafala* system existing today are predicated on previous sets of interregional networks, institutions, and legal contract systems. Vitalis, and Secombe and Lawless' research, also illustrate this matter.[28] These scholars begin their studies in the early rather than mid-twentieth century, and take a broader historical and geographical view of the development of the Gulf's labor regimes and transnational labor migration. Their works provide a compelling account of how the Gulf's hierarchical and racialized systems of labor emerged with the development of the region's oil industries. These studies underscore the importance of Western influence, specifically British colonial and American Jim Crow labor regimes, in shaping the racial and ethno-national bases of labor differentiation and discrimination that developed in the Gulf. They foreground the ongoing role played by Western expatriates, transnational corporations, and government officials—actors and organizations often elided in existing accounts of labor assemblages and in the Gulf—in mediating between citizens and *kafeel* on the one hand, and foreign residents on the other.

Other historical and contemporary forms of socio-political relations and belonging

Besides labor relations, historical interregional connections shape and point to other forms of relations that exist between Gulf nationals and foreign residents today. The most evident form, one that has the potential to fit within existing Gulf nationality codes, consists of genealogical and kinship ties. The

[28] I.J. Secombe and R.I. Lawless, "Foreign Worker Dependence in the Gulf, and International Oil Companies: 1910–50," *International Migration Review*, 20:3 (1986), pp. 548–74; Robert Vitalis, "Black Gold, White Crude: An An Essay on American Exceptionalism, Hierarchy, and Hegemony in the Gulf," *Diplomatic History*, 26:2 (2002), pp. 185–213; Robert Vitalis, *America's Kingdom: Mythmaking on the Saudi Oil Frontier* (London: Verso, 2009).

specific examples of the "Bombay Kuwaiti-wallah" and the Kuwaiti-Indian families residing in Mariam's neighborhood, and more generally the ethnographic work of Leonard, Ho and Osella and Osella,[29] attest to the longstanding marital ties that exist between Gulf communities and other parts of the Indian Ocean. Sailors, traders, functionaries and others contracted marriages amongst their families and communities to bolster and perpetuate the relations that constituted this ecumenical realm. From the late 1960s onwards, the extent and density of these kinship relations diminished and became publicly downplayed through processes of Arabization and with Gulf national belonging becoming more exclusionary and hierarchical.

These connections set a historical precedent for a more recent phenomenon: the development of marital ties and intimate relations between Gulf nationals and foreign residents in the contemporary period.[30] Mariam's stories again prove illustrative. Late in life, after living in the Gulf for over thirty-five years, Mariam took *shehadeh*, the Islamic testament of faith, and became a practicing Muslim. As part of her efforts to further her understanding of Islamic precepts and practices, Mariam began taking courses at one of the women's centers of Kuwait's Islamic *dawa* movement. There she studied alongside a number of other foreign resident women from a dizzying number of places, including North America, Europe, Indonesia, the Philippines, India, Lebanon, Eritrea and China. Some of these women were born Muslim. Others had converted to Islam. A subset had married Muslim men in Kuwait, including Khawla, a Filipina woman with whom Mariam forged a strong friendship.

Khawla had migrated to Kuwait fifteen years earlier after taking up a position as a nurse at one of the country's public hospitals. Through her work, she befriended a Kuwaiti doctor. The two developed a close relationship and eventually married. Khawla's husband set her up in a separate household;

---

[29] Karen Leonard, "Construction of Identity in Diaspora: Emigrants from Hyderabad, India," in Carla Petievich (eds), *Expanding Landscapes: South Asians in Diaspora* (Delhi: Manohar, 1999); Karen Leonard, "South Asian Women in the Gulf: Families and Futures Reconfigured," in Sonita Sarkar and Esha Niyogi De (eds), *Transstatus Subjects: Gender in the Globalization of South and Southeast Asia* (Durham, NC: Duke University Press, 2003). Also see footnote 25.

[30] Sharon Nagy, "'This Time I Think I'll Try a Filipina': Global and Local Influences on Relations between Foreign Household Workers and Their Employers in Doha, Qatar," in *City and Society* Annual Review (1998): pp. 83–103; idem, "The Search for Miss Philippines Bahrain—Possibilities for Representation in Expatriate Communities," in *City and Society* 20 (1): pp. 79–104.

however, on weekends and holidays, the two spent a great deal of time social-izing with his family. In conversation, Khawla described how her husband's family and other Kuwaitis she interacted with compared her situation to non-Arab Kuwaiti wives of previous generations. They expected Khawla to adapt and subsume her own upbringing, culture and language to that of her husband's family. Following patrilineal principles of descent and affiliation, Kuwaitis considered Khawla's children to be a part of their father's family, and to be inherently Kuwaiti, rather than aligned with her own background. The Kuwaiti state granted her children citizenship when they were born, and after she had married and resided in Kuwait for ten years, eventually to Khawla as well. Khawla and her children were considered to be a part of both the family and the nation, but were treated as different, if not of a lesser status than other Kuwaitis.

Although there are historical continuities, there are also important differ-ences that characterize contemporary forms of intimate relations and marriages between Gulf nationals and foreign residents. In the past, these marriages devel-oped largely through trading and interregional networks, and were contracted between families that comprised these networks. Although those who were a part of these networks placed emphasis on the patrilineage of the family,[31] rela-tions between the families were relatively egalitarian. In the contemporary period, rather than interregional trade, the broader socio-political system in which these relations develop is the labor assemblage that disciplines foreign residents as temporary labor migrants. Individuals rather than families enter into these intimate relations and marriages, with authority and power decidedly in favor of Gulf citizens. Another important point of difference relates to gen-der. In the past, it was predominately men from the Gulf who married outside their immediate familial and geographical circles, a circumstance illustrating their greater physical mobility, and the overall patrilineal and patriarchal nature of familial and socio-political forms of organizing. In recent years, a significant number of Gulf women have also married non-citizens, mainly Arab, Iranian and Western expat men. Underscoring the gendered nature of exclusion and citizenship in the Gulf, the state grants neither their children nor their hus-bands citizenship. Gulf states and nationals consider both to be a part of the husband's familial and national grouping rather than the wife's.

The forms of socio-political belonging and identification that foreign resi-dents develop in the Gulf are not just articulated through their labor, histori-

---

[31] A notable exception being the Koyas as discussed by Osella and Osella: see Filippo Osella and Caroline Osella, "'I am Gulf,'" pp. 323–55.

cal interconnections or marital and kinship ties. These relations are entwined with but do not determine another realm of activity foreign residents engage with in the Gulf—a realm Arendt refers to as "action". Even though foreign residents have no recourse to citizenship, to *de jure* belonging, they develop *de facto* forms of socio-belonging and identification in the Gulf. Their acute awareness of the Gulf's cosmopolitan past and present, and their recognition of their own contribution to the region's development, shape other socio-political imaginaries, and provide a basis from which they claim to be in and of the Gulf. The work of Osella and Osella,[32] and that of Vora,[33] prove especially instructive in this regard. In their examination of the form of cosmopolitanism practiced by the Koyas of Kerala, Osella and Osella argue that through their longstanding and intensive linkages to the Gulf, linkages whose forms have changed over time but which remain of great salience to them, the Koyas consider "the Gulf [as] actually part of Kerala, and not at all a separate *nadu*."[34] The "specific and bounded Koya culture," the Osellas explain, "is made up of many strands from the sedimented past and contemporary experience: in all of this, encounters with Gulf Arabs are right at the heart of what it means to be a Koya."[35]

Vora, in her research on middle and upper-middle class South Asians of Dubai, also pays careful attention to new possibilities of being, and configurations of belonging, forming in the Gulf. As the South Asian population grows and continues to reside in Dubai for extended periods of time, it develops socio-cultural networks and spaces that thicken with meaning, activity and vitality. Vora's work points to the different ways in which South Asians' diasporic consciousness and community forms. She argues that the hierarchical exclusions they experience in the Gulf quicken, rather than restrict, the formation of South Asian identifications and belonging. The *kafala* system and labor assemblages disciplining foreign residents as "temporary labor migrants" spur the development of a racial consciousness that undergirds the development of South Asian diasporas. Vora's work also points to broader

---

[32] Filippo Osella and Caroline Osella, "'I am Gulf': The Production of Cosmopolitanism in Kozhikode, Kerala, India," in Edward Simpson and Kai Kress (eds), *Struggling with History: Islam and Cosmopolitanism in the Western Indian Ocean* (New York: Columbia University Press, 2008), pp. 323–55.

[33] Neha Vora, "Producing Diasporas and Globalization: Indian Middle-Class Migrants in Dubai," *Anthropological Quarterly* 81:2 (2008): pp. 377–406.

[34] Filippo Osella and Caroline Osella, "'I am Gulf'," p. 350.

[35] Ibid., p. 351.

economic relations besides labor through which South Asians diasporas are formed, including consumer practices (what she refers to as consumer citizenship) and business ties between well-heeled South Asians and Dubai's elite. Her work also draws attention to the way emergent higher educational institutions and new media in the Gulf, most notably the internet, blogging, and social networking sites, provide novel spaces of interactions between citizens and non-citizens, spaces generative of new horizons of identification and belonging.

The elision of foreign residents' social reproduction in the Gulf

Residing in Kuwait for so long, Mariam developed a small, tight-knit circle of friends. Most of her days she spent with her Kuwaiti family, her everyday life entwined with theirs. Periodically, though, she would venture to the *souk* to meet with friends and shop, or visit with them at their homes. This routine changed somewhat when Sumit, the son of one of her relatives, migrated to Kuwait. Mariam began inviting him to her home for tea on Fridays, the one day of the week he did not have work. When the weather was clement, she would meet him at one of Kuwait's public parks. These interactions provided Mariam with an alternative vantage point from which to assess her experiences in the Gulf. In our conversations she often compared her situation to that of Sumit. In contrast to Mariam, whom Abu and Umm Ibrahim recruited individually, a construction company recruited Sumit with other "bachelor workers" en masse. As with Mariam's situation with Umm and Abu Ibrahim, Sumit's company was responsible for providing him with room and board, but whereas Mariam lived with her employers, Sumit along with his fellow construction workers, men from throughout South and Southeast Asia, lived in dormitory accommodation on the outskirts of the city.

The differences between the work Mariam and Sumit perform, and their living conditions, not only underscore the gendered nature of foreign residents' experiences in the Gulf.[36] They also point to a further issue: the importance of disentangling "social reproduction," another of the three activities that

[36] The work of Nasra Shah carefully documents the gendered nature of foreign residents' experiences. See: Nasra Shah, "Asian Women Workers in Kuwait," *International Migration Review* 25: 3 (1991): pp. 464–486; Nasra Shah *et al.*, "Foreign Domestic Workers in Kuwait: Who Employs How Many," *Asian and Pacific Migration Journal*, 11:2 (2002): pp. 247–69; Nasra Shah, "Gender and Labour Migration to the Gulf Countries," *Feminist Review* 77 (2004): pp. 183–5.

constitute Arendt's *vita activa* from "labor." An overemphasis on labor elides, and makes it difficult to recognize, the gendered nature of difficulties facing foreign residents with respect to "social reproduction." In this section, I examine this issue in relation to the experiences of the two largest populations of foreign residents in the Gulf: "bachelor workers" and domestic workers.

A theme running through Mariam's and Sumit's conversations, one that arose repeatedly while I interviewed and visited "bachelor workers" over the course of my research,[37] related to "frustrations of living in the Gulf," as Sumit once put it. Here, they were not referring to their experiences of being overworked or underpaid, or to the other irregularities and discrimination they faced at their workplaces—although these too are important dimensions of their experience, which they and others draw much needed attention to.[38] Rather, these "frustrations" related to their "living" or lifestyle in the Gulf. Specifically, as the term "bachelor worker" implies, these men live without their families in the Gulf, outside of household contexts. This situation necessitates their undertaking of cooking, cleaning, laundry, and other forms of socially reproductive work these men were previously not involved with. One of my interlocutors, Anil, described his experiences as follows:

and Fridays...our one day off, there is still work and more work. I wake up early, well before I want to wake up, and do the washing; my pants, my shirts, everything. It takes a while, you know, because I do it by hand. And then after the stores they open, I buy the groceries and make food. The food they give us is ok, but not good, and we must cook too. I cook. And then we have to keep our place tidy, clean it. This work, I don't do it in the village...my sisters or mother do it, not me, not the men, not us...

Bachelor workers' experiences of living in the Gulf thus entailed a double burden of responsibility and work, a burden they understood as integral to the hardships they experience in the Gulf. They are responsible not only for laboring in their workplaces, but also for the ongoing work necessary to their everyday functioning. These men often associated socially reproductive work with women, a gendered coding that points to how in undertaking this work, these men further experienced the Gulf as a space in which their previous gendered roles and understandings came into question.

---

[37] I have conducted ethnographic research in Dubai (June-July 2004), Qatar (September 2009–July 2010) and Kuwait (July-August 2004, January 2006–July 2007, March 2008, June 2010), and during this period have interviewed and visited dozens of "bachelor workers."

[38] For an insightful example, see Gardner, *City of Strangers*.

In contrast to "bachelor workers," Gulf nationals hire domestic workers to undertake socially reproductive work. An overwhelmingly female population, one that constitutes the largest group of female foreign residents in the region, domestic workers are hired to cook, clean, care for children and the elderly, and undertake other work necessary to the everyday functioning of Gulf households. For instance, when Abu and Umm Ibrahim first hired Mariam, her work largely consisted of cleaning and cooking. As the family's children married and settled into their parents' extended household, Mariam became responsible for the care of the children. Other domestic workers, initially ones from India, and then Sri Lanka, Nepal, and the Philippines, were eventually hired. Although none of these women experienced any difficulties within Abu and Umm Ibrahim's extended household, and they were paid their proper wages on time and treated respectfully, Mariam and the others knew that the situation of other domestic workers in Kuwait, and the Gulf more generally were not as fortunate. Every day in both the Gulf and international press, reports appear about the abuse and exploitation of domestic workers. These reports often present two explanations for domestic workers' experiences of mistreatment. First are Orientalist and racist accounts that portray Gulf nationals as inherently violent, lascivious and oppressive. Other accounts attribute domestic workers' precarious situation to their legal situation: in the Gulf existing labor laws do not cover domestic workers.

My own research points to another explanation, one requiring us to account for how domestic workers' work fits awkwardly under the category of labor. This slippage between "social reproduction" and "labor" leads to a number of juridico-political complications and contradictions that characterize domestic workers' situation in the Gulf. Mariam and other domestic workers occupy a unique juridico-political position in the Gulf. Unlike other foreign residents in the Gulf, who fall under visa categories that designate them as working in the private or public sectors, migrant domestic workers fall under a visa category particular to their sector, the domestic work sector. Existing labor laws do not cover those who fall under this visa category. These workers, however, are not without legal recourse. If they experience problems, they can seek redress through criminal law in situations of physical or sexual abuse, or through civil law in cases where their contract stipulations are not being met, for example if their pay is being withheld. This situation is not specific to migrant domestic workers in the Gulf. The juridico-political status of domestic workers is precarious globally. With few exceptions—a notable one being the United Kingdom—domestic workers do not fall under the purview of existing labor laws, and in other countries as in the Gulf's *kafala* system, employers must sponsor migrant domestic workers in order for them to obtain work visas and residency permits.

The question of why domestic workers are excluded from labor laws, and whether their inclusion will redress the unfair treatment and exploitation many experience, opens up a series of questions long examined by feminist scholars. A rich body of literature—starting with the works of Engels and continuing with contemporary scholarship focused on questions of immaterial and affective labor[39]—examines the reasons why socially reproductive work is not considered labor. These works point to the gendered historical and social processes whereby socially reproductive work has been relegated to the private or domestic sphere, and understood in terms of use value rather than exchange value. Socially reproductive work, in other words, has historically eluded commodification, exchange through market economic relations, and legal recognition. As work that comprises and is centered on the household, social reproduction has historically exceeded and been excluded from waged labor.

Cumulatively, these works sound a cautionary note about assumptions, often taken for granted and held as doxa, that including socially reproductive work under existing labor laws will redress the problems experienced by domestic workers. These works raise an important question: if labor laws are predicated on gendered understandings of labor that *necessarily* preclude important dimensions of socially reproductive work, how effective will extending these laws to domestic workers be? This question points to yet another limitation in examining foreign residents' experiences solely in terms of labor. As feminist scholars demonstrate, conventional conceptions of labor

---

[39] Friedrich Engels, *Origins of the Family, Private Property and the State* (New York: Penguin Press, 2010 [1884]); M. Dalla Costa and S. James, *The Power of Women and the Subversion of the Community* (Bristol: Falling Wall Press, 1972); E. Malos, *The Politics of Housework*, rev. ed. (Cheltenham: New Clarion Press, 1995); L. Sargent, *Women and Revolution: A Discussion of the Unhappy Marriage of Marxism and Feminism* (Boston: South End Press, 1981); E. Leacock, "Women in Egalitarian Society," in R. Bridenthal and C. Koontz (eds), *Becoming Visible: Women in European History* (Boston: Houghton Mifflin, 1977), pp. 11–35; Kathi Weeks, "Life Within and Against Work: Affective Labor, Feminist Critique and Post-Fordist Politics," *Ephemera* 7:1 (2007): pp. 233–49; Bridget Anderson, *Doing the Dirty Work? The Global Politics of Domestic Labour.* (London: Zed Books, 2000); Barbara Ehrenreich and Arlie Russell Hochschild, *Global Woman: Nannies, Maids and Sex Workers in the New Economy* (New York: Henry Holt and Co., 2002).

are predicated on gendered understandings and exclusions. To assume and conceptualize domestic workers' socially reproductive work as labor—conflating these two terms—precludes critical examination of these points of gendered contradiction and conflict.

Conclusion: Labor's limits

Accounts and analyses of foreign residents in the Gulf often deploy two generalized, almost archetypal figures: the hard-pressed bachelor worker and the victimized domestic worker. Scholars, human rights workers, and policy-makers describe these figures' experiences to illustrate labor assemblages in the Gulf—an array of actors, institutions, and processes that discipline foreign residents into "temporary labor migrants." As people arguably most subject to the region's racialized, hierarchical, and exclusionary socio-economic and political systems, the figures of the hard-pressed bachelor worker and the victimized domestic worker underscore negative aspects of the Gulf's labor assemblages. In this chapter, rather than these archetypal figures, I use the stories of one of my interlocutors, Mariam, to discuss dimensions of foreign residents' experiences that are related, but not reducible to their laboring. I draw on Mariam's narratives not to debunk other portrayals of foreign residents, so much as to complicate them. Mariam's experiences—of being part of networks with long-standing ties to the region, of migrating to the Gulf, spending years working with a Kuwaiti household, eventually becoming a part of the family, developing social networks and community in the Gulf—both resonate and contrast with the experience of other foreign residents in her Gulf. Her narratives instantiate in practice what Arendt's discussion delineates in conceptual terms: the importance that labor has come to play in defining foreign residents' experience needs to be historically contextualized, and other forms of activity that are elided by our focus on labor need to be accounted for. Together, Mariam's and Arendt's accounts provide us with analytical space to examine foreign residents' longstanding interregional connections to the Gulf, the novel forms of identification and belonging they are developing in the region, and their socially reproductive work—all vital realms of foreign residents' experiences in the Gulf that are elided by an overemphasis and exclusionary focus on their labor.

3

Why Do They Keep Coming?
Labor Migrants in the Persian Gulf States

*Andrew M. Gardner**

By some estimates, labor migration to the Persian Gulf states comprises the third largest migration flow in the contemporary world. In comparison with the scholarly literature concerning the larger migration flows to North America and Europe, our collective understanding of migration to the Gulf states remains in its infancy. Nonetheless, within the tidy scholarly literature concerning this transnational flow of labor one can discern a small constellation of nascent themes. One theme that threads through several decades of scholarly analysis concerns the problematic and exploitative labor relations that

* Grateful acknowledgment goes to the Center for International and Regional Studies, Georgetown University School of Foreign Service in Qatar, for providing research funding for this project. I am grateful to all the members of the Center for International and Regional Studies Migrant Labor Working Group for the comments and questions that greatly improved this chapter, and to the migrant laborers in Qatar who so willingly shared their perspectives and experiences with me. Special thanks also go to the cohort of research assistants I employed for this project, including Deependra Giri, Yogamaya Mantha, Tara Thompson, Ramesh Pandey, and Nive Das.

seemingly characterize the experiences of many of the poorest transnational labor migrants who spend time in Gulf States.[1]

The starting point and unexamined premise of this chapter, then, is that unskilled or low-income labor migrants typically face significant challenges and problems during their sojourn in the Gulf states. This premise remains an ethnographic assertion—one backed by a substantial ethnographic literature, an abundance of anecdotal support, and occasional contributions derived from small or localized surveys of particular migrant labor populations in the region.[2] Although the parameters of these challenges and difficulties are well documented elsewhere, a brief review will be useful to the reader. To summarize, the analytic focus of these works is typically centered on the coupling of the transnational labor brokerage system with the *kafala* or sponsorship system, by which foreign migration is managed and governed in the Gulf Cooperation Council (GCC) States. In this system, many migrants receive less pay than they were contractually promised; many migrants work longer hours than their contracts originally indicated; non-payment of promised wages

---

[1] E.J.A.M. Spaan, "Socio-Economic Conditions of Sri Lankan Migrant Workers in the Gulf States," in F. Eelens, T. Schampers and J.D. Speckmann (eds), *Labour Migration to the Middle East: From Sri Lanka to the Gulf* (London: Kegan Paul International, 1992); Anh Longva, *Walls Built on Sand: Migration, Exclusion and Society in Kuwait* (Boulder: Westview Press, 1997); Anh Longva, "Keeping Migrant Workers In Check: The Kafala System in the Gulf," *Middle East Report* 211 (1999): pp. 20–22; Michele Gamburd, *The Kitchen Spoon's Handle: Transnationalism and Sri Lanka's Migrant Housemaids* (Ithaca, NY: Cornell University Press, 2000); Anisur Rahman, *Indian Labour Migration to the Gulf: A Socio-Economic Analysis* (New Delhi: Rajat Publications, 2001); Staci Strobl, "Policing Housemaids: The Criminalization of Domestic Workers in Bahrain," *British Journal of Criminology* 49 (2009): pp. 165–83; Andrew Gardner, "Engulfed: Indian Guest Workers, Bahraini Citizens and the Structural Violence of the Kafala System," in Nicholas De Genova and Nathalie Peutz (eds), *The Deportation Regime: Sovereignty, Space, and Freedom of Movement* (Durham, NC: Duke University Press, 2010), pp. 196–223; Andrew Gardner, *City of Strangers: Gulf Migration and the Indian Community in Bahrain* (Ithaca, NY: ILR/Cornell University Press, 2010).

[2] See, for example, Silvia Pessoa, Marjorie Carlson, Hanoof Al-Thani, Samiha Kamel, Hicham Nedjari, Ramsey Ramadan and Karim Watfa, *The State of Migrant Workers in Qatar: The Workers' Perspective*, Final Report, QNRF Undergraduate Research Experience Program Project, No. 07–12–03, 2008; Silvia Pessoa, Rooda Al-Neama and Maha Al-Shirrawi, *Migrant Workers in Qatar: Documenting their Current Situation*, Final Report, QNRF Undergraduate Research Experience Program Project, No. 05–09–71, 2009.

remains widespread; sponsors typically confiscate migrants' passports, thereby significantly impeding their ability to leave problematic employment situations; living conditions are often extremely overcrowded and difficult; socio-spatial segregation is the norm; and, for a variety of reasons, migrants have significant difficulty asserting their basic rights in these foreign states. This brief list is not comprehensive, but it does include many of the threads that weave through both the existing scholarly literature and many of the stories that will be presented later in this chapter.

For nearly a decade, my scholarly work has been focused on labor migration in the Gulf states, and as an ethnographer, my conclusions have been aligned with the framework I have just described: in sifting through the lived experiences of the hundreds of men and women who have shared some portion of their life with me, my analyses perennially focus upon the structural and systemic aspects that undergird the often exploitative relations encountered by many of these migrants when they enter into a contract for work in the Gulf.[3] These conclusions about the extraordinary challenges many labor migrants face in the Gulf coexist with the fact that a vast flow of remittances streams from the Gulf to the countries from which these labor migrants come. In popular sentiment, these two facts are often portrayed in tandem: labor migrants yield a certain portion of their rights and render themselves vulnerable to exploitation in order to secure the economic opportunities provided by work in the wealthy Gulf states.

What this explanatory configuration obscures is the fact that the vulnerability and exploitation foreign migrants often encounter in the Gulf are unequally borne by the poorest members of that transnational population. While the aggregate Gulf remittance figures are astonishingly large, in my own ethnographic fieldwork amongst the unskilled population of labor migrants I have repeatedly encountered men and women for whom a sojourn in the Gulf states has been a financial catastrophe: by entering into an agreement to travel to the Gulf, these men and women enter into a system that is fully capable of separating them from the tiny fortunes they and their families have invested in sending them to the Gulf in the first place. In William Walters' analysis of illegality and deportation in Europe and North America, he discerns a "deportation industry," including not only police and immigration personnel, but also airline executives, pilots, stewards, and, perhaps more important, a constellation of private companies that profit from detention

---

[3] See Gardner, "Engulfed", pp. 196–223; Gardner, *City of Strangers*.

and deportation.[4] Borrowing this idea, I suggest we conceptualize the migration system in the Gulf—including the money lenders in South Asian villages, the labor brokers in sending countries, the manpower agencies in the Gulf states, the citizens who sponsor foreign labor, and managers and supervisors who serve as these sponsors' proxies—as a migration industry that is not only geared to aggrandizing profit from the labor of foreign migrants, but also capable of deriving profit from the migration process itself.

As noted, these conclusions about unskilled and semi-skilled labor migration to the Gulf states serve as a starting point for this chapter; the more detailed arguments by which I support this position can be found elsewhere.[5] In presenting these findings and conclusions at various conferences and meetings over the years, I have encountered one recurring question, paraphrased as follows: "If things are as bad as you say, then why do migrants keep coming?"[6] This chapter endeavors to answer that question. While the fieldwork informing my answer spans a series of projects conducted in Saudi Arabia, the United Arab Emirates (UAE), Bahrain, and Qatar, I rely specifically upon the findings of a research project funded by the Center for International and Regional Studies at the Georgetown University School of Foreign Service in Qatar.[7] Through this particular project, I was able to follow a diverse group of ten low-income labor migrants through a year and a half of their lives in Qatar. I conducted monthly interviews with these men and women, and those interviews collectively provided me with their nuanced perspectives on the challenges and dilemmas they faced in their everyday lives in Qatar, as well as a perspective on the strategies they devised to overcome many of the challenges

---

[4] William Walters, "Deportation, Expulsion, and the International Police of Aliens," *Citizenship Studies* 6 (2002): pp. 265–92.

[5] Gardner, "Engulfed", pp. 196–223; Gardner, *City of Strangers*.

[6] Out of respect to the colleague who first presented me with this line of inquiry, I refer to this as the "Bruce Mann question."

[7] The basis of this paper is field-based research conducted in Saudi Arabia (1999), the United Arab Emirates (2002), Bahrain (2002–03) and Qatar (2008–present). These various research projects were supported by the Saudi Arabian Meteorological and Environmental Protection Agency, the Foreign Language Area Studies Program, the Fulbright Program, the Wenner-Gren Foundation, Qatar University, and the Qatar National Research Fund. While these various projects form a backdrop to the analysis presented here, I rely specifically on the ethnographic data gathered under the project entitled "A Longitudinal Analysis of Low-Income Laborers in Contemporary Qatar," funded by the Center for International and Regional Studies at the Georgetown University School of Foreign Service in Qatar.

encountered. The project also allowed me the opportunity to visit these migrants' families and communities in Nepal, India and Sri Lanka. Through those interviews and conversations with migrants and their families, I began to discern an answer to the aforementioned question, and in the ethnographic tradition, I use their experiences and their words to illustrate my arguments. That answer, in three sections, comprises the remainder of this chapter.

From economic poverty to structural violence

Economic concerns obviously play a key role in the impulse to depart one's home for the opportunities offered by employment in the Gulf states. While I will eventually complicate the simplistic logic underpinning this statement, it is undoubtedly true that salary levels in the Gulf represent the primary attraction of employment in the region for many migrants. For example, Ram,[8] a forty-year-old migrant from the hilly regions of Nepal, left his village at the age of fourteen to make his way in the world. He worked in many different jobs in Nepal and India—for years he worked in a Chinese-owned leather tannery in Kolkata, earning IR 2500 ($54) monthly, but eventually he left because of the dangerously unhygienic conditions of the factory work. He later found work as a driver in India, earning IR 7500 ($160) a month minus expenses, but by then he was married with children, and was unable to make ends meet. In 2008, his brother-in-law arranged for work as a driver in Qatar, with the promise of a monthly salary of QR 600 ($165) with expenses paid, and the possibility of earning even more. In Ram's particular case, that promise proved to be a mirage—upon arrival in Qatar, he received only QR 500 ($137), and, as I will explain later in the chapter, his sponsor withheld several months' wages to cover the costs of driving instruction. Despite the problems he encountered, it is clear that the contractually promised wage levels in the Gulf states remain competitive in South Asian terms, and often substantially surpass salary levels in the poorer nations from which many migrants come. Because this economically grounded justification for migration is so widespread in the migrants' narratives about the decision to come to the Gulf, it certainly represents the first answer to the question of why, in the face of such difficulties, men and women continue to stream to the region.

The ethnographic approach, however, provides a good opportunity to complicate this simple logic, for the interviews I conducted contained stories and

[8] All the names that appear here are pseudonyms selected by the participants in the study.

explanations that suggested a wide variety of extra-economic explanations for labor migration to the Gulf. Like Ram, Roshan was another of the ten migrants I spent time with between 2008 and 2010. In early 2008, conflicts between the Tamil Tiger rebels and the state forces reached a crescendo in the region surrounding his small village in the northern reaches of Sri Lanka. Despite growing up amidst a veritable civil war, Roshan had been an adept student, and his family worked hard to stay beyond the social and political margins of the conflict. In the spring of 2008, however, rumors began to spread that his sister's fiancé was an agent for the Tamil Tigers; later these rumors evolved into a contention that Roshan's future brother-in-law was a double agent of the state. On the eve of the young couple's wedding, masked motorcycle-borne gunmen shot and killed the young groom outside his pre-wedding party. The family subsequently spiraled into crisis. Roshan, eighteen at the time, seemed a likely target as well, although the family was unsure if it was the government forces or the rebels whom they should fear. Like many other families in the area, they feared Roshan's walk to school would be the last time they would see their son, so his education ceased. Weeks later, he was detained by the police, beaten, and, by his own account, charged with suspect dealings. Following the paths of many others enveloped in the Sri Lankan conflict, the family arranged for the young man to migrate to Qatar. I first met Roshan a week after his arrival in the Gulf.

Roshan's family is a poor family, and their financial problems were only compounded by the violence in the region. The economics of migration certainly played prominently in the context of their decision; after all, there were jobs in Qatar. But in my ongoing conversations with Roshan and, later, with his family in northern Sri Lanka, it became increasingly clear that it was the safety and survival of their son that drove them to mortgage farmland and pawn the household matriarch's jewelry to fund his trip abroad. Similar stories emerged in my discussions with members of the Nepalese contingent of migrants in Qatar, for many of them had arrived with stories of becoming embroiled in the Maoist insurgency sweeping through the low Terai plain found along Nepal's southern border. Divendra, another labor migrant, described how corruption in the Nepalese government left the small country with only an intermittent supply of electricity, and connected this corruption to his own decision to migrate to the Gulf. Recalling his own failed attempt to build a computer training institute, he noted that,

The main problem came when we were getting a lot of problems with the electricity. The electricity would be cut for six or seven hours. My business was totally dependent on electricity. If there's no electricity for six or seven hours, especially in the daytime, then no one will come. How can I operate the computers? And I don't have enough money to buy a generator, because the cheapest generator in Nepal costs one lakh [$1340]. So I cannot think about that. I was managing to run the institute, but when the electricity ... first it was five to six hours, then it was seven or eight hours—finally I thought it's no good. So I had to close the institute. I shut down my business and came here.

The recurrence of these sorts of stories with many of the migrants in my small study and, perhaps more tellingly, amongst many of the other men in the camps I frequently visited, displaces the economics of migration from its central place in the rational calculus driving migration to the Gulf. Certainly the calculations in the migrants' heads often involve money, debt, and prevailing wage levels, but the conditions they face in their home countries are often connected to socio-political forces that spill outside a strictly economic calculus. The concept of structural violence provides a more theoretically comprehensive angle on the forces driving out-migration—the widespread economic penury connected to decades of structural adjustment, for example, can be conceptually conflated with the violence and conflict that inevitably produces quasi-refugees dependent upon migration and the remittances it produces.[9]

Roshan's story yields a second point that merits further discussion. Like almost all of the South Asian men I have encountered in the Gulf, Roshan arrived in the Middle East not as a rational and individual economic agent, but rather as the emissary of a household livelihood strategy. In Roshan's case, all the arrangements were made for him by his family, and this was the case for many of the South Asian men I encountered in Qatar and Bahrain. The money needed to migrate as an unskilled laborer (typically $1,500 to $3,000) is generated at the household level from resources controlled by the family's patriarch; the decision concerning which member of the family will migrate

---

[9] See Johan Galtung's seminal work and the subsequent articulation of the concept by Paul Farmer and Nancy Scheper-Hughes. In previous work, I have also used Eric Wolf's notion of structural power to expand the definition of structural violence to encompass the forces that produce highly exploitative relationships between migrants and citizen-sponsors in the Gulf. See Johan Galtung, "Violence, Peace and Peace Research," *Journal of Peace Research*, 6 (1969), pp. 167–91; Paul Farmer, "An Anthropology of Structural Violence," *Current Anthropology*, 45 (2004), pp. 305–25; Nancy Scheper-Hughes, "Dangerous and Endangered Youth: Social Structures and Determinants of Violence," *Annals of the New York Academy of Sciences*, Volume 1036 (2004), pp. 13–46; Eric Wolf, *Envisioning Power: Ideologies of Dominance and Crisis* (Berkeley: University of California Press, 1999); Gardner, *City of Strangers*.

to the Gulf is decided at the level of the extended family; and the remittances generated by that individual's labor while abroad are often under the control of the migrant's parents. Vasu, for example, was a young labor migrant from a rural village in south India. He had worked as a driver in that village. His uncle, already at work in Qatar, helped arrange for him to come and work as a tea-boy for a company that serves one of Qatar's large government ministries. In describing that decision, Vasu explained his family's rationale:

My parents, my brother, my wife, my daughter and I were living in a very small house ... It's a government house. The government allots houses to farmers in our area. We don't own any property. We don't have land to call our own. Now, since I'm married, we need a bigger house. So we took a loan of IR 80,000 [$1,704] plus interest from a riatu [a wealthy landowner] ... I don't know exactly what the agreement was because my father arranged the loan.

As his concluding statement suggests, Vasu was entirely unaware of the economics of his migration. Indeed, his entire working life had been directly enmeshed in the interests of the extended family. Vasu had originally dropped out of school to begin to work so that the family might assemble a dowry for his younger sister. As the family's finances continued to sputter, they sought a strategy that might allow them to eventually build a larger house or perhaps purchase some land. And as with most South Asian migrants, Vasu's remittances were largely controlled by his father. In the end, his and his family's hopes for a better future were dashed in a horrific accident that left his uncle dead and Vasu severely injured. During his long recovery, the company stopped paying his salary and the money stopped flowing home. Finally, his visa was cancelled, and as Vasu scrambled to find a new job that might accommodate his new disability, his family descended into a financial cataclysm.

As this section suggests, part of the answer to the question of why migrants keep flowing to the region requires that we dissemble some of the premises that underlie that question. One of those premises is that the migrant fits the mold of *homo economicus*—in other words, that she or he is an individual, rational economic agent. As these men's stories suggest, the unit at work in the decision process to migrate to the Gulf is typically not the individual but the family (and, in the case of South Asia, the extended family). While that family may or may not have perfect information about the wages and conditions migrants potentially face in the Gulf states (issues I will deal with more directly in the remainder of this chapter), it is often not the migrant himself who is making the decision about the migrant's sojourn. This social fact complicates the logic of Gulf migration: in many cases, migrants keep coming because their families insist upon it. I have also contended that the economic rationale for migration, while certainly important, is often not the only factor involved in the decision to migrate. Utilizing the concept of structural violence, we can begin to connect the low wage levels and lack of opportunity many of these potential migrants face in their homeland with a much wider array of social and political forces that are intricately intertwined with the decision to migrate to the Gulf.

Contractual deception and the search for ignorance

When one looks for patterns and recurring events in the lives of the unskilled and semi-skilled laborers who arrive in the Gulf states, deception—particularly contractual deception—seems to occupy the center stage in their narratives. Many of the men in this study (and many of the men I have encountered over the years in the Gulf) arrive to a job that is substantially different from the position described to them in their home country. Most commonly this deception involves salary levels, working hours, and type of employment. While this deception is widespread, locating a particular juncture at which responsibility for it can be pinned is an impossible task: as the narratives I will present describe, this disinformation can come from a variety of parties who comprise the migration system connecting Qatar and the other Gulf states to the sending countries of Asia, Africa and the Middle East.

Ram, the Nepalese driver whom I introduced in the previous section, built upon his years of experience as a driver in India when he departed for Qatar. Through a friend already in Doha, Ram was able to arrange for a visa enabling him to work as driver for a Qatari family. Arriving in Qatar, he was given QR 100 ($27.50) for food and expenditures, and taken to a room in a labor camp within a mile of his sponsor's home. Very little happened in the first few months, and Ram struggled to understand his circumstances. He received no salary, but in the second month his sponsor gave him another QR 100 for food and other expenditures. The Qatari sponsor promised that he would receive his salary once he passed the driving exam, but the chain of events leading to that endpoint was formidable: Ram had to pass the medical exam, obtain an official ID, enroll in a 40-day driving course, and pass the driving exam, in that specific order. At the conclusion of his second month in Qatar, only the medical test was complete, and Ram finally confronted his sponsor. Shortly after that confrontation, he described his situation to me:

I am very much worried because I have not received any of the salary promised to me, and my sponsor has delayed my entry into the driving school. I complained to him that I have received no salary and haven't been enrolled in the driving school, and so within a few days he produced my official ID. At least now I can enroll in the driving class. But I still won't receive any salary for several months. What can I do? How can I send my family the money they need?

The weeks following our conversation were equally difficult. Other migrants reported that he needed to pay the driving instructor extra money in order to pass the exam, but Ram had no extra money to give. He finally found another migrant willing to loan him QR 2,000 ($550), but opted to send this home to his desperate family rather than use it for the driving instructor. He felt lucky when he received notice that he had passed the driving exam. His sponsor, however, informed him that his pay would be QR 500 ($137), not QR 600 ($165). By his own estimation, Ram had been working twenty hours a day on average, and for much of that time he endured various gardening and cleaning duties on top of his work as a driver. He confronted his sponsor several times in the following months, and while he was eventually able to obtain the QR 600 salary originally promised to him, he received no pay for the first three months of his time in Qatar. As his sponsor contended, over QR 3,000 ($824) had been spent for the driving course, identification, medical test, and other costs—the sponsor was carrying this debt for Ram.

Such scenarios were common in the small pool of participants I followed in Qatar. Ramesh, an enterprising young migrant from the Nepalese Terai, was promised a job as a supervisor, but arrived to find he would work as a tea-boy at a significantly lower pay level. Rao, an Indian migrant from Andhra Pradesh, had both trained and worked at a welder in India, and departed for Qatar under the impression that he would be welding there as well. Upon arrival, however, he was demoted to welder-helper and its lower salary level. Divendra, Binod and Sanjay—three other participants in the project—arrived to jobs that roughly resembled those described to them in their homes (Nepal, Nepal, and India, respectively), but simply went unpaid for much of their time in Doha. Their companies were three or four months behind the promised salary schedule. The last of these three migrants, Sanjay, simply gave up on his company and returned to Kerala after his third month in Qatar. As all of this suggests, labor migrants frequently encounter misinformation and deception in their journey to the Gulf.

No single conduit shuttles labor to the Gulf. As the above stories suggest, some migrants arrange their sojourn in the Gulf with the help of relatives or friends with some connection to sponsors in the GCC states. Others work through a system of labor brokers that connects most regions of South Asia,

Africa, and Southeast Asia to the opportunities of the Gulf states.[10] This brokerage system may include subagents who move from village to village in search of potential migrants (and therefore profit). These agencies may or may not be registered with the state. Legitimate brokers, whether registered or not, may or may not have good information about the jobs they purvey. For example, in discussing the working conditions the men he had sent to the Gulf face, one labor broker in south India clearly articulated how little he knew about the working conditions in the Gulf:

I don't know much about the working conditions in Doha. It depends on the company and the type of work and also the post of each worker. For example, a supervisor doesn't work under the sun the whole time. On the other hand, a welder works under the sun for about 8 hours a day. Not more than that. I don't think they work for 10 or 12 hours a day. All I know is that the companies who contact us are reputed and legitimate. And Qatar is a desert so the workers know what to expect. During the training session we make them work under the sun for a few hours ...

While labor brokerage firms and other formalized conduits play an important role in migration to the Gulf states, chain migration remains a vital conduit for tens of thousands of migrants to the Arabian Peninsula. As a result, migrants often find themselves complicit in the contractual deception that commonly occurs. By the end of his first year in Qatar, for example, Divendra's employer, a small construction company, faced a desperate labor shortage. Attrition (largely driven by the non-payment of promised wages) had left the company with too few drivers for the various trucks that served as the basis for the small business. Despite the fact that his company owed him and the other employees over three months of back wages, Divendra, who through hard work and extraordinary diplomacy had gained the trust of his Egyptian manager, was asked to utilize his networks in Nepal to bring a cohort of new truck drivers and laborers to Qatar. This put Divendra in a quandary. Could he live with the burden of bringing new migrants into such a problematic situation? The men would certainly blame him if things went awry, and from his experiences in the company, that was almost assured. At the same time, his own contract was approaching its conclusion, and if he did not keep his manager happy, it was entirely possible that the manager would significantly delay his

---

[10] See Gamburd, *The Kitchen Spoon's Handle*; Rachel Silvey, "Transnational Domestication: State Power and Indonesian Migrant Women in Saudi Arabia," *Political Geography*, 23 (2004), pp. 245–64; Prema Kurien, *Kaleidoscopic Ethnicity: International Migration and the Reconstruction of Community Identities in India* (New Brunswick, NJ: Rutgers University Press, 2002), pp. 62–4.

departure. Divendra stalled for several months, but then the manager's tone became more urgent. Describing the situation, Divendra noted that,

Whenever the managers ask me to find replacements, I make up excuses and tell them that most of the Nepali men I know are going to Dubai soon ... My general manager told me to put an ad in the newspaper in Nepal for heavy duty drivers, and he told me that I would be responsible for everything. It would be my responsibility to shortlist the candidates so that he could issue visas for them. I'm very confused right now. I don't know what to do. There are only five months left on my contract. I think I have to play a game so that I can listen to the general manager and at the same time save the people in Nepal from entering his trap.

"[Andrew] How will you do that?"

I have a friend in Kathmandu. I will tell him to send an official email as XYZ manpower agency. I will send an official email to the make believe agency, and say that the company needs a few workers and I will tell my friend to reply. I will tell him to say that it would take about four months to recruit these men in Nepal so that I can buy some time with the general manager. After four months, it will be time for me to return and I will tell the manager that I would send him the CVs as soon as I go back to Nepal. Then when I finally go back, I will disappear. That's my plan.

As Divendra delayed, the general manager found a way to sweeten the offer. The manager suggested that Divendra and his Nepalese co-worker, Sam, would be welcome to extract (and keep) a QR 1,500 ($413) or perhaps even QR 2,000 ($550) fee from each of the thirty successful applicants. For Divendra and Sam—young men earning a salary of $330 a month, most of which was directed to the moneylenders who financed their journey in the first place—this was an extraordinary amount of money. Divendra and Sam had already expressed an ethical concern with the proposal, for any men they brought to the company would face the same verbal abuse, non-payment of wages, and exploitation that had led to the current attrition in the first place. As we explored these issues further, however, Sam put a more practical frame on their decision to avoid facilitating more Nepalese migration:

[Sam] I said okay, I will try my best to find some new drivers in Nepal with the licenses for driving heavy trucks. But in truth I will not do this for the company, because these people, they are very bad and the company now has a very bad reputation. If I bring these people here, then certainly these people will face many problems. So I don't want to bring anyone here ...

[Andrew] So let's see ... that would be [calculating] ... QR 37,500 or so. That's $10,000! That's big money!

[Sam] Yes, I could earn that much money from these twenty-five or thirty visas. But the main problem is when these people face the real problems here in Doha with a company like this, they will tell all the truth about those problems to their family members and their parents in Nepal. And now the situation in Nepal is very bad. Again the Maoists are going to strike, and if by mistake anyone speaks of this to the Maoists, they will kill me. So why would I knowingly bring this trouble to myself?

[Divendra] $10,000 he would be getting, but he would be facing a $50,000 problem at home.

In the next section of this chapter, I explore the role that migrants themselves play in the representation of the Gulf and their experiences there. In this section, I have used the experiences and perspectives of several participants in this project to portray the complexities of this migration system and the multiple junctions at which deception is purveyed. In answering the question as to why migrants keep coming to the Gulf, I contend that we must also look to the complexities of a system that produces misinformation and disinformation across the transnational divide. As I have suggested, labor brokers provide one of the most visible links in this chain, but they are often working with poor information about the working conditions in the Gulf, and as Divendra's and Sam's experiences make clear, migrants themselves are often called upon to participate in this process and, for profit, represent employment in the Gulf in ways that differ significantly from the reality on the ground.

Labor migrants and the image of the Gulf

In late 2002, I was conducting fieldwork in Bahrain and, for bureaucratic reasons, I required another dozen passport photographs for the various forms and badges associated with my host institution. I made my way to a small photography studio at the end of the street, and after a brief discussion with the photographer/clerk I was ushered into the studio itself, located in the back room of the building. In that room were all the various accessories one would expect to find in a photography studio, along with an office desk located prominently on the stage side of the room. Next to the desk was a clothes pole with various sports jackets, button-up shirts, and clip-on ties. On the wall I could see examples of photographs that made use of this stage, set and props. I asked the proprietor about these photographs, and he described the reality of the situation in very straightforward terms: men who work menial and socially demeaning jobs burnish their image by sending home photographs of themselves sitting behind this desk in suit and tie. Across the transnational divide, custodians become office workers, tea boys become accountants, and clerks become managers.

Over time and years of fieldwork, this episode from 2002 evolved from an odd juncture in my fieldnotes to the central example of an interconnected web of observations that collectively point to the widespread and systemic generation of disinformation about working and living conditions in the Gulf. Without a doubt, migrants themselves are actively engaged in the production of this disinformation. These are pre-eminently understandable actions—men and women seek to protect their reputations, to assuage their worried families, and to shape their social identities in the publics to which they will eventually return. As Filippo and Caroline Osella have described, migration to the Gulf also produces subjectivities aligned to a set of pre-established identities (like the "Gulfie") constructed in an earlier era when the association between Gulf migration and wealth was more assured.[11] Collectively, however, these actions contribute directly to the misrepresentation of conditions in the Gulf, and are therefore another integral component in the answer to the question at hand.

In the current decade, images have come to play a central role in the processes I seek to chart. The proliferation of camera phones and digital cameras means that even at the lowest echelons of the transmigrant workforce, images play an integral role in transnational communication and identity construction. The men and women I tracked in Qatar all had access to camera phones and/or cameras, and the production of images was one of the primary activities during their days off. Middle class denizens of Qatar and the other Gulf states are familiar with the sight of workers photographing one another in the green landscaped sites in front of shopping malls, in traffic circles, or along the Corniche. Perhaps what is less clear is that these sites are carefully selected by the migrants, and contrast sharply with the sites these men and women omit from their photographs. As Divendra described:

If we visited our camp today, and if I just stood in front of the apartment where you park your car, and we just took a photograph and sent it to my family, how would they feel? They would feel worried. They would think, if their accommodation is like this, what must their food and room be like? They often ask for photographs of where we stay, of the food, of the rooms, of the kitchen. They want to see it. They want to know what it's like where we stay. We just tell them that we don't have a camera, or that it's broken. I just keep telling them I will take photographs and I will send them to you later. These are the things that we do ... so when we send these photographs of us in these friendly and beautiful places [like shopping malls and parks], they will be happy for us.

[11] Caroline Osella and Filippo Osella, "Migration, Money and Masculinity in Kerala," *Journal of the Royal Anthropological Institute*, 6 (2000), pp. 117–33.

As Divendra notes, his portrayal of his life in Qatar to family and friends is heavily edited. He carefully avoids including any images that might raise the concerns of his family, and present a carefully managed image of his time abroad.

Beginning in 2008 and 2009, many of the men in the labor camps I visited were seeking to purchase low-end netbook computers with any savings they could accrue during their work abroad. These netbooks are the latest entries into the lexicon of symbolically laden goods associated with successful migration to the Gulf (earlier it was Ray-ban sunglasses, gold chains, mobile phones, and digital cameras). In addition to their symbolic function, the presence of these netbooks in the labor camps gives many of the men access to Facebook and other social networking sites where more comprehensive portrayals of life in the Gulf can be articulated and tended. Like the images they send home, the portrayals amassed on Facebook and similar sites portray a green, leisurely, and high-consumerist life in place of the harsh realities many migrants face in their day to day lives in the Gulf.

While many of the men and women who migrate to Qatar and the other Gulf states depart their homeland with an image of the Gulf as a bountiful land of opportunity, they face significant challenges once in place in those states. Across the board, one of the most common difficulties they face is underpayment and non-payment of wages. With families and friends receiving only the sanitized version of the Gulf experience produced by the images and stories that travel back home, many migrants who face underpayment or non-payment of wages often begin to borrow money to keep up appearances. Ram, the driver I introduced early in this chapter, went four months without salary—he was receiving driving instruction, and his sponsor deducted the costs of the course from his salary—while Ram's family continued to plead for money. As noted earlier in the chapter, Ram finally borrowed QR 2,000 ($550) from friends and remitted the money to his wife in Nepal. Similarly, Binod, a heavy truck driver from Nepal, was engaged in a protracted legal battle with his sponsor for much of 2009 and 2010. In the midst of that legal battle, the company stopped paying Binod, and Binod stopped working. He spent his days alone at the camp, and while he was very careful with his spending, his debts nonetheless slowly mounted. By the time his case was settled in June of 2010, he owed various friends thousands of Qatari riyals. Much of that money had been borrowed to send home to his family, and was part of his attempt to present a story of seamless and successful earning while abroad.

The carefully managed images of life in the Gulf became a particularly acute concern in planning my trips to visit with the families of the migrants I tracked in Qatar. While all of the labor migrants were happy that I would visit their families and communities in South Asia, further discussions and pre-travel planning revealed concerns about potential damage I might cause to the images of life and work they had so carefully constructed from afar. In the interviews preceding my visits to Nepal, Sri Lanka, and India, I worked carefully with these migrants to grasp the limitations they wished to impose on my interactions with their families and, more specifically, on my descriptions of their life in Qatar. Many of these restrictions focused on the conditions in the labor camp: many of the camps lack running water and secure electricity connections, and many migrants live in extremely crowded and unhygienic conditions. The migrants sought (and received) my complicity in hiding these often difficult living conditions from family and friends in their home communities.

As I have already noted, these are certainly understandable actions: as the migrants themselves describe, they are mostly interested in protecting the emotional state of their loved ones back home, and the edited versions of life in Qatar and the other Gulf states are intended to insulate their family and friends from concern over the harsh realities many migrants face in the Arabian Peninsula. In aggregate, however, tens of thousands of migrants engaged in the production of a sanitized image of life in the Gulf fuel out-migration from these sending countries, for that image omits many of the exploitative and challenging aspects of the typical migration experience. To answer the question as to why migrants keep flowing to the region in spite of the often-challenging conditions they potentially face, we must accommodate the fact that migrants themselves, along with the labor brokers described in the previous section, construct an image of life in the Gulf that disguises or omits many of the significant challenges transnational labor migrants typically face.[12]

[12] In her examination of the Mexican/American flow of migrants, Balli provides an answer to this question as well. As one migrant described, "We get too carried away with the success stories we hear about in the United States ... We go there and pursue wayward lives. We cheat on our wives and ignore our children. And then we rent expensive cars and jewelry when we visit so that our families in Mexico will think that we have made it. We entice others to come back across the border with us, telling them lies about how good and easy it is. We tell them they can stay in our homes, but once they're around we get tired of them eating our food." Cecilia Balli, "The Border is Wide: Guarding the Southern Flank of the American Dream," *Harper's Magazine*, 313 (2006), p. 67. Similarly, George Packer quotes Folarin Gbadebo-Smith, the chairman of a district of Lagos Island, who also describes the

Conclusion

To recapitulate, in answering the question as to why unskilled and low-skill migrants continue to stream to the Gulf states in spite of the difficult conditions and exploitative labor relations many of them encounter in the region, I have argued that a variety of factors are at work in the calculus of Gulf migration. First, there is no doubt that the salary levels in the Gulf states remain competitive in the global context, and that the economic calculations these salary levels drive are a primary motivation for the continuing strength of these migration flows. Behind that simple fact, however, is the much more complicated mechanics of Gulf migration. I have argued that a variety of extra-economic concerns often play a central role in the decision to migrate, and that the decision to migrate often does not belong to the individual migrant, but rather to the familial unit. These factors complicate simplistic portrayals of the migration decision, and as I have argued here, these factors also foster the proliferation of poor information in the migration process.

In my close examination of the lives of a small set of labor migrants in Qatar, I have also begun to delineate the multiple junctures at which misinformation and disinformation are purveyed within this transnational migration system. Subagents and labor brokers in the sending countries often have poor information about the contracts they arrange, and profit incentives often become aligned with the purveying of disinformation about the challenges and difficulties men and women often face in the Gulf. Manpower agencies, citizen-sponsors and their proxies in the receiving states similarly benefit from the ongoing flow of migrants with incomplete or incorrect information about labor conditions in the Gulf states. With the scale of this migration flow in mind and the profit that is drawn from the migration process itself, I have contended that we can envision this system as a "migration industry" that uses

---

distorted picture that flows back to the village: "Come Christmas, everybody in Lagos—the successful and the unsuccessful—packs their bags and goes off to the rural areas to show off what they have achieved," Gbadebo-Smith said. "Some achievements are real, for some it's just a mirage, but everybody's there showing off. So the young people in the villages very quickly come to the conclusion that 'Hey, I've got to go to Lagos, make enough to be able to come back here, and to show off.'" In this way, the West African countryside is being rapidly depopulated. Cecilia Balli, "The Border is Wide: Guarding the Southern Flank of the American Dream," *Harper's Magazine*, 313 (2006), pp. 63–70; George Packer, "The Megacity: Decoding the Chaos of Lagos," *The New Yorker* (November 13, 2006).

poor information and disinformation to extract profit from the flow of unskilled migrants to the region.

Finally, I have contended that migrants themselves undoubtedly play a role in burnishing the image of the Gulf sojourn. By carefully grooming the portrayal of their time in the Gulf, individual migrants collectively contribute to the production of an image of the Gulf that often omits the primary challenges and difficulties that unskilled laborers experience in the region. These omissions are often tied to their desire to maintain their social status or placate worried families; however, through chain migration, the migrants' transmission of disinformation can also become tied to the profitable junctures of this migration industry.

Altogether, these multiple and overlapping factors complicate and problematize some of the fundamental premises underlying the question driving this chapter. The long tradition of *homo economicus* portrays humans—and migrants—as self-interested agents who make rational choices from the constellation of options presented to them. While the arguments presented in this chapter pose no challenge to the rationality of the Gulf migrant, that rationality faces a blizzard of misinformation and disinformation that renders that rationality almost meaningless. Nor is the migrant best conceived as a rational individual actor: more typically, I have noted, the migrant is the emissary of a familial livelihood strategy, and the purportedly rational decision to migrate is diffused within the extended family. As this suggests, analyses of this migration industry need to more directly apprehend the connection between imperfect information and profit.

4

Socio-Spatial Boundaries in Abu Dhabi

Jane Bristol-Rhys

The states of the Persian Gulf are characterized by varying degrees of dependence on foreign workers, and while there are many commonalities born of the rapid development of the petrochemical industry, concomitant urbanization, small indigenous populations, and a dearth of education and training, there are significant differences that require situated analysis. While the cities of the Gulf all have substantial populations of migrant foreign workers, the living conditions that the migrants experience and their ability to circulate and socialize on the city streets, and the ways in which they perceive their social position, vary significantly. The experience of a migrant working in Jeddah is very different from that of one working in Muscat, Dubai, or Abu Dhabi. In fact, repeat migrants, those who have completed labor contract periods in more than one Gulf country, articulate these different experiences clearly and advise prospective migrants to choose their next destination carefully. An Egyptian, now living in Abu Dhabi after spending six years in Saudi Arabia, articulated his experiences as he gave advice to a younger man who was contemplating taking a job in Saudi Arabia:

You won't like it there; they treat Egyptians very badly in Saudi. Don't think that because you have an education that the Saudis will respect you; no, they will treat you like a *farash* (a cleaner) who is of little importance. You are just a body that works and the fact that you are Muslim and an Arab is not taken into account. Egyptians they know will just take the abuse and keep working because we need the money; we are the poor of Saudi. It is better here for you. There are some Emiratis who are arrogant and flaunt their riches in our faces but generally they are polite and can be quite generous.

Ahmad, the man speaking, had been living in Abu Dhabi for seven years. He had worked for two different educational institutions as a college professor. Over the course of several interviews Ahmad expressed opinions which were echoed by many others who talked to me:

Each of the Gulf countries offers work but the working conditions and the living conditions are very different. Some say that Kuwait was best before the Iraqi invasion, but now it is difficult there for Arabs. Here (the UAE) has been good for me and for most Egyptians. Emiratis are easier to work for; they respect that we are also Muslim and treat us well. But my experiences are not the same as a young man who comes with no training, like a driver or a guard. Those people I know have problems and they are often not paid what they were promised and rarely are they paid on time.

This chapter examines migrants' experiences in one Gulf city, Abu Dhabi. The information presented here is the product of ethnographic research conducted from 2001 to 2010. Ethnographic research, as I am using it here, means extensive, often multiple interviews; direct observation of behavior and action in public venues; participant observation in which I engaged with migrants at social clubs and centers, and on outings; observation of migrants interacting with government officials; and, when interviews could not be conducted, question and answer periods with migrants on the streets of Abu Dhabi. For some of the questions and interviews, notably those in Urdu, Malayalam, and Hindi, it was necessary to have the translation help of friends and acquaintances. I have also been able to contrast my experience as a foreign migrant, working and living in Abu Dhabi, with those communicated by my interlocutors. Additionally, I have had multiple opportunities to observe the vacillating levels of attention, courtesy and service that are meted out to migrants of different nationalities and socio-economic strata. My research has also included an examination of the socio-historical context in which foreign labor has become so necessary and dominant. Dependency on imported foreign labor has evolved over time, and in the case of Abu Dhabi, a part of the evolutionary track has been a reaction to increasing numbers of migrants, not a proactive strategic management of labor requirements or indeed of the requirements of the laborers.

The organization of the chapter is somewhat chronological as I begin with a review of the socio-historical context of pre-oil Abu Dhabi. I then consider how the organic evolution of the city and its increasing numbers of foreigners have constructed spatial divisions that effectively separate certain classes of migrants from the rest of the urban population. A part of this consideration includes an examination of the different categories of migrants that are in current use and the manner in which laborer and worker have become qualitatively distinct from "bachelor" and "expat." This is followed by a description of the spatial divisions that divide Abu Dhabi into "no-go zones" for some migrants and have resulted in some public areas, such as parks and beaches, being considered "foreign" areas to be avoided by Emiratis. Emirati or Emarati (the *nisbah* adjective formed from al Emarat al 'Arabiyah al Muttahidah) describes an individual who is a citizen of the United Arab Emirates (UAE). Strictly speaking no Emiratis existed before the formation of the country in 1972; however, I use the term here to denote also the native population before that time, in preference to "indigenous" and "native." Finally, I examine the social and behavioral elements that separate migrants from each other and from Emiratis.

The Gulf city

In addition to the shared characteristic of dependence on foreign labor, all Persian Gulf states have also experienced rapid urbanization. Most commonly this occurred within the context of existing port cities, such as those of Dubai, Manama, and Doha.[1] In order to understand the explosive growth that transformed Abu Dhabi, it is useful to review the development of Gulf cities generally.

"The Gulf city" is a particular type that evolved from the late 1950s when oil was discovered in the region. The rapid post-oil development of Gulf cities occurred within a set of circumstances that are unique to the political economy, geography, ecology, society and demography of the region.[2] Certainly there is an element of fascination associated with the growth and development

---

[1] Nelida Fuccaro, *Histories of City and State in the Persian Gulf: Manama since 1800* (Cambridge University Press, 2009).

[2] Janet Abu Lughod, "Urbanization and Social Change in the Arab World," *Ekistics*, 50 (1983), pp. 223–32; Ian J. Seccombe, "Labour Migration to the Arabia Gulf: Evolution and Characteristics 1920–1950," *Bulletin of the British Society for Middle Eastern Studies*, 10 (1983), pp. 3–20.

of the cities of the Gulf because it all happened so fast. A man who worked in the planning department in Abu Dhabi in the late 1960s described the experience as something akin to being "asked to build Manhattan in seven days."[3] Indeed, many of the people I have interviewed who were involved in the first rush to develop Abu Dhabi shake their heads and wonder "how we ever kept up with the plans and in some cases we couldn't, by the time we went to inspect a plot of land to give the building permission, the house was half-built."[4] One of the most apt descriptions of the rapid change is Abu Lughod's: "for seldom has the world seen a more striking experiment *in situ* of instant urbanization and hot house forced social change."[5]

So rapid were the changes that urbanized the towns of the Gulf that it is difficult to compare their development to environments elsewhere. They are known as the petro-urban cities of the Gulf.[6] They are urban centers that, while not industrial in themselves, manage all aspects of the political economy of the oil generated wealth and, as such, are considered distinct from urban forms found elsewhere in the industrialized world and those evolving in developing countries.[7] The urban oil-rich Gulf societies have each emerged with a particular type of oil city, not an industrial oil city but one in which oil wealth has shaped both the physical structure and social composition.

Khalaf identifies phases of development that are common to the Gulf cities.[8] The first phase marks the beginnings of development from coastal towns and villages organized traditionally (usually along tribal lines) to cities that could accommodate the people, equipment, services, offices and banks necessary to initiate oil production and export. The next phase of development included rapid growth of what were now becoming urban centers with an influx of oil workers, engineers, planners, bankers, advisors, and all who

---

[3] Ahmad Salah Al Harbi, "Interview," ed. Jane Bristol-Rhys (Abu Dhabi, 2004).

[4] Bin Brook Al Hamiri, "Interview," ed. Jane Bristol-Rhys (Abu Dhabi, 2005).

[5] Lughod, "Urbanization and Social Change in the Arab World," pp. 223–32.

[6] Ibid., pp. 6–12.

[7] Ibid., pp. 223–32; Fuad Khouri, "Urbanization and City Management in the Middle East," in H. Riviln and K. Helmer (eds), *The Changing Middle Eastern City* (Binghamton: SUNY Press, 1981); Mohammad Riad, "Some aspects of Petro-urbanism in the Arab Gulf States," *Bulletin of the Faculty of Humanities and Social Sciences* 4 (1981), pp. 7–24.

[8] Sulayman Khalaf, "The Evolution of the Gulf City Type, Oil and Globalization," in John W. Fox, Nada Mourtada-Sabbah and Muhammed al Mutawa (eds), *Globalization and the Gulf* (London: Routledge, 2006), pp. 244–65.

were needed to design, construct and install major segments of infrastructure: roads, ports, desalination plants, electrical plants, hospitals, schools and airports. This rapid phase began in the late 1960s for Dubai and in the early 1970s for Abu Dhabi. For both cities throughout the 1970s, development and construction continued at a remarkable pace as hospitals, schools, colleges, hotels, housing, shops and warehouses were built to accommodate the exploding population of expatriates and the booming, though considerably less dramatic, growth of the urban Emirati population as people moved into the cities to take advantage of new opportunities and services. A significant feature of these cities is the monumental architecture of palaces, sports arenas, exhibition grounds, hotels and mosques, constructed as one means of distributing oil revenues to the citizenry, but also as visible articulations of the beneficence of the welfare states through the construction of an "image of unlimited good" for their citizens.[9] Rapid urbanization continued until the late 1980s, after which there was a phase of somewhat slower growth and development that was necessary to keep up with the growing population, improvement of services and the infrastructure of roads and telecommunications.[10]

Development in the region since 2000 has been anything but gradual. The opening of Dubai's Burj al Arab hotel in 1999 seems in retrospect to mark the beginning of a new phase of urban development. This latest phase might well be called the "global phase" as each of the prominent cities of the Gulf—Dubai, Doha and Abu Dhabi—are being redesigned as cities that can compete on the global stage in terms of architecture, lifestyle and amenities, in addition to their already considerable integration into the global economy.

Abu Dhabi's socio-history

Abu Dhabi has waxed and waned with changing economic circumstances since it was settled in the 1790s. Established then as the official residence of the ruling family, al Nahayan, the little settlement was composed of Qasr al Hosn, the fort that served as the ruler's residence and was the locus of power, and a series of clustered 'arish or palm-frond houses that stretched out along the beach. As with other Gulf port towns, Abu Dhabi's fort guarded a fresh

[9] Sulayman Khalaf, "Gulf Societies and the Image of Unlimited Good," *Dialectical Anthropology*, 17 (1992), pp. 53–84.

[10] Khalaf, "The Evolution of the Gulf City Type, Oil and Globalization," pp. 244–65.

water source and the approaches from the sea. As Fuccaro notes, over time these proto-urban forts attracted the settlement of client tribes and non-tribal protégés.[11] Abu Dhabi was not a trade emporium like Manama or Dubai: fishing and pearling were the main occupations and the residents of the island traded for dates and livestock with their kin inland at the Buraimi and Liwa oases as well as with nomadic tribes. In 1903 the German explorer Burkhardt described Abu Dhabi as a little town with separate bazaars in which the Indian merchants both worked and lived.[12] Up to the first decades of the twentieth century Abu Dhabi thrived. Wealthy tribal entrepreneurs constructed coral and stone houses, two schools opened and the population grew. However, in 1929 the city's fortunes changed when the austerity of the Depression lessened the demand for Persian Gulf pearls and, as if that were not bad enough, then the cheaper Japanese cultured pearls effectively slashed the demand for natural pearls. Abu Dhabi plummeted into poverty.[13] From 1930 to the late 1950s it suffered under extreme poverty. By 1953 drinking water was sold by the glass and the water needed to mix concrete to build anything, including a house for the first European to live in Abu Dhabi, a British oil man, had to be shipped down the coast from Dubai.[14] The markets noted by Burkhardt fifty years earlier had shrunk to a cluster of some forty stalls that was housed in the area of town where members of al Qubaisat tribe lived, although none of them or any other members of Trucial States tribes worked in the market: it was run by Indians and Hule, Arabs from across the Gulf both of which populations had long and strong trading ties with the cities on the southern coast of the Persian Gulf.[15] There were no roads, just expanses of sand between family settlements that were reserved for future expansion as sons married, and the town was a place of palm frond houses built on sand among the trees.[16] Toward the end of the 1950s a few buildings

---

[11] Fuccaro, *Histories of City and State in the Persian Gulf: Manama since 1800.*

[12] Hermann Burkhardt, "Ost-Arabien von Basra bis Maskat auf Grund eigener Reisen," in *Zeitschrift der Gesellschaft fur Erdkunde* (Berlin, 1906).

[13] Mohammed Mattar Al Asi, *The Progress of Education in the United Arab Emirates* (Dubai: Matabi' al Bayan al Tijariyyah, 1993); Muhammad Morsy Abdullah, *United Arab Emirates. A Modern History* (London: Croom Helm, 1978).

[14] Susan Hillyard, *Before the Oil: A Personal Memoir of Abu Dhabi 1954–1958* (Blakewell: Ashridge Press, 2002); Peter Lienhardt, *Shaikhdoms of Eastern Arabia* (London: Palgrave, 2001).

[15] Lienhardt, *Shaikhdoms of Eastern Arabia.*

[16] Lienhardt, *Shaikhdoms of Eastern Arabia*; Donald Hawley, *The Trucial States* (London: Allen and Unwin, 1970).

had been constructed to support the activities needed to search for oil, but it was not until oil was first exported in 1962 that the town was able to stir out of poverty. Immediate improvements included building a new jetty, laying a water pipeline from distant Buraimi, completing a power station and two water distillation plants and beginning work on roads.[17]

With oil revenues bringing in cash and a new ruler, Sheikh Zayed, the town exploded with growth and development in 1966. The first of many projects initiated by the ruler was the construction of housing for the families of Abu Dhabi. The people's houses, *buyut as shabbiya*, were built of concrete in areas that roughly corresponded to the recognized tribal areas of town.[18] The *'arish* or palm frond houses vacated when people moved to the new dwellings were given over to the Indian shopkeepers and the growing number of non-native workers now living in and around the town. The building boom was such that in two short years, 56 percent of Abu Dhabi's population was foreign and there was a housing shortage.[19] Fully 40 percent of the town's workforce was devoted to construction as a whole city was being built. With the construction work grew a service sector to accommodate the workers. The service sector employed more foreigners in "restaurants, bakeries, barber shops, newsstands and entertainment places which catered to the different ethnic groups."[20]

In order to capitalize on the financial blessings promised by oil, great influxes of foreigners were needed because the indigenous workforce was too small and, after years of grinding poverty, woefully lacking in the education or technical training required by the petroleum industry. Once the workers initially needed for oil extraction and exportation arrived, they then had to be housed, fed, transported and serviced with banks, communications, homes, medical facilities, laundries and entertainment. All that construction and development was soon followed by the arrival of more foreign construction workers to build roads, airports, and seaports that were necessary to import the food and goods now needed and, in the case of the airports, to bring in even more foreigners.

The native population of Abu Dhabi, estimated at 4,000 to 5,000 people in the early 1960s, was soon surrounded by foreigners in the tens of thousands.

[17] Hawley, *The Trucial States*.

[18] Frauke Heard-Bey, *From Trucial States to United Arab Emirates* (London: Longman, 1982).

[19] Aqil Kazim, *The United Arab Emirates A.D. 600 to the Present* (Dubai: Gulf Book Centre, 2000).

[20] Ibid.

This was made worse by the fact that the first waves of migrants were exclusively male. A small, tribal society that was organized consanguinally with marked separation of genders and affines was suddenly surrounded by males of various ethnicities and religions. Where should these men live? The first answer was "away from us." Those men who worked in oil and construction were housed in dormitory-style housing constructed on the outskirts of town; these were the precursors of today's labor camps. The men who worked in the now thriving service sector in the expanding town slept in the shops as they were built (a phenomenon that persists today with construction laborers sleeping on completed floors as the building rises), and when they could, in the backrooms of bakeries and restaurants, or in buildings rented to them by Emiratis as they had sixty years earlier.[21]

More and more money now flowed into the city and Emiratis were benefitting from all the activity and the expansion of the government and ambitious development plans. One such government plan was the distribution of land and financing for the resident tribes to build houses and commercial buildings. Emiratis chose to build their new homes in undeveloped areas of the island like al Batin and al Mushref, away from what was becoming a congested and foreign dominated city core. The original *buyut as-shabbiya*, people's houses, were soon vacated and rented out to foreign workers.[22]

Increasing numbers of commercial buildings, banks, oil company offices, car dealerships, and apartments for well-paid foreigners, spread down the beach in both directions from the old fort, Qasr al Hosn, and what had been the core of the old town. The Emirati population moved away from the beach, inland toward the Maqta'a crossing to the mainland. The first and rather organic solution to house the city's growing number of working foreigners was to put them close to where they worked, often by subdividing small retail spaces to accommodate sleeping quarters, or using spaces that were not being used or that had been vacated by the owners. In part this solution seems to reflect the pervasive notion that migrant workers were temporary; they were not here "to stay" and so no permanent solution was needed. Anecdotally, the

---

[21] Khalaf, "The Evolution of the Gulf City Type, Oil and Globalization"; Heard-Bey, *From Trucial States to United Arab Emirates*.

[22] The concomitant development of the *kafāla* system by which individual Emiratis could obtain residence visas for foreigners who would work in their homes, businesses, and on large projects, meant that in most cases the abandoned houses were rented to workers who were in the employ of the owner.

idea that the demographic imbalance is provisional and will be corrected in the near future persists. For nine years I have been teaching a course on the socio-economic and cultural changes in the UAE to Emirati university students in Abu Dhabi. An integral element of that course is to critically examine the factors that have and continue to shape life in the Emirates. Each semester I ask the students to list the three most important issues that they think the country must confront in the coming years. The results of this biannual straw poll are fascinating because while the students typically include the phrase "demographic imbalance" or "too many foreigners," they all express confidence that this problem will go away soon. These students are not unusual; throughout the Gulf, as Dresch points out, the phrase "demographic imbalance" connotes a temporary situation; it suggests that balance is achievable and that the "problem" will go away sometime in the future.[23]

The result of Emiratis moving inland, while the core of the city grew ever more densely populated as high-rise apartments reached higher and higher, was to establish an exclusionary boundary that still functions today. Emirati neighborhoods are removed from the congestion of the now seriously overbuilt and overpopulated city. The urban plan drawn up for Abu Dhabi in the 1970s was based on a projected population of 700,000; the current population is over 1.5 million.

Navigating Abu Dhabi's boundaries

There are multiple boundaries in Abu Dhabi that separate its disparate populations. Although there are few gated communities in the city, and those that do exist are relatively recent developments, the markers that designate no-go areas for migrant laborers are as clearly recognizable as a guarded gate. There is also a grammar of migrants that is used to distinguish laborers from workers; workers from expats; and all migrants from Emiratis. This grammar uses nationality, ethnicity, socio-economic status and job to categorize and effectively pigeon-hole the hundreds of thousands of foreigners in the city. The social boundaries—which groups and individuals may interact and which or who should not—are normative constructions that are reproduced within the many migrant societies. It appears that each new migrant, regardless of origin, is quickly acculturated and can recognize where the boundaries of access lie.

---

[23] Paul Dresch, "Foreign Matter: The Place of Strangers in Gulf Society," in John W. Fox, Nada Mourtada-Sabbah and Muhammed Al Mutawa (eds), *Globalization and the Gulf*, (London: Routledge, 2006), pp. 200–22.

Illustration 1.

Source: Google Maps.

A grammar of migrants

Knowing who is who is essential in Abu Dhabi. First and foremost, Emiratis must be recognized immediately and approached cautiously, if at all. This, I am told, is common sense because Emiratis can have people deported immediately if they are angered. I have not yet spoken to a person who actually knows someone who was deported by an angry Emirati, but the vast majority of my interlocutors were utterly convinced that it happened frequently and could happen to them. Elsewhere I have considered this widespread paranoia to be an outcome of the *kafāla* system in which individual Emiratis wield the power of the state with the ability to grant and revoke residence/work visas.[24] Migrants, especially those who do not fully comprehend the complexity of sponsorship, have generalized that power and assume that any Emirati is capa-

---

[24] "Divided and Disciplined: Migrants in Abu Dhabi. Paper presented at the Gulf Research Conference, Cambridge University, July 2010.

ble of deporting any migrant should they so choose. Effectively this has created a very oppositional situation in which all Emiratis are possible threats and a migrant must be constantly on guard. For the migrants I interviewed, this was the case for female Emiratis as well; in fact, many men said that it was more dangerous to "cross" a woman than a man, and so they were extremely self-conscious when near an Emirati woman, even if only passing her on the street.

The migrants with whom I spent time also viewed Western foreigners with great suspicion and not a little apprehension. Western "expats" were perceived to be incredibly rich, and for the migrants richness equals power. The men also assumed, quite erroneously, that Western expatriates socialized with Emiratis, and so they thought that provoking a Westerner in some way was tantamount to displeasing an Emirati. Other assumptions the migrants made about Westerners included arrogance, a refusal to make eye-contact (which they perceived as a rudeness that dehumanized), and generalized notions about dissolute lifestyles.

Non-Western migrants who drove cars and wore Western-style clothing were highly problematic for many of the men I interviewed. None perceived

Illustration 2.

Source: Image received via BlackBerry broadcast message.

co-nationals—or even aggregated South Asians, as in the case of Indians, Pakistanis and Sri Lankans—to be a source of danger as Emiratis and Westerners were seen; rather, each group looked down on the other. Shared language and citizenship were, as one man put it, of little value because "they don't see us as being the same people at all, we are the poor people and we have no power in our country so why would they help us here?"[25] All of my interlocutors agreed that they would have to be well and truly desperate to approach someone from their own country for any sort of assistance, even for directions. "They would be upset if we spoke to them because to talk to us is to be associated with us. I think they all think we want something from them, like beggars."[26] This was not true for the men working in small shops throughout the city; those people could be approached easily, according to the laborers. "They are closer to us, they come from villages too and so don't have the idea that they are different or better."

The grammar of foreign migrants at play here distinguishes laborers from workers on the basis of the type of employment that the migrant undertakes. Laborers are those who work in construction, broadly construed to include buildings, roads, and landscaping. Workers are those who do everything else: street-cleaning, window-washing, retail sales, restaurants and hotels; essentially the entire service industry. The fundamental distinction that splits all migrants into one of two categories is the type of work visa: contracted or sponsored. Only laborers and workers are contracted in the way that word is used in the UAE, despite the fact that all non-GCC (Gulf Cooperation Council) passport holders, including those in professions such as engineering, architecture, medicine, and higher education, must have employment contracts in order to qualify for a residence visa. Contract laborers are employed in construction, municipal cleaning crews, building maintenance, agriculture, and road works; they are Pakistani, Indian, and recently—but in smaller numbers—Nepalese and Chinese. Contracted laborers are assumed to have been recruited by labor agencies in their home countries and to have little education; they must live in labor camps and are transported to and from job sites. Workers also may be contracted to an industrial cleaning firm or a municipality, but the majority of those who live in Abu Dhabi city are sponsored through the *kafāla* system that allows Emiratis to obtain visas for employees, both real and putative. They live in the older areas of the city, most commonly

---

[25] Confidential interview conducted by author, Abu Dhabi, 2004.
[26] Confidential interview conducted by author, Abu Dhabi, 2004.

renting a sleeping space in an apartment that may house as many as twenty men. Laborers are always male but workers are often female; they work in shops, drive taxis, serve food in restaurants, and sell sex. Domestic workers, both male and female, usually reside with the sponsoring family, be they Emirati or foreign. The salary range in this category goes from the low end of 600 or 700 dirhams per month (roughly $160 to $190) to several thousand per month. All foreigners who have residence visas in the UAE are sponsored workers, but in common use "worker" refers only to individuals who are from non-Western countries and earn less than 8,000 dirhams ($2,100) per month. "Worker" immediately denotes a South Asian, Arab, Asian, or African nationality. By contrast, individuals from Western countries are referred to as "expatriates," regardless of salary. An Egyptian or an Indian must earn much more, and be sponsored by an institution such as a university, to be called an expatriate. It is interesting to note that the origin of the word, at least according to my Indian interlocutors and friends, is in the phrase "Indian Expatriate" which has now been replaced by "NRI" or "Non-resident Indian". The word expatriate has been disconnected from "Indian," at least in English. Expatriates generally, and this does include all professionals regardless of nationality, do not consider themselves to be migrants in any sense of the word. They are "living abroad and working," but are not migrant workers. Interestingly, Emiratis rarely use the term "expatriate" to refer to an employee, professor, or doctor. Emiratis normally use the word "foreigner" to denote the upper-level range of migrants (that is, expatriates); all others are workers. Emiratis do use nationality to distinguish between foreigners. Therefore, "the Indian doctor" and the "Lebanese barber" are common, while just as often Arabs from Lebanon, Jordan, and Syria are lumped together as *zalamat*, a normally innocuous word for man that is actually used quite pejoratively to give the meaning of "interchangeable and replaceable." In the final analysis, that word could be applied to all foreign workers in the UAE, because since naturalization occurs only in exceptional cases, all of them work under contracts of varying lengths and are both temporary and replaceable. I consider the case of "expat" relationships with Emiratis, as well as the increasing frequency of ethnocentrically derived abuse directed at Arabs from other countries, in another context; here our focus is on laborers and workers.[27]

---

[27] Jane Bristol-Rhys, *Future Perfect: Societies in the Emirates* (New York: Columbia University Press, 2011).

Spatial boundaries

The first and most insurmountable spatial boundary that separates laborers and some industrial workers is residence. Labor camps and the new Worker Villages are, as they were in the past, all located off the island, most prominently in Mussafah and Mohammad bin Zayed City, close to the airport. They are isolated from the city in various ways. First, laborers are transported to and from their work sites on a company owned (or contracted) bus. Second, taxi fares from these outlying areas are prohibitively expensive for these men. There is now the beginning of a transportation system in Abu Dhabi, but it does not serve the labor camp areas and it is doubtful that it will in the future. The laborers have one day off per week, Friday. On Fridays, the same buses that shuttle them to work carry them into the city before *dhuhr*, the communal prayer. After prayer the laborers are allowed to stay in the city to shop and socialize. Shopping is minimal as most laborers send the bulk of their salaries home to families. Phone cards, spices and medicines are the most commonly purchased essentials. Socializing often means spending the money to buy a cup or two of tea, but that too is described as an essential.

Workers live in the city. Rather, workers live in certain parts of the city: in the areas in which buildings are considered old. Laughably, this means older than 15 years. As mentioned above, workers share apartments in these older buildings. Apartments built for one family are now occupied by a score or more of single men, often referred to as "bachelors," who each pay for sleeping space.[28] Often a two-bedroom apartment is home to six or eight individuals. Larger apartments will house as many as twenty. In some cases, when workers have alternate shifts, sleeping spaces are rotated so that fifteen men sleep during the night and another fifteen take over the mattresses and pads during the day. Such compound tenancy is illegal, and while a recent crackdown has targeted villas that have been subdivided into separate and discrete rental units, no similar focus has affected the overcrowding of apartments.

Abu Dhabi's skyline of soaring opulence along the Gulf is bordered by a new Corniche that embodies the city's public image as it is captured on postcards, websites, and brochures for tourists. The scope and pace of development in Abu Dhabi intensified in 2005, after the death of Sheikh Zayed bin Sultan

---

[28] Jay B. Hilotin, "Smiles that veil misery," *Gulf News* (Dubai, February 7, 2008); "Abu Dhabi Construction," *Gulf News* (Dubai, August 14, 2003); "Civic body cuts power supply to villas housing bachelors," *Gulf News* (Dubai, September 4, 2006).

al Nahayan, when it seemed that his sons were no longer content to invest quietly in Dubai.[29] Indeed, whereas previously Abu Dhabi's strategy was to sit comfortably astride massive investments and calmly contemplate growth ideas for the future, competition grew fierce between Dubai and Abu Dhabi in 2006 and 2007.[30] The competition ended when Dubai needed Abu Dhabi's financial backing to survive.

Behind the gleaming glass façade of the new skyscrapers stand quarters of the city that have devolved into decay while the new construction has moved to the periphery of the island, or—as in the cases of the Saadiyat Island complex with the Guggenheim and Louvre Abu Dhabi, eco-tourism developments and the Yas Island Formula One racing venue—onto adjacent islands. These quarters are a visibly disagreeable result of the large number of migrant workers who live crowded together in the city's older buildings that have become *de facto* urban labor camps. Soaring inflation and the shortage of rental units have combined to create a desperate housing situation for many of these workers. These areas have no place in Abu Dhabi's stylized image; indeed, they are ignored rather like the large elephant standing in the middle of the room that no one will mention.

The cities of Dubai, Abu Dhabi and Doha are marketing actively as destinations for upscale tourists and wealthy investors. They are branding themselves not only as "pearls of the Gulf" but also as the new "world" cities. Indeed, Abu Dhabi announced in September 2007 that it was pursuing the title of "global city."[31] Exactly what "global city" denotes depends on one's perspective. Some focus on the socio-economic functions of these cities in the world economy as global economic hubs, while others examine the transnational, hybrid characteristics of these urban centers.[32] A third perspective, a part of ongoing research at Loughborough University, considers that there are mandatory features for a global city to achieve international recognition. These are nota-

---

[29] Christopher Davidson, "The Emirates of Abu Dhabi and Dubai: Contrasting Roles in the International System," *Asian Affairs*, 37 (2007): pp. 33–48.

[30] Davidson, "The Emirates of Abu Dhabi and Dubai"; Zvika Krieger, "Buying Culture," in *Newsweek*, CL vols, International ed. (2007), pp. 20–5.

[31] Samir Salama, "Abu Dhabi reveals long term urban plan," *Gulf News* (Dubai, September 21, 2007).

[32] Saskia Sassen, *Cities in a World Economy* (Thousand Oaks: Pine Forge Press, 1994); Saskia Sassen, *The Global City* (Princeton University Press, 2001); Nezar Alsayyad, *Hybrid Urbanism: On Identity Discourse and the Built Environment* (Westport, CT: Praeger, 2001); David Clark, *Urban World/Global City* (London: Routledge, 1996).

ble and distinct architectural forms, cultural venues, sports arenas that can host international events and iconic public spaces.[33] Abu Dhabi appears to have not only consulted this list of must-have urban features but incorporated all of them into its strategic planning.[34]

Dubai, Abu Dhabi and Doha are creating towering developments, post-modern urban enclaves and designed mini-cities that are primarily on the periphery of the existing city. In the case of Dubai, the stretch of open beach and desert from Jumeirah to Mina Seyahi and on to Jebel Ali is one such area, as are the thousands of desert hectares that will be Dubailand. The most famous peripheral development in Dubai is, of course, the man-made islands. Abu Dhabi, an island itself, is building on the smaller, naturally occurring islands close to its shore. Saadiyat Island will house the "cultural quarter" made up of the Guggenheim, Louvre, galleries, and restaurants. Reem Island will offer primarily towering residential apartment developments such as Shams al Abu Dhabi.[35] The largest of the planned developments, Raha Beach, stretches 17 kilometers down the mainland coast toward Dubai and will be a conglomeration of themed communities linked by shopping malls and marinas.

Relatively little development energy is being spent on the existing city centers. There are exceptions of course, like the Central Market complex underway in Abu Dhabi and the bridge and road works in Dubai. Building out new construction in areas away from existing structures and sections of the city is not a new phenomenon in the Gulf, nor is it simply a by-product of the size of the new developments. In the case of the "new, global Abu Dhabi" the city may be redefining itself, but it is doing so by following a pattern established when the first public housing, *buyut as shabbiya*, was constructed in the 1960s. This pattern involves two interrelated factors: the preference for building anew in pristine areas, and the subsequent decision to abandon old construction in the older areas of the city for the foreign workforce living in the city. These foreign workers, primarily Indian, Pakistani, and Filipino, work in offices, shops, cafés and restaurants throughout the city and drive the taxis that still constitute the city's public transportation system. City workers, as I

---

[33] The University of Loughborough's Global and World Cities Network website (GaWC) regularly publishes new research and perspectives on global cities. It can be accessed at http://www.lboro.ac.uk/gawc/in_resea.html.

[34] Council, "Policy Agenda 2007–2008 The Emirate of Abu Dhabi," ed. Executive Council (Abu Dhabi, 2007), p. 79.

[35] AME, "Sorouh launches The Gate at Shams Abu Dhabi," in *City and Society* (Dubai: AME Info, 2007).

have noted, represent a different class of migrant from the thousands of men who work as contracted labor and who live in labor camps situated on the far outskirts of the cities. In Abu Dhabi these camps are off the island, in the Mussafah industrial area with new sites, now called "villages", being built near the new towns of Khalifa and Muhammad bin Zayed. The Dubai labor camps are rather more notorious for strikes and protests, which have drawn a considerable amount of negative publicity internationally. The crowded and unsanitary conditions in these camps are being rectified as the governments of Dubai and Abu Dhabi draft and enforce new regulations.[36]

However, inside the cities similar crowded and unsanitary conditions exist to such an extent that areas within Abu Dhabi look very much like slums. This is rather amazing considering that few buildings in the city are older than thirty years. Nevertheless, sections of the city are in decay and buildings crumble under the weight of neglect. Mold first stains the inner walls of these buildings while the window sills and ledges corrode, loosen and then spill dislodged concrete on to the street below. Single room air-conditioning units, markers of older buildings, sometimes shimmed and propped in place with wooden frames, punctuate the outer walls and drip water onto the sidewalks. Laundry dries on every balcony, windows are covered with newspapers, and on the street level tiny tea and food shops, barbers and vegetable stalls serve the men who live in these buildings.

The streets in these areas are difficult to negotiate as the sidewalks are often broken, and those sections that are not have been appropriated by shopkeepers as merchandise display areas, or have been taken over as additional seating for the small restaurants or as social space for the residents of the crowded buildings. When new, these buildings housed migrants of a different sort, most of whom were considered "expatriate." These were the professional and clerical staff that came to work in offices, banks, schools and government ministries. This type of migrant arrived with family members and was given housing and furniture allowances, and either located or was assigned living accommodation commensurate with their contract and salary. When I arrived in 2001 I was assigned an apartment in a new building that was "Western" style and given the money to furnish it according to my personal tastes. As an Emirati explained it to me shortly after I arrived, "streets and buildings here have several lives." "They start new with high rents and Western professionals and

---

[36] Himendra M. Kumar, "Aldar builds permanent labor camp," *Gulf News* (Dubai, January 29, 2008).

sometimes young Emirati couples, then after five years or so the building ages and the rents go down accordingly. For the next three or four years Arab and Indian families move in and out, but by eight years the building is in bad shape and the landlord turns it over to rental agents who fill the building by renting out not apartments but sleeping space."[37] As these buildings fill with males living in all-male communities the shops on the streets transform as well, reflecting the needs of the new residents: laundries, tailors, tea shops, hot-food shops, barbers, newsagents who charge for calls to family back home and who can write a letter when necessary.[38] The buildings are usually filled with members of the same or similar ethnic groups, and in the case of Pakistanis, who figure disproportionately in this equation, often tribal affiliation is taken into consideration. Languages, dialects, dress and food preferences are reflected on the streets and in the nicknames given to certain areas such as "little Karachi, Peshawar West" and, in Indian and Sri Lankan enclaves, "Kerala land" and "Tamil town."

Often these areas are separated from major city streets by only a block or two. They are hidden from view until one leaves the main street and enters into a grid of smaller, connecting streets. In some of the worst areas, tea bags and other rubbish litter are left on the paved sidewalk, and the streets are generally impassible because of the cars parked illegally down the center lane; there are no brightly lit grocery stores or retail chain shops. The few shops that do exist are geared exclusively to meet the needs of the migrant men now living in the neighborhood with the usual repetition of barber, tea shop, laundry, used furniture shop and newsagents/sundries store. These are marked by signs in Urdu or Malayalam, not in Arabic.

Access to the city

As I noted, laborers have limited access to the city: one day a week and only for five or six hours. Being in Abu Dhabi does not imply that the laborers have access to the entire city. "The bus stops near where we pray, I don't know the street but it is the same place on every Friday," says Nur, who is a laborer working for a large irrigation company. Nur and the other eight men sitting on a grassy area in the wide sidewalk on Airport Road all work together and live in a camp in Mussafah. Their description of a typical Friday in Abu Dhabi echoes

[37] Interview with Ahmad Salah Al Harbi, conducted by author, Abu Dhabi, 2004.
[38] Interview with Gul Khan, conducted by author, Abu Dhabi, 2003.

what I have heard from other laborers. Nur, who seems to enjoy being questioned, continues: "We pray and then we gather outside and wait to see if we will see any of our family in town that day. Most of us have brothers and cousins working in the UAE and so we try to meet after praying so that we can talk and perhaps share the news of our homes if someone has been on the telephone." I ask him how they spend the rest of the day. "We have no money, you know," he says as a matter of fact. "We will find a teashop close by and each of us will get a small plastic glass of tea. Then we look for a place to sit and talk, especially if we have met family. That is hard to find because everyone is looking for the same places to sit. We don't want to walk too far; we are tired from our work every day and want to sit and rest together." I ask the group if they have ever walked down to the Corniche and sat in the new parks that line the road. "No, no, that is too far and it is also too difficult! The police watch you very closely down there, we have been told, because they don't want all of the men from the camps crowding the area. We were told by our company that we should not go there at all."

Other laborers were not warned off the area, but many that I have spoken to express the same misgivings about being there. One man, Shahid, told me that he and his four co-workers had once gone there rather by accident as they were looking for a pharmacy in which someone's rather distant cousin worked as a stock boy. "It was in January so it was cool and we didn't mind walking to find this place. We walked down one of the main ways, I don't know which one, but we found ourselves in a park with grass and trees so we sat down and spent some time there. I was nervous sitting there and I wanted to leave. I told the others that we shouldn't sit too long on the grass because there were no other Pakistani men in that place, only we five men and we must have been very easy to see." The parks are for the public, are they not? I asked. Shahid asked what I meant by the word public. I said that I meant people, all people, that the parks were for the people of the city and open to all. "No, Madam, no, this is not the case because we are not people of the city, we live in the labor camp and are not public."

Some parks are clearly identified as "family parks," which in the parlance of the city means that the only men allowed in the area are those in the company of their wives, sisters or mothers. This effectively excludes all laborers and probably fifty percent of the "bachelor" workers in the city. The rationale behind this is that single men—of any ethnicity and class—might behave inappropriately in the proximity of women and children. Some of these family parks have been successfully appropriated on the weekends by families from other Arab countries, who spend the day barbequing and playing football. The parks not designated for families, such as the Formal Park, the City Park and other, smaller unnamed parks, are usually a mix of ethnicities, which occasionally includes a small group of laborers. Interestingly, recent renovations along the Corniche, including building of cafés and restaurants along with small retail shops that offered beach clothing and accessories, rental bicycles, and large public art installations, were accompanied by building of protective fences and charging of entry fees to certain parts of the beach areas. These measures exclude all laborers and most of the workers because they cannot afford the ten-dirham entry fee. The fence that divides the cycling, jogging and walking lanes along the road from the sandy beach also discourages watching sunbathers and swimmers. One area of the restricted entry beach is also designated as "families only," which further excludes the wandering single male.

Until two years ago access to more far-flung areas of the city was difficult because the only transportation available were taxis which the laborers could not afford, except perhaps in the case of an emergency. Now Abu Dhabi has bus transportation that traverses the island east to west and north to south, and from the mainland areas such as Shahamma and Mussafah, and out to new construction on Yas Island. The buses are cheap and they are popular with workers and laborers alike. Workers, most of who live in the city, have a distinct advantage because they know the names of areas and streets, whereas the laborers are unfamiliar with both. Bus stops on Friday are crowded with men who are going to ride around the city for part of their day's entertainment. No one to whom I spoke had an actual destination in mind: "We will just ride for a short time in the cool air of the bus. We don't know where the bus goes but we will ask if it is a good place to go. We don't want to go too far because we will have to come back here." The buses have become so popular with men that women complained to the authorities that the buses had become, in short order, unsafe or at least unsavory for women to ride. The city responded with "women only" areas in each of the buses. On Fridays no one enforces that rule and consequently few women ride among the laborers in the city for the day.

Parks are not the only areas that are perceived by laborers to be off-limits to them in Abu Dhabi. Only three of the several hundred men I interviewed and questioned had been inside of one of the larger shopping malls. The big malls, Marina, Abu Dhabi, Wahda, and Khalidiya, were all described as too expensive to purchase even a cup of tea, and most men related concerns that they would be harassed by security if they did try to go inside those malls. Indeed, the entrances to all of those malls are monitored by security officers and I have observed them stopping laborers—in fact all males wearing *shalwar khameez*, the Pakistani national dress—and, in most cases, refusing the men entrance. I inquired about the rules of entry at each mall and was told that "all people who have a reason to come into the mall are allowed to enter." What about laborers? I was told in various ways that laborers have no money to spend and therefore no reason to come to the mall. Several of the security guards told me that they had been instructed to keep the laborers out because they would just sit on benches and stare at women. "That is a bad thing and Emiratis will not tolerate that," said one of the guards. The rules seem to have relaxed somewhat recently—or the guards are ineffective—because laborers, usually in twos or threes, have been observed in two of the malls on Fridays. They were not sitting and they were not staring; they were window shopping.

Emirati residential neighborhoods are strictly off-limits to laborers as well. In fact, any neighborhood in which villas predominate is usually bereft of laborers and all workers other than domestic workers who reside there. There are few attractions in these areas other than well-maintained grassy places to sit, and so there is no real reason to be there. However, it appears to be common knowledge among the laborers and many of the workers who live in the center of the city that it is not wise to be seen on the streets around the large villa compounds. A young man who worked in a shop in the city told me that he had been let out of a taxi coming from Dubai because the driver was not familiar with Abu Dhabi and was afraid of becoming lost if he drove further into the city. "He left me on the road in Al Mushref, near to a co-operative (grocery) store but there were no taxis and I had to walk. I walked in front of gates and walls and yet still the workers from inside challenged me. They called out in Urdu to me telling me that I should not be here, that this was not a place for walking." Another Pakistani man told me about his cousin, Hussein, who was accosted by drivers and gardeners in a similar area as he walked to the medical place on Khaleej al Arabi (Gulf Diagnostics) when he had an illness. "Hussein was asked what he was doing there at least one time on every street and it was always by workers from the big homes. It was very strange to Hussein that other Pakistanis would question him in that way."

On the western side of the island are the President's palace and a string of sumptuous villas belonging to members of the ruling family and very wealthy Emiratis. This area is completely off-limits for laborers and workers and, in fact, for most Westerners as well. The palace and palatial villas are guarded and the streets are regularly patrolled day and night. I was pulled over by the Abu Dhabi police one evening for doing nothing more suspicious than circling one neighborhood. I was looking for a student's home to which I had been invited for an engagement party and was having trouble locating it; driving up and down the same street was enough apparently to have aroused the suspicions of the cruising police. The police officer was kind enough to escort me to the house. He was also kind enough to answer my questions about why he stopped me and what rules governed whom he stopped, quite candidly. It helped that he was an Egyptian whose village, Zagazig, I knew well. "The first rule is that no one is expected to be seen walking here! Emiratis do not walk; they drive their cars so there should be no one walking. If I see someone walking I stop them immediately, *ya'anni alatool*. The second rule is that cars drive through the area on the main road; they don't drive around looking. That is why I stopped you. No one should be looking inside these walls at all. This area is for Emiratis and they don't want to see foreigners. No foreigners at all, doesn't matter where they come from, they are not welcome here." The irony of his job was not lost on him. "Yes, I am the *khawāga* (outsider) who keeps out all other *khawāgaat*. This is the Emirates."

Social boundaries

It has been difficult to keep the spatial boundaries distinct from those that are socially constructed, and in the above descriptions there have been several that overlap. One example is making eye-contact on the streets. The laborers told me repeatedly that people never make eye-contact with them when passing on the street. They thought this was because Westerners were arrogant and other South Asians were class conscious and, in my words, uptight. They avoided making eye-contact with Emiratis because they thought Emiratis would be angered by that. Then why, I asked, were they so conscious of others not making the same contact? The responses were quite interesting and lead me to think that the major Friday entertainment has now become a competition to see who will make eye-contact on the streets with laborers. "We do try to look people in the eyes. Why not? We are people walking on the streets too are we not?" To what end, I inquired. "It is a game, a game that costs nothing. We are not trying to frighten people; we just want to see who will look at us." Very few people did look at them, it seemed. "We see how people turn their faces away when they see us in the buses that take us to work; we see that we are nobodies that people don't want to acknowledge; we are invisible people. On Friday, when we can wear our own clothes (not the jumpsuits provided by their company) and walk about like men, we want to be seen, we want to be recognized."

Knowing who is a Pakistani laborer is easy; the ubiquitous light colored *shalwar khameez* is instantly recognizable. For other ethnic groups employed as laborers it is more difficult to identify them as laborers and to attribute ethnicity. Chinese, Indian and Sri Lankan laborers tend to wear Western-style clothing on Fridays and their status as "workers" is therefore somewhat camouflaged. This is a good thing for many of them. "We just blend in with all the other people on the streets," one young man from Andhra Pradesh told me. "We don't want to be laborers all the time; we are more than just our jobs." In fact, among the workers who live in the city, except for Pakistanis, clothing does not function as a marker. Language and behavior are more important. "We hear Malayalam spoken everywhere on the streets! We then know who is from Kerala. If we hear other languages like Hindi and Gujarati we know that we are with other Indians and that is good but not as good as being with people from our state."

Suresh, a Kerala Indian whom I have interviewed a dozen times over the course of five years, has told me that it is often the manner in which migrants group together that marks them as laborers or workers, even if clothing and language do not help. "Many of those men who live in Mussafah are frightened in Abu Dhabi because this is the first big city for them. They don't know where to go, what to do and they are afraid of getting lost. That is why they group together; they feel safe in a group because they can protect—and guide—each other. But that is not how others see it. They see a large group of men doing nothing." This is echoed by Emiratis who, it must be said, are more than a little disquieted by the large numbers of men on the streets, especially on Fridays. One woman described them as gangs of laborers and added that she thought the police should prohibit such gatherings. "Why are they all together walking? There are often thousands sitting on the ground all around the Medina Zayed area and it is very uncomfortable to drive through because they are all staring." The area she refers to is in the center of the city, and is very popular with the Friday-visiting laborers because it abuts areas that are predominantly Indian and Pakistani. It also boasts the gold *souk*, which, perhaps unsurprisingly, is one of the shopping areas in which the laborers are welcome as they do purchase gold jewelry to send or take home.

In conversations with Emiratis about the numbers of migrants in the city it becomes apparent that many confront the issue only when they are shopping or driving through areas that they would not normally frequent. When, as on Fridays, they encounter thousands of men who are not on scaffolding, not laying paving bricks, not digging ditches along the side of a road, they are disquieted. This is, according to several acquaintances who work with the Abu Dhabi police, exactly why the city has over 30,000 officers. "They don't work in traffic, they monitor the single male population of the city; that's who makes us nervous." Abdullah is an officer who is frequently assigned to what he calls "street patrol" during which it is his job to drive through particular areas of the city very slowly and rather menacingly, as if looking for someone in particular. That, he says, is usually sufficient to make the groups of men nervous and they break up into smaller groups and move away from each other. "I think part of the problem is that we see the groups of men and while we don't immediately assume that they are up to no good, seeing them in force

Illustration 3.

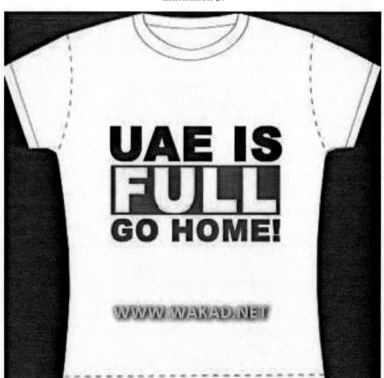

Source: uaesm.maktoob.com. This T-shirt was sold online and is quite popular with Emiratis.

makes us exceedingly nervous. It is one thing to know that there are millions of foreigners in the country and another thing entirely to see so many in one place. Seeing them makes me wonder if the price we are paying for modern development is too great; we have given our country away to foreigners."

Many Emiratis would concur with Abdullah's comments and there appears to be increasing public articulation of discomfort with the number of foreigners and complaints about the behavior of foreigners in public. Often it is the behavior of Westerners that draws criticism, specifically about clothing that Emiratis consider to be inappropriate. Just as frequently heard are complaints about the manner in which foreigners have ruined the city "with their dirty ways of living" and foreign mores. I am frequently told by students not to go to a certain area of town, like Tourist Club, because it is both unsafe and unsanitary. A T-shirt slogan "The UAE is full. Go Home" has become very popular with younger Emiratis as are others that underscore the rights of citizens in contrast to migrants. There are quite a few stories—urban myths really—told about maids who steal pictures of family members, usually the wife, in order to have some sort of curse put on her or some spell cast that will end with the maid getting paid more for doing nothing. Filipinos are often the culprits in these stories and they are now known for the "power" of their black magic. I have not yet encountered a maid who has been successful through black magic but I remain hopeful.

Emiratis express intense feelings about the fact that English and Urdu are more commonly spoken on the streets of Abu Dhabi than Arabic. In what ways this discontent will be manifest in the future remains to be seen, but most of the Emiratis with whom I have spoken seem to think that hostility toward foreigners is on the rise and will get much worse.

For the migrant laborer and worker who have come to work in order to support families back home, Abu Dhabi is a strange and often perplexing place that harbors more dangers than rewards. Pay is often late or withheld entirely to pay off debts accrued for housing, food, uniforms and transportation. Negotiating the strange city is a frightening challenge that is best to face with co-workers and, to be safe, it is best to take heed of all warnings about people and places. The good fortune to land a job in the city is sometimes illusory as the cramped and crowded conditions that workers share are hideous and illegal—punishment being meted out to the "bachelor" men, not the landlord. And yet, as Emiratis point out, still they come to work. As Gardner discusses in this volume, the reasons why migrants continue to work in the Gulf is a complex dynamic that often involves family strategies and, sadly, the politics of rebellion and war. Many Sri Lankans returned home from the UAE when the Tamil Tigers had been crushed. Some of those people have come back to Abu Dhabi because their home country is, in their words, "still not okay for making a good living." In the last four years or so, Filipinos have begun to dominate certain sectors of the service industry. They are a constant presence in restaurants, hotels, bars, shops and some medical centers (as nurses primarily) and it is usually an English-speaking Filipina who answers service phone calls. The increase in the number of Filipinos has occurred despite the fact that domestic workers must be now paid a minimum wage according to the Government of the Philippines.[39]

Conclusion

The spatial boundaries that separate foreign migrants from Emiratis in Abu Dhabi were laid down early in the history of the city. Non-tribal clients, merchants, and the few workers in markets and pearling were physically segregated from the tribally organized areas around Qasr al Hosn. When the town exploded with oil activity, that pattern of separation shaped the growth of the city. Some forty years later, Abu Dhabi has outgrown the island and is expanding onto adjacent islands and the mainland. But some forty years later, too, Emiratis still talk about being dependent on foreign labor temporarily despite overwhelming evidence to the contrary. In many ways, it has been that refusal to acknowledge the ever-increasing number of foreigners that has resulted in years of ad hoc responses that have shaped the core of Abu Dhabi.

Abu Dhabi officials now seem to be facing up to the reality of the labor situation and are constructing new labor villages on the peripheries of the many new developments off the island. These areas will be new, however the same pattern of separation and segregation is being reproduced. In fact, these new areas will be more separated from the Emirati population than ever and, it seems reasonable to predict, they will most likely become foreign ghettos. The spatial boundaries are being deepened.

---

[39] Bassma al Jandalay, "Basic wage of Filipino maids double," *Gulf News* (Dubai, May 3, 2009).

5

Informality and Its Discontents

Mapping Migrant Worker Trajectories into Dubai's Informal Economy

Pardis Mahdavi

"I am an illegal migrant, that's why people think they can abuse me," said Surri, an Indonesian domestic worker who moved into the informal economy[1] of commercial sex work after suffering abuse in the formal economy of domestic

[1] Throughout this piece I use the term "informal economy" to refer to labor that takes place outside of formal structures such as taxation, or, in the case of the UAE, outside of the *kafala* or sponsorship system which structures labor laws and regulations in the Emirates. The work conducted in the informal economy is not always illegal, but it is the nature in which it is conducted ("off the books") that makes it informal and unregulated. Some work in the informal economy is illegal (such as buying and selling drugs or, in some countries, commercial sex work), much is not (domestic work, childcare, etc.). The distinction made between the formal and informal economies is along the lines of regulation. Some work in the informal economy because they do not have legal permits in the countries in which they reside, others are conducting illegal work. For more on the informal economy, see Phillippe Bourgois, *In Search of Respect: Selling Crack in El Barrio* (Cambridge University Press, 2002).

work. Surri decided to leave Indonesia after her husband left her in debt and with two children. "I found that I am alone, no money, no food, nothing. Nothing for me and my babies," she recalled. After a few weeks of looking for work and seeking out help from family and friends, she encountered a friend of her cousin who told her he could help her find work abroad in Dubai as a nanny and domestic worker. Wary of migrating through an unknown channel, Surri first decided to seek out official migratory options through the Ministry of Labor in Jakarta. When immigration officials found out that she was under the age of 30 and no longer married she was turned away. "I was told I was not a 'desirable candidate,' because I am a woman not married," she explained. Frustrated at the response she received from ministry officials, and in need of a job, Surri returned to her cousin's friend to ask for his assistance. "I didn't trust him, but I thought, I have no choice. If I stay here, death for my family and me. At least I must try to go, try to find work to send money home to my family," she said.

But migration, even through back channels, was not that easy. Her "recruiter" charged her the equivalent of US$1,000 (which she had to borrow), and then was not able to procure legal working papers for Surri. She was placed illegally (meaning she did not have a legal work permit) in the home of an Iranian family, which was supposed to pay her $500 a month. "I was told I would get that money, and that I would work 8 hours a day and live with the family," she explained. When she arrived, however, she was made to work 16–18 hour days, cleaning the house, caring for the three children, and often was sent to the homes of friends of her host family to assist others with cleaning and childcare. In addition, she was only paid $250 a month, and on occasion her wages were withheld. After about six months, Surri, worried about her family back home, worked up the courage to confront her employer. "I tell them, I need my money. I want my money! I tell them I work too hard, not fair!" she said, her ordinarily fair complexion flushing red. She took a deep breath and smoothed her long hair back into a bun before continuing. "But that is when the beatings began," she said.

Because Surri had migrated outside the formal structures of legal migration (meaning that she did not procure legal working papers and did not migrate under the auspices of the Ministry of Labor), and was working in the informal economy (due to the lack of a work permit), she felt that she had no avenues for recourse. She could not go to her embassy or to the police for fear of deportation or arrest. In addition, she owed a large amount of debt to her recruiter that she had not yet worked off. After several more months of abuse,

Surri finally ran away and found shelter through an ad hoc religious group that provides services to migrants in need regardless of their visa status. When I met her, she was staying at the home of one of the volunteers and trying to calculate her next steps.

Adechike, who preferred to be called Ade, was also working in the informal economy of Dubai and struggling to make ends meet when I met him. "I'm a hustler now, you know what that means?" he asked me, somewhat rhetorically. "Do you know what it is to sell everything you have? Leave everything you know behind, and come to a different country, only to realize you are an illegal?" he continued. Ade had left Nigeria in search of employment in the United Arab Emirates (UAE). He met a recruiting agent in Lagos on one of his trips to see his father who worked in the capital. The agent told him that if he went to Dubai, he could earn up to US$2,000 a month working as a salesperson in a car dealership. When he told his father about this opportunity, his father was thrilled and encouraged him to go. The only catch was that he would have to pay $2,000 to the recruiter to facilitate his travel. Encouraged by his family, Ade sold his belongings and borrowed some money from his parents to pay the recruiter and packed his bags.

"I was so happy, so excited to go! I thought, now I'm makin' it, now things are going to be different for me, and I can make my family proud," he recalled. But once he arrived in Dubai, things quickly began spiraling downward. As he was attempting to pass through immigration, the officials at the border held him back, telling him that his visa was fraudulent. "Can you believe it? The guy, the guy who had pretended to be my friend, he had sold me a fake visa! Now what to do?" Ade reflected. After a few hours of sitting in the airport, Ade called his father to ask for advice and assistance. His father was outraged and told him to stick it out in Dubai, to find some form of work, and not to return home empty handed. "I'm thinking, I'm stuck in the airport, no job, no money, no visa. And no way to go home. No money to go home, and dad saying I'm not welcome there without gold in my pockets," he explained. Ade then spent the next five days living at the airport, begging for food and money from travelers, digging through trash cans, and trying to find a way out. After a few days of living like this, Ade met another Nigerian man, on his way back to Dubai from Nigeria, who had been working in the informal economy of Dubai selling handbags, wallets and other items in tourist hotspots. He entered on tourist visas and regularly over-stayed his visa. This man helped Ade to leave the airport by smuggling him out in a duffel bag, and inducted him into the informal economy of selling stolen goods on the street. "So, now

I'm a hustler. But I always have to watch my back because them cops, they are always on me. Last month one of them caught me and wrestled me to the ground, but I'm no fool, I fought back. Bloody lip and all, I busted that cop real good and I got away. But I don't know how much longer I can go on like this. I just want to go home," he said.

Elyse, a domestic worker from Ethiopia who is now working as a commercial sex worker in Dubai, also told me she wanted to go home, but was not willing to return empty handed. Elyse had migrated legally to Dubai to work as a domestic worker. She had contracted with an official agency in Addis Ababa who had facilitated her migration to Dubai and placed her in the home of a Jordanian family. After a few months, the female head of the household began abusing Elyse. "She threw things at me, made me sleep on the floor, wouldn't let me out of the house," Elyse remembered. She was locked in the house for days on end, sometimes without food or water. When she tried contacting her embassy she was placed endlessly on hold, and then told that as a domestic worker she had limited rights. Frustrated with the fact that she was held to the standards of labor laws as outlined in the UAE's sponsorship system (*kafala*), but did not enjoy the attendant benefits,[2] she decided to run away and file a complaint at the police station. When she managed to find a policeman, he was very violent with her and arrested her on the spot. She was held in jail for 24 hours until her employers were called to come and take her home. After that, she suffered several beatings from the male and female heads of household, who told her they would never give her back her passport or support her desire for another job.

After enduring several days of punishment without food or water, Elyse ran away once again, but this time was determined to work in the sex industry. Having heard from her friends at the local church (which she was permitted to attend once a month) that many Ethiopian workers were able to earn significant amounts of money through transactional sex, Elyse decided to abscond from the formal economy of domestic work to seek out commercial sex work in the informal economy. For her, the informal economy offered more earning potential, and a way to make money free of the abuse of her employers. "I thought to myself, why take the abuse, be locked up in that

[2] Domestic workers must adhere to laws in sponsorship system but are not protected by these laws and thus cannot assert their rights under this system. See laws 155 and 167 of the UAE Labor Law. For further information on the status of domestic workers in the UAE see Pardis Mahdavi, *Gridlock: Labor, Migration and Human Trafficking in Dubai* (Stanford University Press, 2011).

house? I can make more money this way, and yes, maybe if I become a prostitute I will be abused. But if I stay a maid, I will be abused for sure, and never see my money," she explained.

Elyse ran away and managed to find her way to Little Ethiopia in the northern part of Dubai. There she met many other women who had, like her, absconded from work in the formal economy in favor of employment in the informal economy of sex work. "I don't regret my decision, even though this work is hard," she reflected. "But this way, I have control over my life. Who will protect me when I'm a maid? But in here (the space of the sex industry) we all watch each other's backs. And maybe I can make more money and go home sooner, right?"

These narratives are just a few examples of the increasing numbers of migrant workers that I met during my time in the field who are moving from the formal into the informal economy of Dubai. While some of this movement can be attributed to the declining economy in the region, the rise in informal labor also coincides with a combination of stringent labor laws (that operate in favor of the employer rather than protecting the employee) as well as the global moral panic about "trafficking."[3] Of the three stories presented above, perhaps the only one that would fit popular imaginings of 'human trafficking' would be the experience of Elyse. But even she does not fit neatly, and would only be considered trafficked due to her work in the sex industry. While only Elyse would be considered trafficked, all three of these individuals have experienced some form of force, fraud or coercion which forms the core of the official definition of trafficking under the United Nations Protocol to Prevent, Suppress and Punish Trafficking in Persons (referred to as the Palermo Protocol).[4] Although the definition of trafficking is broad enough to encompass many forms of abuse, the popular understanding and implementation of legislation on trafficking tend to focus narrowly on women in the commercial sex industry. This often results in unwanted hyper-scrutiny of female commercial sex workers, while erasing instances of force or coercion experienced by men and women working in other areas outside of transactional sex.

Unfortunately, all three of the individuals introduced above have been adversely affected by global and local policies on labor and trafficking that are

---

[3] This term is placed in quotations to indicate its contested nature as a term that at once claims too much and too little according to scholars such as Nicole Constable, Carole Vance and Julia O'Connell Davidson.

[4] For a full text of the United Nations Protocol to Prevent, Suppress and Punish Trafficking in Persons, see http://www.unodc.org/unodc/en/treaties/CTOC/index.html.

serving to the detriment of those they are designed to protect. In this paper, I show how policy directly affects the lived experiences of migrant workers in the Gulf. Migrant narratives about their trajectories into the potentially abusive space of the informal economy help to highlight the direct impact of policies and discourses on migration. A closer look at migrants' narratives and experiences reveals not only the disjuncture between policy and lived experience, but it can also indicate areas where policies might be reformed to meet their needs. Local labor laws (in the form of the *kafala* system) are in desperate need of reform, but the global discourse on trafficking has focused the issue on sex trafficking, thus eliding the problems of forced labor. Currently, policies designed to reduce "trafficking" and the irregular flows of migrant workers are having the opposite effect. While these policies could be used to protect migrants' rights and reduce forced labor, the interpretation and implementation of the policies are hindering the positive application of these laws. The discourse and application of trafficking policies are resulting in larger numbers of people migrating illegally or into the informal economy, while at the same time thwarting civil society efforts and grass roots organizing to meet the needs of migrant workers. Broadly speaking, a re-conceptualization of trafficking within the context of forced labor and migration is needed.[5] Furthermore, current trafficking policies operate under a criminalization framework, and can be re-harnessed within a rights discourse.[6]

The data presented in this essay draw on five years of qualitative fieldwork in the UAE. Between 2004 and 2009 I made several extended trips to Dubai and Abu Dhabi to interview male and female migrants working in various industries such as domestic work, construction work, sex work and service work, who came from a variety of countries such as the Philippines, Iran, Ethiopia, India, Pakistan, Sri Lanka, Bangladesh, and Indonesia. I also spent several months interviewing government officials in the UAE about labor, migration and trafficking policies, in addition to returning to the US to interview members of the State Department who work on international trafficking policy.[7]

[5] D. Brennan, "The Labor of Trafficking." Paper presented at the University of California, Los Angeles, March 2010.

[6] C. Vance. "Re-Thinking Human Trafficking." Paper presented at the Woodrow Wilson Center, Washington, March 2010.

[7] This study received IRB approval from Pomona College. The data in this chapter are part of a larger study: see Mahdavi, *Gridlock*.

Good intentions gone wrong? Global policies on trafficking

Forced labor and migration are global realities with historical precedence. I do not mean to make the argument that instances of forced labor have increased in the UAE due to recent conversations about human trafficking that have taken center stage in the last decade. I acknowledge that migrants have faced instances of force, fraud and coercion in the UAE for many decades. Similarly, activists within the Gulf as well as in sending countries have been lobbying for the protection of migrants' rights in the UAE for many years. What I wish to highlight, however, is that current laws on human trafficking might be used to assist in this activism and could provide a protective mechanism for many migrant workers in the Gulf and globally, but that unfortunately, rather than improving the situation for forced laborers in the UAE and encouraging a reform of the *kafala* system and increased rights for workers, global policies and rhetoric on trafficking have currently provided increased challenges to migrants and forced laborers in the region.

Global discourses about human trafficking (as evidenced in films like *Taken* or *Human Trafficking*, or in the essays of Nicholas Kristoff) are markedly focused on sex trafficking and have constructed the issue (in the minds of the public and policy makers alike) in specifically gendered, raced and classed ways. The archetypal trafficking victims are women, minors, or female minors who have been tricked or forced into "human slavery," almost always for the explicit purpose of sexual exploitation. Alternatively, men are rarely seen as vulnerable to trafficking. The dominant conception of masculinity refuses the possibility that they are "weak" enough to end up victims of trafficking. Men are understood either as voluntary, capable, and consenting migrants, or as being implicated in the root causes of trafficking, cast as predatory consumers of commercial sex services or as ruthless middleman recruiters. Women outside the sex industry are also not imagined as "trafficked" and thus cannot access the attendant rights that could come with being placed in this category.

Trafficking seeks to account for migratory experiences characterized by the elements of force, fraud, and/or coercion. To be labeled a "trafficking victim" theoretically entitles one to a particular legal status and its attendant benefits. Borne out of an understandable sense of indignation regarding the types of abuse and exploitation that seem all too common in migrant women's worlds, the concept has been expanded beyond reasonable or feasible limits, becoming both conceptually and juristically obtuse, while being narrowly gendered, sexualized and racialized at the same time. Trafficking rhetoric and policies, as articulated by Euro-American policies and discourses (such as the US-based TVPA or Trafficking Victims Protection Act passed in 2000) have both narrowed and broadened this definition to fit their political motivations.

The official definition of trafficking as stated in Article 3, paragraph (a) of the Palermo Protocol prepared by the United Nations Office on Drugs and Crime (note the disjuncture in the UN agency designated to monitor human trafficking—an agency dedicated to organized crime and drug trafficking rather than the human rights arm of the UN) is as follows:

the recruitment, transportation, transfer, harboring or receipt of persons, by means of the threat or use of force or other forms of coercion, of abduction, of fraud, of deception, of the abuse of power or of a position of vulnerability or of the giving or receiving of payments or benefits to achieve the consent of a person having control over another person, for the purpose of exploitation. Exploitation shall include, at a minimum, the exploitation of the prostitution of others or other forms of sexual exploitation, forced labor or services, slavery or practices similar to slavery, servitude or the removal of organs. The consent of a victim of trafficking in persons to the intended exploitation set forth [above] shall be irrelevant where any of the means set forth [above] have been used.

Though the definition of trafficking as outlined in the United Nations Palermo Protocol broadly refers to many types of forced labor and migration, the discourse on trafficking has largely focused the issue on transnational sex work. The ambiguity embedded in the Palermo Protocol definition (which was necessary for the resolution to pass) enables multiple, selective, and contradictory understandings of just what human trafficking does or does not entail. This has directly impacted research conducted on the subject. The numbers offered by different sources can vary significantly, and these discrepancies in data reflect the political convictions and motivations that shape and generate such investigations. Unproductively polarized and politicized human trafficking discourses often depend upon differing quantitative grounds to stake their claims. For this reason, it is imperative that trafficking should be examined through qualitative, ethnographically based research methods that enable migrants themselves to address, contest, and inform current discourses, policies, and gaps in our knowledge.

The unfortunate reality is that current policies on trafficking are actually marginalizing those they are designed to protect, and leading increasing numbers of migrant workers (at least in the UAE) into the potentially abusive space of the informal economy. The Trafficking in Persons Report (TIP), the highly influential foreign policy component of the United State's TVPA (the

INFORMALITY AND ITS DISCONTENTS

major piece of US domestic legislation on trafficking), casts the UAE as a major site of sex trafficking, but it does not equally address abuses due to labor violations which in fact constitute the majority of rights violations given the challenges of enforcing labor laws with such a large and diverse migrant population in Dubai.[8] In so doing the TIP Report, written and researched by members of the US State Department, silences the many narratives that challenge this narrow conception of human trafficking in the UAE. In Dubai, and worldwide, one can find both sex workers who choose to migrate in search of better economic opportunities (who view sex as a form of labor and not an identity) and many men in the construction or service industries (such as taxi drivers, or hotel employees) who suffer serious violations of their rights, very possibly "tricked" into their current employment situations. Furthermore, perhaps the majority of women in the service industry of Dubai in particular seem to seek out employment of their own volition, but upon arrival, or during the course of their stay, face instances of unexpected abuse with no avenues to turn to for redress. It is important to re-conceptualize our approach to human trafficking in order to provide support to and serve the needs of all migrant workers, regardless of the industry into which they are migrating or their complicity in the migratory process. While many migrants consent to move for employment, no one consents to instances of force, fraud or coercion (the three elements that define human trafficking as outlined in the United Nations Palermo Protocol).

Power in policy

The TIP report ranks countries according to perceived responses to human trafficking within their borders. These rankings, designated by US officials who typically spend no more than a few days in a country and base their recommendations on limited conversations with Embassy staff,[9] seem arbitrary both to casual observers and to officials within the UAE with whom I spoke. Many felt that a country's ranking had nothing to do with its labor situation or efforts to address the needs of trafficked persons and everything to do with

[8] For more information and copies of the TIP report see http://www.state.gov/g/tip/rls/tiprpt/.

[9] L. Agustin, "Trafficking Reconsidered" and R. Parrenas, "Re-Thinking Human Trafficking." Both papers presented at the Woodrow Wilson Center, Washington, March 2010.

how the United States perceived the country.[10] Some activists in the UAE with whom I spoke felt that as long as the UAE was profitable for the United States it would be ranked no lower than Tier 2, with the prospect of being upgraded to Tier 1 as an incentive. When the economy began to crash, two activists said, the UAE was no longer considered a friend.

Officials and citizens in the UAE were frustrated and embarrassed when the UAE was moved to the Tier 3 (2005) or Tier 2 Watch List (2007) level. The official public response to the TIP reports of 2008 and 2009 was the issuing of statements from the office of the Sheikhs publicly denouncing sex trafficking, the passage of Federal Law 51, an increase in media coverage in outlets such as *Gulf News*, and a temporary increase in brothel raids. Shortly after the 2009 TIP report was released, stories appeared in the major UAE newspapers such as *Gulf News* about the arrest and prosecution of a number of "traffickers," who were immediately jailed and some deported without trial. A series of stories also appeared about brothel raids and the deportation of a number of sex workers who were also convicted and deported without trial. These types of stories faded within weeks, and it is not known whether further raids and arrests were conducted. What is known is that in 2008, 10 persons were prosecuted for crimes related to trafficking, and in 2009 this number doubled to 20, though the exact nature of their crimes is not clear.[11] The responses of the UAE focusing on arresting and prosecuting perceived "sex offenders" keeps the country from falling to the dreaded Tier 3 ranking within the report. Thus, the attention of the government is focused on raids and arresting sex workers, rather than reforming labor laws to protect migrants in a variety of industries.

All three of the individuals introduced at the beginning of this essay have been affected by global policies on trafficking that make migrants in the Gulf *more* vulnerable to instances of force, fraud or coercion with limited avenues for redress. The global moral panic on sex trafficking has resulted in local policies that focus attention on arrest and prosecution of members of the sex industry. The TIP encourages "tightened borders" and "increased police" (TIP report on the UAE 2009) as a strategy to ameliorate the problem of trafficking within the UAE's borders. What the TIP author's failed to recog-

---

[10] See Gargash's statement responding to the 2009 TIP: http://www.wam.ae/servlet/ Satellite?c=WamLocEnews&cid=1241072976464&pagename=WAM/ WAM_E_Layout.

[11] Ibid.

nize, however, is that the UAE must import members of law enforcement bodies (as citizens make up less than 8 percent of the population of Dubai),[12] and these officials are often not trained to work with trafficked individuals. Many of the women I spoke with (women such as Elyse) during my time in the field reported that the majority of abuses they experienced came from these imported law enforcement officials who arrested and detained them (and sometimes raped and abused them in the process) in street or bar raids, or at times where women would come to them for assistance. Other women like Surri reported a fear of the police and indicated that they would avoid them at all costs due to rumors of abuse that circulate amongst migrant circles. Rather than encouraging the UAE to import *more* untrained officials (thereby increasing the numbers of potential abusers), it might be more prudent to recommend that the current members of law enforcement receive some type of training and are held accountable for their actions.

The issue of tightened borders, as encouraged by the 2009 TIP report that recommends tightened borders for both sending countries (such as Indonesia and the Philippines) as well as receiving countries (such as the UAE and Saudi Arabia), is one that has led many migrants directly into the informal economy, as they are not able to migrate through legal channels. Tightening borders (or increasing restrictions on migration in home and host countries) typically results in an increase in the numbers of people (specifically women) who migrate illegally or through unofficial channels.[13] While many do not seek to migrate into the informal economy, a variety of events can lead them to that sector, such as fake visas, illegal migratory patterns, and a lack of laws to protect laborers such as domestic workers when in the host country. Laws that seek to restrict out-migration, especially those that do not create alternative employment opportunities in home countries, do not decrease migrants' desire or need to migrate to earn an income, but rather make them more vulnerable to trafficking as they become increasingly dependent on middlemen brokers and recruiters. Enterprising migrants who have had to make the difficult decision to migrate will do so by any means necessary. When sending countries impose stricter regulations and increased bureaucracy to regulate migration, or when receiving countries seek to tighten their borders, many migrants, women especially, turn to informal routes of migration that can be quicker and seem simpler, but in reality are often more expensive—resulting in migrants incurring high debt to recruiters—and possibly abusive.

---

[12] According to the Dubai Statistics Center, 2009.
[13] Parrenas, "Re-Thinking Human Trafficking."

Policies in sending countries have been affected by global discourse and laws on trafficking as well. The TIP report, which ranks sending countries such as the Philippines, Indonesia, or Ethiopia on a watch list, has encouraged sending countries to tighten their borders and work to regulate migration, specifically migration of women. The problem is that many of these countries have sought to increase restrictions on females who are leaving in search of employment elsewhere—women such as Surri and Elyse—but simultaneously maintain economic development strategies that depend on remittances. Countries such as Sri Lanka, Indonesia, and the Philippines that simultaneously embrace both types of policies have created an environment rampant with contradictions and difficult for their citizens to maneuver. When development strategies depend on remittances, women (and men) are increasingly reliant on jobs outside of home countries for income generation. In 1997 the remittances just from the Middle East to Sri Lanka totaled over $1 billion, which outweighed the trade deficit of $0.7 billion. In 1999, remittances to the Philippines totaled roughly $5 billion.[14] As Ray Jureidini notes, "Asian governments pursued active policies for overseas employment, partly to alleviate unemployment and partly to generate foreign income."[15] This increasing dependence on labor exporting for national income generation means that migrants have fewer choices when looking for employment at home. If countries focused more energy on development strategies that relied less on remittances and more on creating jobs at home, this could help lead to a situation in which those who migrate for work are doing so more out of choice than out of a lack of choices in the home country. It is often the case that these sending countries are suffering from the aftershocks of structural adjustment programs and global economies in transition. Many times they do not have the resources to create sustainable employment programs at home, and thus continue to rely on remittances. These economic dependencies should be examined more closely when crafting bilateral agreements that seek to prevent women's migration from home countries to receiving countries in the Persian Gulf.

The trouble is that TIP recommendations are often misguided, and they lead countries such as the UAE down a difficult path. Specifically, in this case, the strong emphasis on sex trafficking obscures the larger issue of migrants' rights. Currently, the largest challenge facing migrant workers in the UAE is

[14] According to the Philippines Overseas Employment Agency.
[15] R. Jureidini, "Migrant Workers and Xenophobia in the Middle East" (Geneva: United Nations Research Institute for Social Development, 2003).

the structure of the *kafala* or sponsorship system that provides the legal frame-work for all documented migrants working in the formal economy in the UAE. This system works in favor of the employer and has led to poor working conditions in the cases of many migrant workers. The *kafala* system is in desperate need of reform as it is often the exploitative conditions of labor created under this system that lead migrants into situations of trafficking. In 2004 and 2005 government officials in the UAE were willing to work with migrants' rights groups to reform the *kafala* system (inspired by the example of their neighbors in Bahrain who have recently shown interest in reforming the system and worked to provide more protections for laborers).[16] When the UAE was placed in Tier 3 on the 2005 TIP report, however, attention was directed away from *kafala* and turned toward the issue of policing sex work. Unfortunately, the focus of the TIP being on sex trafficking directs attention away from the larger context of migrants' rights, and focuses often unwanted hyperscrutiny on one group of migrant workers in the informal economy—sex workers. Furthermore, one reason that the UAE was given a low ranking in the TIP is a lack of civil society.[17] The erasure of civil society efforts that do exist in the UAE, as alluded to in the TIP report, ignores the many informal groups that form the civil society created to work on the issues of migrants' rights within the UAE and the region. The fact that these efforts have been overlooked presents a direct challenge to those who have worked so hard to build this type of momentum. It also directs attention away from one of the most productive ways of addressing instances of force, fraud, or coercion—through services and outreach provided to abused persons.

Labor and law

Migrant labor in Dubai is structured by a *kafala* or labor sponsorship system. Those migrating into the formal economy must operate on the basis of their contracts and work with a sponsor. This system is unique to the GCC countries and structures the lived experience of migrant work in the formal economy. Under the *kafala* system, each migrant worker is tied to a sponsor, or

---

[16] See "Bahrain commended for sponsorship reforms," *Gulf Daily News* (Bahrain, April 30, 2010); "Bahrain introduces job switch visa rules," *The National* (United Arab Emirates, August 1, 2009); "Bahrain scraps foreign labour sponsorship scheme," www.arabianbusiness.com (May 5, 2009).

[17] According to a TIP officer I interviewed in 2009.

kafeel, who also functions as his/her employer. Residence and legal working papers for the migrant depend on the relationship with the sponsor. In the case of disputes with the sponsor-employer, migrant workers can be left without legal permits to remain in the UAE.[18]

As Andrew Gardner has noted in his thorough study of male migrant workers in Bahrain and later Qatar, the *kafala* system leads to extreme variability in the experiences of workers, in that the governance of the individual depends entirely on the sponsor. While some sponsors are quite accommodating and committed to protecting their laborers, others are exploitative and abusive.[19] Migrant workers with whom I spoke noted that once they were able to speak to their sponsors, their problems were quickly solved; however, communication with the sponsors is not always easy, as middlemen managers (often of the same ethnicity and language group) can present barriers in accessing help from the sponsors. Disputes with sponsor-employers—or even managers—can result not only in job loss, but in making the migrant worker an illegal alien. In addition, while in theory either party can break the contract at any time, doing so forces workers to pay for their return tickets, often a restrictive price further augmented by the debts that many migrants incur in order to migrate.[20] Many workers who choose to break employment contracts attempt to stay in the country as illegal aliens—a better option for them than returning home empty handed. Certain labor laws allow workers to take employers to court for the violation of labor contracts, yet during the proceedings workers become and remain undocumented and are often forced into the informal economy to make ends meet. Indeed, collapsing employer and sponsor into a single category may be the root of the problem. Migrants have no place to turn because the law is written to protect the employers rather than the migrant workers.

Other challenging aspects of UAE labor laws include the fact that contracts are typically written in Arabic. The challenge presented by this is that neither employees nor those who seek to provide them with informal social services typically have a strong enough command of Arabic to decipher the contracts. Though middlemen in home countries may purport to be well-versed in the

---

[18] For more discussion of the *kafala* system, see Andrew Gardner, *City of Strangers: Gulf Migration and the Indian Community in Bahrain* (Ithaca, NY: ILR/Cornell University Press, 2010); and A. Longva, *Walls Built on Sand: Migration, Exclusion and Society in Kuwait* (Boulder, CO: Westview Press, 1999).

[19] Gardner, *City of Strangers*.

[20] Longva, *Walls Built on Sand*.

ways of the host country, they frequently mislead their recruits regarding the contracts, which seldom acknowledge the rights of the workers.[21] Among other aspects of the labor laws that structure the lived experiences of migration, domestic workers and agricultural workers are excluded from the protections of labor laws.[22]

While I argue that the articles of the law outlined above need serious revision, there are, in fact, a series of articles that in theory protect laborers' rights, but lack enforcement. Articles 65–73 outline appropriate working hours and the need to give workers time off at regular intervals. Similarly, Articles 80–90 outline a long list of occupational hazards and diseases that the employer must provide treatment for, both in the short and long term. These laws protect migrants' time and health, but are often not adhered to, due to the lack of inspectors. According to a Human Rights Watch Report, "though a decree in 2006 asked for at least 2000 new labor inspectors, the number currently stands at just 48."[23]

The 1990 UN Convention on the Protection of the Rights of All Migrant Workers and Members of Their Families has not been signed by the UAE, and this convention is the only available international instrument able to protect domestic workers, since even the ILO Convention excludes contract workers recruited under the *kafala* system. Migrants in the domestic work industry and those employed in the agricultural sector in the Gulf are unprotected by the labor laws. The legal domain of domestic work remains a highly contested issue across the globe, and in the Gulf the fact that this type of labor is outside the system of labor laws has been problematic. As they work within the private homes of citizens, any dispute between domestic workers and their employers are viewed as "private matters" or "matters of the home" and not to be resolved in a court of law.

Many migrant workers and scholars with whom I spoke while in the field emphasized the need to reform the *kafala* system to make it more favorable to employees. This reform includes the need to provide rights and benefits for domestic workers and other migrant workers who are subject to rules of *kafala* without enjoying its attendant benefits. Indeed, it is the potentially exploita-

---

[21] Article 2 of the General Provisions of UAE Labor Law, www.uae-embassy.org (last accessed April 2010).

[22] Articles 3 and 72 of General Provisions of UAE Labor Law.

[23] Human Rights Watch Report, "Building Towers, Cheating Workers: Exploitation of Migrant Construction Workers in the United Arab Emirates" (New York: HRW, 2006).

tive situations caused by the system's structure that render many workers vulnerable to situations of trafficking whereby wages are withheld and abuse can occur. It is for this reason that activist groups within the region have been pushing for a reform of the system and have been frustrated at the international community's focus on sex trafficking without contextualizing trafficking within the broader frame of migration.

Perverse integration and the informal economy

Due to a combination of tightened borders and a lack of labor laws to protect migrants in sectors such as domestic work or agricultural labor, some of my interviewees indicated that the potentially abusive space of the informal economy became more attractive to them. Women such as Elyse who were confronted with abuse in the formal economy of domestic work with no avenues for redress, or people like Ade who realized that they were defrauded in the migratory process but could not return home empty handed, or migrants such as Surri who made a difficult decision to migrate through an illegal channel due to the "tightened borders" resulting from global policies, all found themselves in the space of the informal economy. For some, like Elyse, moving into the informal economy was a decision made as a result of a lack of rights in the formal economy. "I can make more money as a working girl, and I have more freedom," she explained, referring to the fact that as a domestic worker her movement was restricted by her employers who often withheld her wages. Surri's experience reflects the structural inequalities that result in many migrants feeling that they must leave their home countries, through any means necessary, to find employment and support their families.

It is no wonder then that some migrants might find the space of the informal economy a comparatively desirable alternative to facing abuse in the formal economy, or to not being able to support their families or pay back their migratory debts. In assessing the trajectory of some migrants from the formal to the informal labor sphere, the concept of "perverse integration" can be particularly helpful. The term "perverse integration" was perhaps first used by Manuel Castells in his book *The Rise of the Network Society* to refer to people's preference for work in the informal economy. Castells describes the "fourth world" as a group of people, located in multiple geographies, who are economically and socially marginalized and seek out work in the informal economy.[24]

---

[24] Manuel Castells, *The Rise of the Network Society: The Information Age: Economy, Society and Culture* (Hoboken, NJ: Wiley Blackwell, 2009).

Castells notes that "the process of social exclusion and the insufficiency of remedial policies of social integration lead to a key process of perverse integration referred to the labor force in the criminal economy."[25] He goes on to add that in the absence of new forms of integration for those who are marginalized members of the fourth world, the integration will necessarily come in the form of the informal economy. In writing about homeless street vendors in New York City, Mitch Duneier uses the concept of perverse integration to show how homeless men in particular, who find themselves on the outskirts of society, use panhandling and illegal street and drug vending as a way to acquire income within the informal economy.[26] Through ethnographic research with street vendors in New York, Duneier delineates the deliberate decision-making processes by which many men seek out employment in the informal economy. He notes that the perversion of this type of integration is demonstrated by the fact that it becomes a regular source of income for these men, while their integration is made evident by the formal economy's dependency on their labor. A further example of perverse integration can be observed in organized crime, which is illegal, however lucrative. Similar to illegal vending, organized crime also operates and benefits members of the formal economy, making it an integrated part of systems in many countries.[27]

For the purposes of my fieldwork, the concept of perverse integration is particularly useful in assessing migrants' decision making with regard to seeking out employment in the informal economy of sex work. Especially when confronted with structural constraints in the formal economy (in the form of the *kafala* system or limited earning potential), some women are integrated into the informal economy, and find that this labor provides them with higher wages and increased autonomy. These women are perversely integrated in that their work in the informal sphere is illegal, yet allows them more opportunities. Additionally, the demand for their services further integrates these women and the service they provide.

While the informal economy becomes the comparatively desirable alternative to no employment or abuse in the formal economy, the space of this underground economy can be increasingly abusive and illegal workers have no avenues for redress or rights protection or social services. Due to their illegal

[25] Manuel Castells, "Information Technology, Globalization and Social Development" (Geneva: United Nations Research Institute, 1999).
[26] Mitchell Duneier, *Sidewalk* (New York: Farrar, Straus and Giroux, 1999).
[27] For further reading on perverse integration and organized crime see Bourgois, *In Search of Respect*.

status, they often cannot go to the police or their embassies if they are facing abuse due to the fear of arrest or deportation. In addition, there are limited social services in place to meet their needs because this has not been a priority of the "global war on trafficking." As alluded to above, the TIP report does not acknowledge the presence of informal social service providers who have been working to build a migrants' rights movement in the Gulf. While erasing those efforts, official policies also direct the attention of the UAE government away from formalizing these outreach providers in favor of increasing law enforcement. If instances of force, fraud, or coercion are really to be addressed, social services, and groups that provide outreach to migrants regardless of their status (as legal or illegal migrants), are an important step in assessing the scope of the problem as well as the needs of migrants who are facing abuse.

Concluding thoughts: moving forward

Force, fraud, and coercion during the migratory process or in the host country are major issues confronting many migrant workers in the UAE. While the challenges faced by migrant workers in the Gulf are not new, the recent global discourse on "human trafficking" as articulated in policies such as the TIP report or the United Nations Protocol to Prevent, Suppress and Punish Trafficking in Persons (Palermo Protocol) has unwittingly produced a new set of challenges. Rather than harnessing the language of trafficking to provide rights protection to all laborers facing instances of force, fraud or coercion, the discourse on trafficking that focuses on sex trafficking has resulted in more obstacles for migrant workers, leading some migrants into the informal economy. Though the numbers are not available, and it is not possible to assess whether and how many more laborers in the UAE are entering the informal economy now as compared to a decade ago, I noticed a distinct trend throughout my fieldwork. When I began this project in 2004 there seemed to be far fewer numbers of migrant workers entering the informal economy than there were in 2009. Many of the reasons that my interlocutors articulated for entering the economy were directly linked to the disconnect between trafficking policy (which has taken center stage in the region since 2005 due to low rankings on the TIP report) and the lived experience of forced labor and migration.

The language of trafficking policies has the potential to create a framework for the protection of migrants' rights worldwide. However, the current hyperscrutiny on sex trafficking has resulted in a number of measures taken (such as directives to increase prosecution of "sex traffickers" or policies restricting the out-migration of women in particular, rather than policies that encourage promotion of social services and outreach for example) that are leading more workers into the potentially abusive space of the informal economy. When there are increased restrictions on mobility of labor in the formal economy, or when laborers feel that they have no way to assert their rights in the formal economy, the informal economy becomes the comparatively desirable choice for some migrants. If we want to address the challenges faced by these migrants we must hear their narratives and listen to their voices, in order to structure policies that align more closely with lived experience and migrant workers' needs.

6

Migration, Networks and Connectedness across the Indian Ocean

Caroline Osella and Filippo Osella

As anthropologists, we find ourselves drawn into and interested in the many kinds of informal networking practices spread among Indian migrants in the Gulf countries of West Asia; in this paper, we begin to explore comparison and compatibility between Indian and Arab approaches to making connections.[1] We explore the ubiquity of practices of connectedness in Indian society, from extended family networks through to the well-known figure of the *dalal*, or broker, go-between; we also begin to trace ways in which Indian networking styles articulate with the Gulf phenomenon of *wasta*, or advantage via social connection. This pushes us to critique the abstraction of much social science literature on social networks and connectedness, raising questions about normativity, legitimacy and morality.

We have been working since 1989 in Kerala, south India, and in various Gulf states among migrants from Kerala (Malayalis).[2] Kerala is a state in which

[1] We thank Kaveri Qureshi and Vekkal J. Varghese for their comments on early drafts of this article.
[2] Over the years, our ethnographic research has been supported by the ESRC, the

Hindus are, as in India as a whole, the majority population, but Kerala also has substantial populations of Muslims and Christians.[3] The three populations have high concentrations and dominance in geographically specific zones. We have worked in two main field sites: throughout the 1990s in an inland rural area (pseudonym Valiyagramam), split roughly equally between various Hindu and Christian communities, formerly dependent upon rice paddy, in which ties to the Gulf developed only after the 1970s;[4] and since 2000 in an urban coastal town in the zone of greatest Muslim significance, where recorded ties to the Gulf stretch back to the tenth century, known as Calicut or Kozhikode.[5]

State, society and the politics of mediation

The state is accepted as hard to define in general terms,[6] and especially in the Gulf, where the nation is recent and takes on a highly specific form, being built upon the postcolonial remnants of reinvigorated and regrouped tribal formations.[7] But even in India—the world's largest democracy, a mature state, equipped with functioning bureaucracy, codified legal institutions, etc.—still

---

AHRC, the Wenner-Gren Foundation and the Nuffield Foundation, to which bodies we are thankful.

[3] The Government of India Census (2001) records 17,883,449 Hindus; 7,863,842 Muslims; 6,057 427 Christians in Kerala. Data taken from: http://www.censusindia. gov.in/Census_Data_2001/Census_data_finder/C_Series/Population_by_religious_communities.htm (last accessed on November 15, 2010).

[4] Filippo Osella and Caroline Osella, *Social Mobility in Kerala* (London: Pluto Press, 2000).

[5] Filippo Osella and Caroline Osella, "'I Am Gulf!': The Production of Cosmopolitanism in Calicut, Kerala," in Edward Simpson and Kai Kresse (eds), *Cosmopolitanism Contested: The Confluence of History and Anthropology in the Indian Ocean* (London: Hurst, 2007), pp. 323–55; Caroline Osella and Filippo Osella, "Nuancing the Migrant Experience: Perspectives from Kerala, South India," in Susan Koshy and R. Radhakrishnan (eds), *Transnational South Asians: The Making of a Neo-diaspora* (New Delhi: Oxford University Press, 2008), pp. 146–80.

[6] Christopher Fuller and John Harriss, "For an Anthropology of the Modern Indian State," in Christopher J. Fuller and Véronique Bénéï (eds), *The Everyday State and Society in India* (London: Hurst, 2001), pp. 1–30; Thomas Blom Hansen and Finn Stepputat, "Introduction: States of Imagination," in Thomas Blom Hansen and Finn Stepputat (eds), *States of Imagination. Ethnographic Explorations of the Postcolonial State* (Durham, NC and London: Duke University Press), pp. 1–38.

[7] Philip S. Khoury and Joseph Kostiner, *Tribes and State Formation in the Middle East* (Berkeley: California University Press, 1990).

we ask, what is the state and where is it anyway? And yet, while the "state" might remain difficult to define and locate, its presence and effects on people's lives are significant and tangible, especially for migrant labor, as it has to cross national borders, arguably the most tangible expression of state presence. While the Gulf Cooperation Council (GCC) countries have attracted a great deal of scholarly and activist attention for implementing policies which, in liberalizing the circulation of capital, impose stringent regulations on the circulation of migrant labor and significantly curtail labor rights, far less has been said about the Indian state's governance of emigration. The 1983 Indian Emigration Act and the 1967 Indian Passport Act, under the guise of offering state "protection" to the most vulnerable migrants, put substantial bureaucratic hurdles in the way of low and unskilled migrant labor, women in particular.[8] Whether we turn our gaze to one shore of the Indian Ocean or the other, then, we find that migrants have to confront complex migration regulations, hostile bureaucracies, police controls or stringent residency and employment laws on a regular basis. It is perhaps all too obvious that navigating through the bureaucratic quagmires of migration—from acquiring a passport and obtaining an emigration clearance certificate, to securing a visa and getting a job—requires skills, competences and contacts which may not be available in equal measure to all actual or would-be-migrants. The relationship between migrants and state bureaucracies normally necessitates various degrees of mediation.

We should also note at the outset that boundaries between "state" and "society" are, in India and the Gulf (as elsewhere), blurred from the outset.[9] There is a clear tension here between the way the "state" produces itself—and is produced through social theory—as disembedded, reified beyond and above the reach of social relations and interests, and the lived experience of state apparatuses and bureaucracies which are inevitably enmeshed in complex social relations, and hence open to popular examination.[10] Still, despite these

---

[8] Rajan S. Irudaya, V.J. Varghese and M.S. Jayakumar, "Overseas Recruitment in India: Structures, Practices and Remedies" (Trivandrum: CDS Working Paper 421, 2010).

[9] Akhil Gupta, "Blurred Boundaries: The Discourse of Corruption, the Culture of Politics, and the Imagined State," *American Ethnologist*, 22 (1995), pp. 375–402.

[10] Gupta, "Blurred Boundaries" pp. 375–402; Fuller and Harriss, "For an Anthropology of the Modern Indian State"; Hansen and Stepputat, "Introduction" pp. 1–38; Jonathan Spencer, *Anthropology, Politics and the State: Democracy and Violence in South Asia* (Cambridge University Press, 2007).

frankly admitted analytic problems in defining the state and its putative boundaries, much policy work envisages civil society (often reduced to NGOs) as the classic "mediatory space" between the bounded spheres of "state" and "society," which therefore demands research and intervention and becomes the major focus. In development circles, civil society is imagined as the panacea for the shortcomings of (postcolonial) states, the latter characterized as being either too authoritarian and overwhelming or utterly ineffectual (if not altogether absent) in people's lives. Civil society is invested, then, with the task of maintaining and policing the boundaries between "state" and "society," a "disembedding" work deemed necessary to avoid the spilling over or encroaching of one sphere into the other which, if unchecked, would foster at best conflict of interests, if not corruption and prevarication.[11]

Here, we run into an immediate difficulty, in that not only are boundaries between state and society inevitably blurred, but also actual instances of civil society seldom fulfill the predictions of social and political theory. Critics have highlighted its class orientation;[12] others have underscored its linkages to global governance projects[13] and neoliberal capitalism.[14] At the same time,

---

[11] Martin Webb, "Boundary Paradoxes: the Social Life of Transparency and Accountability Activism in Delhi" (University of Sussex: unpublished PhD thesis, 2010).

[12] For instance, Bayat and White note differences between Islamist politics—associated with educated, urbanized middle or lower classes—and the "politics of the poor." The latter is ostensibly informed by pragmatism and driven by the necessity to secure jobs, housing and education. Asef Bayat, "Radical Religion and the Habitus of the Dispossessed: does Islamic militancy have an Urban Ecology?" *International Journal of Urban and Regional Research*, 31 (2007), pp. 579–90; Jenny B. White, *Islamist Mobilization in Turkey: a Study in Vernacular Politics* (Seattle and London: University of Washington Press, 2002). See also Partha Chatterjee, *The Politics of the Governed: Reflections on Popular Politics in Most of the World* (New York: Columbia University Press, 2004).

[13] James Ferguson, *Global Shadows: Africa in the Neoliberal Order* (Durham, NC: Duke University Press, 2006); James Ferguson and Akhil Gupta, "Spatializing States: Toward an Ethnography of Neoliberal Governmentality," *American Ethnologist*, 29 (2002), pp. 981–1002; Brad Weiss (ed.), *Producing African Futures: Ritual and Reproduction in a Neoliberal Age* (Leiden: Brill, 2004); Harry West and Tom Sanders (eds), *Transparency and Conspiracy: Ethnographies of Suspicion in the New World Order* (Durham, NC: Duke University Press, 2003).

[14] Timothy Mitchell, *Rule of Experts: Egypt, Techno-politics, Modernity* (Berkeley: University of California Press, 2002); Julia Elyachar, *Markets of Dispossession: NGOs, Economic Development and the State in Cairo* (Durham, NC: Duke University Press, 2005).

civil society is often open to outright state control and manipulation.[15] Hence, it is utterly unremarkable to find that in Gulf societies the formation of civil society associations is strictly scrutinized, their numbers controlled, their activities delimited and closely monitored. The state may even have direct intervention and input into them, as when Skeikhly patronage and supervision become mandatory or when state employees from various ministries are placed as employees and managers within associations.[16] That in India, as much as in the Gulf, protection and representation of migrants—especially unskilled male laborers and female domestic workers—are taken up by or delegated to a plethora of (often state-sponsored) non-governmental organizations indicates the connivance of "civil society" in the governance of migration. In Kerala, for instance, Overseas Development and Employment Promotion Consultants Limited (ODEPC) and the Non Resident Keralites Affairs Department (NORKA) are government-sponsored initiatives explicitly directed toward regulating informal networks—judged to be inherently corrupt and exploitative—with an eye to shifting mediation entirely to the non-governmental sector. Such entanglement between state and non-governmental organizations is all too apparent to most migrants, who routinely shy away from seeking the help of these organizations—often experienced as another, but less efficient, layer of patronage—and rely instead on less expensive and more secure informal connections to support migration projects.[17]

Our research underscores the centrality of informal networks and interpersonal relationships in allowing people both to engage with state bureaucracies and to negotiate their everyday lives. Networks offer Gulf migrants the first recourse right through the process, from first seeking employment and visas, into arrival and settling into accommodation, and on into dealing with post-arrival problems or a desire to change contract. Networks get done what cannot be achieved through direct approach to institutions.[18]

[15] Asef Bayat, *Making Islam Democratic: Social Movements and the Post-Islamist Turn* (Stanford University Press, 2007), pp. 49ff.; Yael Navaro-Yashin, *Faces of the State: Secularism and Public Life in Turkey* (Princeton University Press, 2002), pp. 117ff.
[16] Wanda Krause, *Women in Civil Society: the State, Islamism and Networks in the UAE* (London: Palgrave Macmillan, 2008).
[17] Irudaya Rajan *et al.* suggest that in Kerala only 25 percent of migrants use formal channels of migration, such as NGOs or GONGOs (Government-Organized Non-Governmental Organizations). Reasons given include that informal networks are more efficient, less costly, friendly and more secure. Rajan, Varghese and Jayakumar, "Overseas Recruitment in India": pp. 26ff.
[18] Ibid.

Neha Vora notes that professional and middle class migrants are vocal in their criticism of the UAE for its failure to live up to the neoliberal and capitalist ideals it claims to espouse—no freedom of movement, of labor, of hiring, and so on, and no market-led salary structure.[19] Networks mitigate some of these restrictions. Another type of migrant criticism takes the far more concrete form of simply trying to evade the severe controls as far as possible. Here, informal networks become critical, and force people into realms of the "illicit." We agree with Andrew Gardner that the state itself actually produces illicitness and lays the ground for the flourishing of informal networks,[20] exactly because of its desire to limit NGO action, control media, and enforce highly restrictive residence and employment regulations. Gardner's recent study of the *kafala* (sponsorship) system[21] in Bahrain follows Eric Wolf's notion of the "orchestration" of power to explore how neoliberal economic regimes of extraction and the *kafala* system come together to "produce illegal workers" and orchestrate structural violence.[22] We push Gardner's analysis further, by noting, firstly, that civil society, inevitably embedded in both "state" and "society," cannot but reproduce the blurring of those same boundaries that it seeks to keep apart;[23] secondly, that an ideological, and uncritical, commitment to formal structures of mediation between people and state bureaucracy not only forecloses understanding of informal networks, but draws an unwarranted blanket of illicitness and criminality over the most significant relationships

[19] Neha Vora, "Producing Diasporas and Globalization: Indian Middle-Class Migrants in Dubai," *Anthropological Quarterly*, 81 (2008), pp. 377–406.
[20] Maegher notes that informal networks "are not defined by their autonomy from the state, but are critically shaped by the nature of their relationship with the state" (p. 226). Kate Meagher, "Social Capital or Analytical Liability? Social Networks and African informal economy," *Global Networks* 5 (2005), pp. 217–38. See also V.J. Varghese and S. Irudaya Rajan, "Migration as a Transnational Enterprise: Migrations from Eastern Punjab and the Question of Social Licitness," unpublished paper presented at the International Conference on "Migrations, Mobility and Multiple Affiliations: Punjab in a Transnational World" (Trivandrum: CDS, 2010).
[21] To work in the Gulf countries, foreigners require a sponsor as a legal guarantor for their residence in the country. For a detailed discussion of the *kafala* system, see Gilbert Beaugé, "La *kafala*: un système de gestion transitoire de la main-d'œuvre et du capital dans les pays du Golfe," *Revue Européenne de Migrations Internationales*, 2 (1986), pp. 109–122.
[22] Andrew Gardner, *City of Strangers* (Ithaca, NY and London: Cornell University Press, 2010), p. 51.
[23] See Webb, "Boundary Paradoxes."

which migrants rely on in their everyday lives. Such "illegalization" of informal networks of migration is central to the working of contemporary global capitalism in that, to use Di Giorgi's words, it "work[s] symbiotically toward the reproduction of a vulnerable labor force, suitable for the most exploitative sectors of the post-Fordist economy,"[24] as it is the case for migrant labor in many Gulf countries.

Producing connectedness across the Indian Ocean

In India, networking practices flourish. The figure of the dalal, or the go-between/broker, is ubiquitous; the dalal is used for nearly everything, from marriage arrangements through to business deals and school admissions, even for the mundane matter of buying an air ticket. We mention two major factors here. First is the vast gap between an arcane and time-consuming postcolonial bureaucracy and a relatively uneducated and even sometimes illiterate population, which has socialized people into expecting that official matters and things requiring "paperwork" will be difficult to navigate alone. But even in Kerala state, with its population boasting full literacy and a high competence in modernity, this hardly seems an adequate explanation. In Kerala, as in the rest of India, one can well apply for a driving license or passport, hunt for a job, buy an air ticket, rent a house directly; yet people routinely turn to others for advice and help, and for many matters they will approach the middlemen—brokers, agents, dalals, "uncles"—who make their living this way.[25]

Hence we also pay attention to a second factor, which is that many Indians are brought into modes of subjectification that produce forms of highly socially connected selves. A non-autonomous self who will work happily around and within forms of family, marriage, and life-decision making (study, job) that do not place all the burden of decision or action upon one isolated individual is what works best, and is widely cultivated. We must make it very clear that no value judgment is being made here. In fact, one might well view

[24] Alessandro De Giorgi, "Immigration Control, Post-Fordism, and Less Eligibility: A Materialist Critique of the Criminalization of Immigration across Europe," *Punishment and Society*, 12 (2010): pp. 147–67.

[25] Emma Tarlo, *Unsettling Memories: Narratives of the Emergency in Delhi* (Berkeley: University of California Press, 2003); Ajay Gandhi, "Vernacular Citizenship and Everyday Governance Amongst India's Urban Poor," http://www.irmgard-coninx-stiftung.de/fileadmin/user_upload/pdf/urbanplanet/identities/ws1/041-Gandhi.pdf (last accessed November 18, 2010).

the autonomy and isolation normatively demanded of the contemporary Northern European or American as nearing pathological in the degree of pressure it places upon the single person. So we do not make a judgment, but simply an observation, made across sociology and psychology,[26] that in much of Indian society, family socialization styles and wider realms of action encourage not individual action, but rather a group-centered and dependent, connected self. This means that it is quite normal and expected—advisable, wise—for anybody needing to do anything to turn to others for opinion, advice, and help. Brokerage is one logical outgrowth of the connected self. Among the lower classes of a highly hierarchical society, to this factor we can also add the widespread subaltern tendency of imagining the self as less skilled or less able in the face of technical or bureaucratic matters than "experts." The groundwork is then done for the rise of a class of "Mr Fixits" who, with a little more education, worldly wisdom and specific experience, can offer to help—for a fee. India is a society in which mature and functioning institutions are criss-crossed by networks.

Work on migration has often focused on the important role that personal connections play in migration strategies and in making migration happen. Theories of chain migration or discussions of the role of kin and friends in passing information and offering practical support to would-be migrants have been a core focus. Recently, Vertovec's sociological overview of transnationalism[27] has identified a general trend away from the abstracted high theory of the 1980s and toward studies of concrete and specific linkages. Vertovec argues for the absolute centrality of networks to various forms of transnational social formations. Examples of phenomena that flow through transnational networks would include internet information and social sites; diaspora politics (which can encompass forms of ethno-nationalistic "new patriotisms" but also cosmopolitan activisms); the continual symbolic work involved in the reconstruction of senses of place or locality; flows of capital (such as migrant remittances or investment capital); and much more.

---

[26] See for example Alan Roland, *In Search of Self in India and Japan: Toward a Cross-Cultural Psychology* (Princeton University Press, 1988); Margaret Trawick, *Notes on Love in a Tamil Family* (Berkeley: University of California Press, 1990); Gananath Obeyesekere, *The Work of Culture: Symbolic Transformation in Psychoanalysis and Anthropology* (University of Chicago Press, 1990); Stanley N. Kurtz, *All the Mothers are One: Hindu India and the Cultural Reshaping of Psychoanalysis* (New York: Columbia University Press, 1992).

[27] Steven Vertovec, *Transnationalism* (London and New York: Routledge, 2009).

In our own work, it has long been clear that from Kerala, access to information, contacts, hospitality, capital, and so on has been critical in people's migration strategies, in a state where the economy is reliant upon remittances and Gulf connections,[28] such that, we have often argued, Dubai is more familiar to many Malayali than is Delhi, and the Gulf could be considered as part of the place that is Kerala. Kerala has been a remittance state for so long that a normative male life cycle has come to be built around a period of Gulf migration.[29] Anxiety about having, maintaining, improving one's connections and information is correspondingly high, so that no chance may be missed or lost out to somebody else, and energetic networking around issues of access to "Gulf" is a central part of Kerala life. In a terrain of neoliberal economies and limited employment chances, Indian would-be migrants are not mere surplus labor waiting to be called, but are actively fashioning themselves: gaining the certificates, connections and so on needed for success, in a highly entrepreneurial manner. The importance of information in the Gulf's ever shifting and fast moving migration scene means that networking takes on a heightened importance, akin to that discussed by Patricia Sloane in her work on Malaysian entrepreneurs and their energetic social and business lives[30] or that found in state-socialist societies where access to scarce resources and speedy passage through labyrinthine regulations is mediated by having the right "connections."[31]

We are not taking here a naïve view of these migrants' networks, as simply instances of demotic resistance to state or to formal, bourgeois associationism.[32] Literature on patron-client relations in India, for instance, has extensively explored the power relations producing and underpinning informal connections,[33] even as recent research highlights how so-called clients might

[28] While direct official remittances have dropped from 25 percent of GDP in 1998 to 18 percent in 2008, the secondary economic development in the form of real estate, sales of consumer goods and so on is hard to estimate but clearly enormous. Rajan, Varghese and Jayakumar, "Overseas Recruitment in India."

[29] Caroline Osella and Filippo Osella, *Men and Masculinities in South India* (London: Anthem Press, 2008).

[30] Patricia Sloane-White, *Islam, Modernity, and Entrepreneurship among the Malays* (New York: St. Martin's Press, 1999).

[31] Mayfair Yang, *Gifts, Favours and Banquets: the Art of Social Relationships in China* (Ithaca, NY and London: Cornell University Press, 1994).

[32] See for example Chatterjee, *The Politics of the Governed*. For a critique, see Meagher, "Social Capital or Analytical Liability?", pp. 217–38.

[33] See for example Jan Breman, *Beyond Patronage and Exploitation: Changing Agrarian Relations in South Gujarat* (New Delhi: Oxford University Press, 1993); Jan Bre-

have considerable leverage in negotiating or resisting patrons' demands.[34] Clearly, favors have to be repaid, in cash or otherwise. Yet these informal networks through which information, jobs, accommodation and visas circulate between migrants and would-be migrants, while entailing various degrees of power inequality and exploitation, do also offer simultaneously a source of necessary connections and social capital.

In other words, our ethnography not only collapses the opposition drawn between patronage and networking—marked in the literature, respectively, as illicit, "primordial" and licit, "modern" forms of social connectivity, but in practice working in analogous ways—but also undermines another dualism: between the alleged morality of socially embedded economic practices and the assumed amorality (or immorality) of impersonal market exchange. Some Gulf-based Malayali entrepreneurs mobilize their business skills and interests to sustain community development back in Kerala; many help by privileging the recruitment of migrant labor from their "own people";[35] while those at the center of informal migrant networks might be driven less by considerations for long-term reciprocity than by ruthless self-interest, as testified by the many instances of "cheating" (some of which we discuss below).

Aware that, in practice, formal and informal networks might overlap,[36] in the rest of the paper we heed Kate Meagher's warning against the essentialism

---

man, *Footloose Labour: Working in India's Informal Economy* (Cambridge University Press, 1996); Pierre Bourdieu, *The Logic Of Practice* (Cambridge: Polity Press, 1990).

[34] Arjun Appadurai, "Topographies of the Self: Praise and Emotion in Hindu India" in Catherine Lutz and Lila Abu-Lughod (eds), *Affecting Discourse: Anthropological Essays on Emotions and Social Life* (Cambridge University Press, 1990), pp. 92–112; Geert De Neve, "Patronage and 'Community': The Role of a Tamil 'Village' Festival in the Integration of a Town," *Journal of the Royal Anthropological Institute*, 6 (2000), pp. 501–19; Filippo Osella and Caroline Osella, "Sneham and the Articulation of Bodies," *Contributions to Indian Sociology*, 30 (1996), pp. 36–68; James Staples, "Disguise, Revelation and Copyright: Disassembling the South Indian Leper," *Journal of the Royal Anthropological Institute*, 9 (2003), pp. 295–315.

[35] Caroline Osella and Filippo Osella, "Muslim Entrepreneurs between India and the Gulf," *ISIM Review*, 19 (2007), pp. 8–9; Caroline Osella and Filippo Osella, "Muslim Entrepreneurs in Public Life between India and the Gulf: Making Good and Doing Good," *Journal of the Royal Anthropological Institute*, Special Issue (2009), pp. 202–21.

[36] Cf. Massimiliano Mollona, "Factory, Family and Neighbourhood: the Political Economy of Informal Labour in Sheffield," *Journal of the Royal Anthropological Institute*, 11 (2005), pp. 527–48.

and cultural determinism of "abstract models of solidarity and connectivity," to focus instead "on the specificities of how particular types of networks operate."[37]

Expanding one's networks

We have observed over the years a range of different styles of social network in operation. Some are based on pre-existing connections, via kinship, friendship and neighborliness back home, as we expect from migration studies.

Sitting along the Kuwait City seafront, Filippo shares takeaway food with a few Malayali friends. It is a heterogeneous group—young migrants and old hands, kin and unrelated, professionals and house servants—who meet regularly because they are all Muslims from the same Kozhikode neighborhood. The conversation soon turns to serious matters. There are two new arrivals: Faizal, who has recently moved from Muscat, where he had to abandon his small haulage business as the result of Omanization policies; and Gafoor, a young man who, after some years in Damam, could no longer stand Saudi restrictions upon "bachelors'" use of public space. Faizal is staying with his sister's husband, an accountant who has provided him contacts with a number of shops and stores that are now hiring him to transport goods using the van he has purchased. He considers himself lucky, although he claims to "have lost a fortune" in the move, and complains that he is hardly making a living. Faizal's brother-in-law, who had arranged the work permit, now negotiates cheap hiring rates for Faizal's van as a favor to some of his own clients. The group listens carefully, but does not have harsh words for the brother-in-law, simply reminding each other that "it is always hard when you arrive in a new place." Concerned, though, about Faizal's reduced income, and what a protracted reduction of remittances to his family would do to his reputation back home, a few—discreetly—offer to lend money. Gafoor has not found a steady job as yet, and is helping out "for time passing" in a supermarket belonging to one of his father's friends. Father, after spending all his working life in Damam, has now retired back to Kerala. Considering his son's lack of employment, he is setting up a shoe shop for Gafoor in Kozhikode. Group discussions of these predicaments tease out a long exchange about how much the Gulf has changed: it is much harder to find a job, salaries have gone down, working conditions are not what they used to be and, in general, there are far fewer

---

[37] Meagher, "Social Capital or Analytical Liability?", p. 226.

"chances" than before. Yes, with the right connections it is still possible to make money, but no one has any illusions about the Gulf anymore. And many of these men will not choose migrants as husbands for their daughters. Newcomers, Filippo's friends argued, have to learn fast that the streets of the Gulf are not paved with gold, as they used to be.

The oldest migrants in this group arrived here in the late 1960s, brought by some Kuwaiti traders who, after many years settled in Kozhikode, had closed their businesses and returned to the Gulf in the wake of the oil boom. Such good connections, built over years—sometimes generations—of trading partnerships across the Indian Ocean allowed Malayalis to find government employment, from post offices to the police. And as the Kuwaiti economy developed, young professionals—engineers, accountants and medical doctors—used longstanding trade connections to enter private and public companies. In the meantime, Kuwaiti and Malayali trading partners used the last boats (dhows) plying the moribund Indian Ocean trade route to "smuggle" migrants—mostly laborers—to the Kuwaiti coast. "They were dropped outside the city, on the beach," Filippo's friends recounted. "There was a Malayali "hotel" which gave shelter to these men, and found them jobs." Over time, as migration became a steady stream, networks diversified. On the one hand, familial, friendship or business relations—often overlapping each other—provided reliable information, contacts and support for would-be migrants. On the other, established migrants doubled up occupation and income by moonlighting as middlemen between Arab sponsors and Malayali "agents," offering their services to those who had no direct Gulf contacts and connections.

Back in Kozhikode, in the Muslim neighborhood (where most households have at least one member working in the Gulf, and where many families now hold three generations of migrants), information on job opportunities, salaries and so on is readily available and discussed on a daily basis. Seldom do would-be migrants rely on "agents", and young men have a good idea of what awaits them in Damam, Sharjah or Doha: the oft embellished tales of some holidaying migrants are tamed by what is heard directly and honestly from relatives or family friends. A decision on whether to migrate or not, then, is taken judiciously. With the help of a tourist visa, men might go and stay with friends and relatives in the Gulf, visiting different locations to find out first-hand what opportunities they will have there. And returning shortly after migrating because a job did not match up to promises is not considered shameful. Shahad, for example, went to the UAE as a teacher in a Malayali-owned secondary school. Missing his family, and finding work conditions too harsh and "demeaning" given his status and educational qualification, he did not hesitate to take the first flight back to Kozhikode. For many youths, migration to the Gulf is not an attractive proposition, and unless they expect a well paid professional job, or are forced by kin, young men would much prefer to stay put in Kerala, or perhaps move to Bangalore. At the same time, many long-term migrants have become weary of extending help to all those who approach them, either directly or via network chains, for help. Having a reputation as a "fixer" or as a patron certainly increases one's status, but it is also time consuming and brings too many responsibilities. If you "arrange" a job for a family acquaintance's son and the employer turns out to be a cheat, paying a much lower salary than promised, then it is your duty to mediate and find a satisfactory solution, or to find alternative employment.

We note here a significant difference between migrant networks in Muslim urban Kozhikode and rural Hindu Valiyagramam, both in the way information circulates and in the manner in which help is extended to support aspiring migrants. In Kozhikode city, with historical trade and religious connections with the Arabian Peninsula and extensive migration to the Gulf countries, we never found locals hanging on the words of migrants, taking as true fantastic stories about glamorous life and easy money that lead to overblown expectations; expectations inevitably proved wrong by first-hand migration experiences. Unlike rural Valiyagramam, in urban Kozhikode, familiarity with the Gulf is such and the transnational information and gossip networks so deep and extensive that masculine boasting about one's good fortune or cunning can be easily disproved and ridiculed.[38] In Kozhikode everyone knows what current salary rates are for different jobs; in which states or cities life is easier and cheaper; how migration laws are changing and where it might be easier to circumvent them; and so on. In Valiyagramam, on the contrary, this knowledge is limited to a few longer-term migrants, who restrict its circulation and cash in on its disclosure, making money and brokerage jobs. At the same time, we also discern a difference between Muslim, Christian and Hindu networks. Specifically, among Muslims, reliable connections are extended well beyond close family members, to include a wider circle of friends, hence limiting the extent to which social mutuality and reciprocity can be turned into patronage, or commoditized as a service offered for a fee, as often happens in the other communities. Non-Muslims sometimes carp at this ethos of mutuality and

[38] Cf. Caroline Osella and Filippo Osella, "Migration, Money and Masculinity in Kerala," *Journal of the Royal Anthropological Institute*, 6 (2000), pp. 115–31.

help and express envy of the wider trust circles which they observe among Muslims, never thinking that all this may have grown up in the first place as a survival response in India's very harsh socio-economic environment, where Muslims are subject to systematic discrimination and disadvantage.[39]

Women, too, play a crucial part in information exchanges and assessment of the *chance*. Back home, at weddings, at dinners, in school lobbies, beauty parlors and all the many other places where women have time to socialize, stay-behind wives routinely share information about where a husband is working and how he is finding the place. With those they trust, they will confide detail. Shabira's husband has been working for ten years as the manager of a small mini-market in Saudi. He is unhappy with pay and conditions and always looking to get out. Shabira quizzes other women about their husbands' situations, and passes back to her husband during their weekly Friday skype video call what she has learnt—usually, that other men are working equally long hours and in no better conditions.

Many migrants who shared their stories with us were first taken to the Gulf by a relative, were given residence in the relative's place, and worked at a job arranged by a relative. This often results in a safe situation, quite unlike the labor bondage described in many studies. Mujib's father's younger brother Aziz (thirty-two years) is an accountant at the LuLu supermarket in Abu Dhabi. Aziz managed to get his nephew Mujib (nineteen years) a job as sales assistant in the electrical department and took him into his own apartment to live. This allowed the lad time to find his feet and look around, ready to move on to look for a better contract or *chance* after two years. People often agree that the important thing is to get to the Gulf—only there can you begin to meet the people you need to know and gather the information you need in order to make your migrancy successful. Even those Malayalis coming "alone" will have two or three names and phone numbers of direct or indirect friends and relatives, and will be able within one week of arrival to insert themselves into multiple networks.

While most therefore come already with some connection, many more contacts are forged in the Gulf itself, and this aspect in particular cries out for further study. This can happen via expansion along the familiar Indian line of working to familiarize the unfamiliar and give oneself a sense of belonging, through making contact with a "friend of a friend of a friend." We often use

---

[39] Thomas Blom Hansen, "The India that does not Shine," *ISIM Review*, 19 (2007), pp. 50–51.

this ourselves as a fieldwork tool; when coming to a new place in the Gulf, we have never contacted NGOs or organizations working with Malayalis, but simply ask around among our Kerala contacts, "Who knows somebody in this place?" Invariably a list of introductions appears, often with requests to carry letters, small gifts, cash or requests for cash, food items and so on along a chain. These chains and networks tend to be narrow, reaching back to homeland roots and hence usually to specific communities or kin groups.

In Dubai there is an apartment building "named" after a residential district of Kozhikode town. By a process of snowballing, a handful of original residents (some related) who found comfort and convenience in co-residence attracted others from the neighborhood, who also appreciated the shared cooking of favorite "home" foods, being able to share and discuss news from back home, and having constant easy access to communication. It is usual practice to avoid the Indian postal system and for letters, cash and small gifts to be sent home by means of other traveling migrants; living among hometown folk makes for an uninterrupted and easy line of transit. Those who work outside the city or in labor camps use this address for correspondence or as a resting place on the rare days off. By now, the existence of the block is well known among hometowners both back home and around the Gulf.

Going to church or mosque affords other opportunities for meeting conationals and making new contacts. An apartment in downtown Karama in Dubai was shared by a group of south Indian Christians who attended an underground evangelical fellowship and had become good friends through church. This bachelor flat was interesting in highlighting the possibilities that shared religious affiliation offers for expanding networks beyond hometown, state and even linguistic groups. Half the men were working in a handbag distribution warehouse, where they had been recruited by a fellow church member and were happy with their working and living conditions. Some of them of course were officially on visas and contracts for different jobs and were "illegals," but they did not seem unduly anxious about the situation, partly because they envisaged making money and then returning to India, partly because they seemed to feel (rightly or wrongly) that the warehouse owner had the *wasta* to ensure that no raids or deportation would take place at the workplace.

Reggie has a small old house in the outskirts of Ras al Khaimah, where he works in management in a mall. His days off inevitably involve energetic moving around the entire UAE, as he pops in to meet with people he already knew back home and who are now settled in the UAE and new people from his home area who have been introduced to him through friend-of-a-friend networks. He may only stay for half an hour, but he tries to keep in regular contact with as many hometowners as he can. Sometimes, he and a few men friends get out on a Friday night to one of the discreet Indian drinking clubs. There, his regular friend group of six or so men will be augmented by friends-of-friends who have been invited along to relax in company. Drinking friends share new Indian songs, movie clips, and pornographic mini-videos on their mobile phones as the evening progresses, and finish up with phone numbers swapped, with new contacts made and everyone's networks strengthened and widened. Bars, like churches and mosques, are spaces where people are sometimes able to make connections and widen networks beyond hometown or direct chain linkages.

But the settling of oneself into a place and into new networks can also happen through contact with one of the many ambiguous "self-interested" new friends one might meet, and such networks are far wider and cross any boundary, so long as the price is right or the mutual advantage good enough. What we have seen of such connections in the Gulf is that they cross boundaries of religion or caste, even of gender and, to some degree, of class, boundaries normally observed in India.

Varghese took us to meet his "very good friend" Abu Awais, in a rundown little office in downtown Ras al Khaimah. Abu, a hugely fat and jovial Somali man, sitting behind a desk littered with many piles of paperwork and with three phones on it, was introduced as one of the long-term Gulfies, someone who had been there since the 1960s. Varghese pointed out to us that Abu knew hundreds of people, understood all the regulations and—more important—how to get round them, had many Arab friends, and also spoke, read and wrote Arabic. Ostensibly acting as scribe and document translator, Abu derived his real income mainstay from acting as the liaison between Indian agents seeking papers or jobs for their Indian clients, and between locals who were looking to make money out of visa sponsorship, offering fake letters of employment, or acting as sitting partners in businesses—real or fake.

One triangle we know, consisting of a local Arab—whom we of course never met, nor did we ever know his identity—a Malayali and an East African, set up and registered a business supplying window frames in Ajman. The enterprise existed, in that there was a yard, some basic equipment, materials, and some window frames being made, but the real business of the yard was to sell work visas with employment with the company. Men back in India who paid for these visas were not cheated, but knew that their offer of employment was fake and simply designed to get them a visa and entry into the

UAE, where they could then seek out employment. A series of officials and the combined *wasta* of all three partners had been involved in obtaining the clearances, premises, and so on needed to set up the business, and would continue to be involved in keeping clear of detection as a "ghost" company. The Malayali partner in the triangle, Shajan, was also involved in many other small networks and money-making opportunities; he did his best never to say no to anybody, to work to connect people and build his reputation as "a man who can."

One evening in the car driving around Dubai, Shajan took a call from somebody who had heard that a labor camp in Al Quoz was unhappy with the price it was paying to its food contractors and was looking for another contractor; he asked menu and price details, and then told his caller that he knew other people who could supply similar menus at reduced prices, and that he would get back within a day or two. He then called somebody and passed on the details, and asked them to get back to him with a price which would beat the existing one. Soon after, he took another call from somebody who had a chance to offer sanitary fittings for reconstruction in Kuwait; they wanted to source second-hand sanitary fittings being removed from bathrooms in hotels under refurbishment in the UAE, and ship them to Kuwait. Again, he promised that he would be able to find somebody who could supply these materials. A third call came from somebody working in an Arab household, who wanted a recommendation for somebody practicing Ayurvedic treatments for diabetes and offering courses of medicinal oil massages. Shajan immediately named two establishments, giving the name of the head masseur, and agreed to "adjust" (give commission to) the caller as thanks for this business when they next met. Shajan himself would of course take commission from whichever Ayurvedic clinic got the business. This is small-time stuff: "lunch money," "drinks money" or "tea money" changes hands in many of these transactions, amounts of cash which would be laughable to Gulf citizens, but which, added together, can scrape together a livable income for a careful Indian broker. It is the extent, size, and heterogeneity of a broker's network that makes success; Shajan receives nonstop calls and makes several small deals a day because he has managed to become known as somebody who is ultra-connected. New arrivals who are doing business in the Emirates are likely to end up with his number in their phones, upon recommendation, as a useful person to know.

Many migrants in the Gulf, like Shajan, actually have as their main business (whatever their official business or job may be) the work of acting as broker or go-between for visas, jobs, contracts, certificates, supplies and whatever else might be needed. Hub points in many overlapping networks, these energetic entrepreneurial types find out about a variety of needs and connect—for a fee or a favor—two or more parties. Some of them open their houses as temporary stop-points for migrants who are in between work contracts or looking to make connections. Obviously, this is not an open service, and one needs to be personally known or be strongly recommended and tightly connected to one of the broker's own close contacts in order to be invited to stay in the broker's home. We reiterate here the point that the domestic sphere is not a sealed off arena that is ring-fenced from the public sphere; it is often a very active hub of migrant networking and activities, and as such may be deeply implicated in the worlds of business and employment.

Dalal and *wasta*

There is, then, continuity and ease for Indians arriving in the Gulf with the way that things get done. They are skilled and accustomed to negotiate their way through personalized relationships, and through networks around which favors, benefits, material gain and information all circulate busily. There is also a personal continuity for some Gulf Indians between the older forms of patronage and networking familiar to them from back home and the new ones operative under *wasta* logics.

Meena's father Babuchan had been a *panchayat* president back home and a "big man" in the village and the immediate neighborhood. Though well educated, he had never taken up formal employment, preferring to maintain the status of "cultivator" of his many hectares of paddy land and to grow active in local politics, as an energetic member of Kerala's Communist Party. His home was always full of people, and he was forever off to meet some block office bureaucrat or Member of the Local Assembly. He helped people sort out problems, liaised with government offices on people's behalf, networked people together for business, marriage, and whatever other connections they were seeking, and was a reliable source of news on what was going on both in the village and immediately beyond. A couple of years after his daughter arrived in the Gulf, she was already working as a broker. She had her fingers in just as many pies as her father did, finding it natural to connect people together for the sake of business. Once, juggling two of her mobile phones, through which she was brokering a deal between a "buyer" and a "seller," she smiled at us and, with a wink, said, "Don't look so surprised. What do you expect? I am Babuchan's daughter!"

When we introduced another Malayali friend of ours to Meena, as we left her house after taking tea along with the usual three or four "house guests" and hangers on, he dismissively remarked, "Oh, I know this type: the typical Kerala Christian, always looking for the main chance, always tricky and on the make, everybody's friend. But you can't trust them—it's all business, business." Having known Meena for many years, we can say that this was a rather unfair assessment, but we can agree that she has excellent skills in networking and doing deals, and that these skills, which she has developed and used now for many years to support her family, have flourished in the Gulf but were initially built up from a habitus learnt at home, at her father's knee. There is a continuity of skill, a set of habits, and—in Kerala idiom—a "social-mindedness" which Meena's father put to good use in local politics and "social work," and which Meena has been able in the Gulf to turn into a basis for income generation.

We can also argue then that, unable to develop her talents back home, hampered by south Indian rural expectations of appropriate gendered behavior, Meena was finally able to realize her ambitions and herself in the Emirates. The Gulf has opened equal opportunities to this sharp, enterprising and energetic woman. Neha Vora (and we ourselves) have previously noted how employment and mobility options are significantly opened up for many Indian women in the Gulf, and how this fact is very much part of what women appreciate about their experience there.[40] We need also to recognize the (ambivalent, to be sure) fact that the same sorts of opening up of opportunity for economic activity, self-realization, social advancement and personal fulfillment are offered within the realm of the illicit economies that flourish across the Gulf.[41]

These cases also confirm the point that those working as broker-hustlers for a living seek to expand their networks indefinitely, and hence often mingle with people whom they would avoid and often disdain back home. We have spent Friday afternoon in a car with a Malayali woman based in the UAE, driving around from mosque to mosque, handing out, ordering and collecting orders for fake work sponsor letters, educational certificates, passports and so on. She is protected by an Indian Muslim policeman. Back home, she would be far more circumspect both in maintaining her public reputation and in

---

[40] Vora, "Producing Diasporas and Globalization," pp. 377–406; Osella and Osella, "Nuancing the Migrant Experience," pp. 146–80.

[41] This is a point made well in Pardis Madhavi's contribution in this volume.

choosing who to interact with. We also note a relative advantage of Muslim and Christian migrants over Hindus. The fixed times and more obligatory and congregational nature of Friday *jumma* and Sunday services ensure a guaranteed meeting place and point for those wanting to make new connections or do deals.

As our discussion of Meena—who developed her father's social networking skills into an entrepreneurial talent and an ability to work in the Gulf's illicit economies—suggests, there is a happy articulation of expectation and practices around *wasta* and *dalal*. Malayalis are used to working through the Indian mode of using go-betweens, and also to the more general idea that working to uncover or forge new personal connections is the best way to get things done. With connections come obligation and favors traded. A connection might run across a frank commercial transaction in which someone claiming better access or knowledge is paid to smooth a process, or can be based on more advanced, ambiguous relationships of friendship, patronage and clientelism. The means used—gifts, hospitality—are predictable. When talking about the success of the Malayali entrepreneur Yusuf Ali, leader of the Emke group which owns LuLu stores across the Gulf, and named as the fourth richest Gulf Indian,[42] many phrased it as a combination of good business sense and an ability to work *wasta*. "He is very good at knowing what the Arabs want," was a typical remark. We have explored elsewhere the way Indian (like Malaysian) entrepreneurs are frank and clear about the fact that their success and their vision of contemporary entrepreneurship are based upon a winning combination of technocratic "know how" and older skills of "know who," whereas it is more common in North America and Europe to cling to the fiction of impersonal institutions, merit, open competition and transparency.[43]

There are of course differences between Indian practices of connectedness and Arab ones. One is that an important element of building *wasta* seems to be public networking: being sure to be seen in the right place and moving

---

[42] http://newfrontworld.com/2010/08/17/richest-indians-in-gulf-br-shetty-no-2-m-a-yusuf-ali-no-4/ (last accessed 12 September 2010).

[43] Again we reference Andrew Gardner's ethnography, this time to note that one of his entry strategies into the field in Bahrain was to join the local branch of Toastmasters, a North American organization dedicated to social networking and providing training in public speaking. In Bahrain, as in the US, the chance to build useful "know who" is a core part of the rationale for joining the organization. Filippo was a member of Calicut Lions' Club in Kerala, another organization providing businesses and professional people with networking opportunities.

among the "right people," such that in Gulf society, things that look like or would be counted as "leisure" in classical Western sociology or society are actually productive in terms of *wasta* logics. Malayalis immediately grasp this, because of a basic shared understanding that it is important to cultivate potentially useful social relationships.

When Gulfar Mohamad Ali's daughter Kadeeja married back in Kerala (a wedding that we also attended), it was a lavish affair. Around 4,000 guests were put up in various hotels around Cochin, from the luxury Le Meridien Hotel and Convention Center (which his own construction company owned and had built) to smaller but still three-star venues. We were told that five hotels had been completely taken over by the wedding party and that 200 guests were flown in from Muscat, where Gulfar HQ and Mohamad Ali's main Gulf residences are. All guests were offered full hospitality, met at train stations and airports by family members, taken by air-conditioned car to their hotel, and invited to a lavish pre-wedding evening *mailanchi* ceremony. This included an extensive buffet dinner, henna hand painting for the bride and all female guests (offered by a team of five professional beauticians), "folk-traditional" style professional singing and dance displays of *oppana*, Kerala's Muslim wedding songs. Next day came the wedding proper. One enormous air-conditioned hall in the Convention Center hosted the event and relayed onto huge screens both close ups of the *nikkah* stage and a view of the arrival door, where a variety of dignitaries flooded in. We noted various entrepreneurs, Kerala state ministers, and members of the Omani state government and ruling family. Beside the main hall, there were around five other rooms, such as luxury air-conditioned cinemas, each with a screen showing the wedding for the overflow who did not make it in time or were not notable enough to get a seat in the main hall. The bridegroom was brought in with great ceremony and *daff muttu*, another Arabic-inspired Kerala Muslim folk art. Before the *nikkah*, the bride's father stood up on the podium and made a speech about the groom's family: how noble they were, how many of the family held MBA degrees, what businesses they were involved in, and so on. The buffet dinner, served by waiters galore, offered an astonishing array of food stalls, including some from chefs brought in especially from the Gulf. We noted Arabic, north Indian style kebabs, Kerala food, salads, pasta, Maharashtrian, Gujerati, Punjabi, Lebanese. The sweet stalls also offered a variety of all the European, Arabic and Indian sweets you could imagine. As Indian weddings go, which are—at every level, from rural peasant to upper elite—always a performance of status, money and prestige, this was exemplary, and was directed no less at the local audience than it was at the visiting Omanis. Here, a transnational business elite mingled and made connections with high-level politicians from both sides of the sea.

Compared to *wasta*, the Indian *dalal* system seems more democratic in its openness, in that the favor-seeker can be simply a very tenuous and hardly known friend of a friend of a friend, can be somebody only just met, with no social depth to the relation, or can even be openly fee-paying. Whether the relationship slides into patronage, exchange of favors, passing of gifts, or openly monetary dealing will be carefully judged and negotiated when the parties meet. So many people are actually reliant on acting as brokers in order to make their own living, acting as hub points—redistribution points—that one can always easily find several paths toward one's goal, and then simply choose the most convenient. Even when patronage or help is cloaked in terms of friendship, with no fee or obvious material benefit accruing to the favor giver, the hierarchy within the relationship is always well understood by both parties, and the "friend" who receives a favor knows that at some point, some sort of payback may be called in. Sometimes that payback is no more than being part of an entourage, or being part of the group which reflects back a big man's glory, to him and to wider society,[44] for the pure satisfaction of the patron and for the maintenance of his reputation and leverage in society as someone who matters and can get things done. Men who seek to augment their masculine status, to stand at the center of many network hubs, and to be recognized as part of a class of hegemonic male, are plenty.[45]

But despite the numerous differences, Indians well used to dealing with a brokerage system find *wasta* easy to understand and work. Shabith, who had worked in administration at a shipping office, told us happily how his boss had, every Thursday, bought *biryani* (actually *machboos*) for all the workers and sat to eat with them, sharing food off the same plate (for Indians, whose normative food practices include avoidance of food sharing beyond family intimates, this is an extraordinary gesture of equality and intimacy). This was clearly understood by Shabith as a pretence at friendliness and equality, as a superficial performance, because of course the boss was still the boss—and an

---

[44] Geert De Neve, "The Workplace and the Neighbourhood: Locating Masculinities in the South Indian Textile Industry," in Radhika Chopra, Caroline Osella and Filippo Osella (eds), *South Asian Masculinities* (New Delhi: Kali for Women & Women Unlimited, 2004), pp. 60–95.

[45] See for example Caroline Osella and Filippo Osella, *Men And Masculinities In South India* (London: Anthem Press, 2006).

Arab as well. But Shabith also understood that the boss was trying to solidify his connection to his workers beyond mere contract, was purchasing loyalty and silence about certain accounting and recording practices, and had, through the Thursday night meals, become in turn somebody to whom Shabith could present his own case for help in case of difficulty—a valuable source of *wasta*. Although Shabith would often have preferred to go off early to friends and free time as soon as his precious weekend leave began, he would stay behind to share food with the boss and co-workers, knowing the value and significance of his participation in this weekly meal. He never interpreted the invite as an innocent offer of hospitality.

The situation of a migrant already in the Gulf and looking to jump contract and find a better deal is quite different from that of the would-be migrant back in India, and Malayalis, with their deep density of population around the Gulf and their skills, Gulf experience and Gulf knowledge, are in a far better position in Gulf states than, say, the Nepali bonded laborer in a camp. While education accounts for part of the general picture, the larger, better, denser, more numerous and deeper history of the average Malayali's networks must also account for a lot of their relative success and ease. We can say that Malayalis have better social capital in this illicit networking field than Nepalis, but we also note, finally, that even as we repudiate normative snap judgments which would speak immediately of "corruption" and "illegality," or refuse to dignify certain networks as "social capital," still we must acknowledge problems in the system, in the form of the degree of inequality in access to *wasta*. We will return to this discussion in our conclusion.

The large literature on networking can also be very useful in avoiding the pitfalls of exceptionalism, so apparent in regional studies. One must avoid the temptation to explain everything in terms of specific Gulf histories or imagine the social morphologies found as region-specific concepts, such as "rentier-state" or "*wasta*." Analyses that do not broaden out from the Gulf and make comparison are in danger of missing some of the wider socio-economic logics at work in favor of narrow explanation. Differences between how *dalal* and *wasta* get things moving are already instructive; studying other examples of societies or portions of society where networking is intense would offer yet another layer. Examples are legion: we have mentioned Sloane's study of energetic Malaysian sociality; *guanx chi* in China brings people together in favors, gifts, and feasting/hosting;[46] the latest change of government in the UK

[46] Yang, *Gifts, Favours and Banquets*, pp. 90–99.

prompted an outpouring of commentary noting the close networks drawing together Britain's new power class,[47] a limited network which however connects into larger and more powerful global ones. We also note here that this last example—indexed by studies such as *Superclass*[48]—however much views are sometimes informed by exaggeration or paranoia, points us toward a phenomenon which even the most conservative commentators cannot deny exists. These studies thereby offer a fast corrective to easy neo-Orientalist assumptions that this sort of mutually advantageous networking is a specifically Eastern practice, by drawing attention to the personalized relationships and the interwoven networks (tight and closed and secretive in some cases) which are implicated in global capital and its power base.

Morality and legitimacy in the informal life

Some networks are benign groupings of people offering help to each other and closely fit a social science category of social capital. Others—many more, we are arguing—are more ambivalent. Cheating, hustling, lying and hiding are rampant in the Gulf migrant economy: the stakes for financial gain or ruin are high, expectations and demands made by those back home upon Indian migrants (in both financial and prestige terms) are enormous, and people act accordingly. We want to underline again that the difference between the types of connection does not map neatly onto a continuum between "trusted familiars and risky strangers." We have observed over and over that one is as likely to be cheated by one's own brother as by a stranger-hustler to whom one has paid cash in hope of a contract or permit.

"Cheating" covers a wide range of events, from plain swindling of money—typically when an "agent," after cashing his fees, fails to deliver a visa and job—to failure to live up to promises made concerning quality of jobs, salaries, accommodation. In Valiyagramam, Baby John built a reputation as a successful businessman, having built, after some years away, a thriving water-bottling plant. He readily offered help to relatives, neighbors and friends, recruiting them to work in his plant. Soon, however, many of those who had joined him

---

[47] See for example the "power maps" at "Who knows Who" at http://whoknowswho. channel4.com/people/Kenneth_Clarke (last accessed 12 September 2010). See also "Cambridge mafia" photograph on http://www.bbc.co.uk/radio4/today/gallery/ gallery_cambridge_mafia.shtml (last accessed 12 September 2010).

[48] David Rothkopf, *Superclass: The Global Power Elite and the World They Are Making* (New York: Farrar, Straus & Giroux, 2008).

returned to the village, complaining that "office positions" turned out to be laboring jobs. Moreover, Baby John was treating them harshly, and, to make it worse, had not been paying salaries, arguing that, "it had cost him lots of money to bring them there." Similarly, Hussein, belonging to a reputed Kozhikode trading family, decided to try his luck in Dubai, accepting the offer made by some old family friends of participation as a partner in their tire dealership. Although he contributed several hundreds of thousands of rupees to the business, after a few months in Dubai he realized that with the excuse that "he had to learn the trade," he was being used as a shop assistant, while receiving no salary, since he was of course not an employee, but a partner. Eventually, he decided to leave, but in doing so he lost all the money he had invested.

Over the years we have collected hundreds of similar stories, revealing not only the aggressive nature of economic life in the Gulf, but also how ambiguous and precarious are the relationships migrants are involved in, especially those involving people whose trust one would hope to take for granted. Ties of reciprocity and mutuality, embedded in kinship and friendship, can easily turn into naked exploitation and deception. But migrants are equally vulnerable back home, once they seek to invest remittances and savings. Ahmedkutty worked for a long time as an accountant in a bank in rural Saudi Arabia, a good job that allowed him to save substantial capital. Getting close to retirement, he joined a couple of long-term friends to buy an ailing brick factory back in Kerala. As the three partners were still in the Gulf, they were happy to leave the deal in the hands of a relative who had proposed and brokered the investment. Money was paid, papers were signed, but Ahmedkutty and his friends soon learned that their partner had simply disappeared with all the cash. As a consequence, Ahmedkutty had to postpone his return for several years. Indeed, where to invest savings, who to trust back home and how to avoid being cheated are issues of great concern to most migrants, especially Muslims, for whom the easy and safe option of simply putting money in the bank and taking interest is forbidden. Malayali Hindu and Christian migrants have long been happy to bypass the problem by investing their savings in life insurance and various bank saving schemes, a fact continually deplored by the Kerala state government which longs to see Gulf savings used in "productive" investment and development.[49] Lately, Islamic banking is offering Muslims a

---

[49] Osella and Osella, "Migration, Money and Masculinity in Kerala", pp.115–31; Caroline Osella and Filippo Osella, "Once Upon A Time In The West: Stories of Migration and Modernity from Kerala, South India," *Journal of The Royal Anthropological Institute*, 12 (2006), pp. 569–88.

welcome get-out from risky small business ventures. But eventually, for returnees of all communities, the commonest (and perceived as most risk-free) form
of long-term investment is buying flats in apartment blocks that are being
built all across Kerala in a property speculation boom.

But we cannot simply identify and deplore the sharp practitioners in the
tales above. For the guy who cheats you may at the same time be doing genu-
ine favors for somebody else. One cannot clearly identify agents as necessarily
"social workers" or "exploiting hustlers": the same person will play both roles
in different moments. It is the nature of the moment, the other agents—the
particular assemblage of circumstances and actors involved—that will flavor
the event. The ambivalent nature of networked connections and personal
relationships highlights the unhelpfulness here of talking in terms of civil
society. It is not so easy then to label or delineate "civil" and "uncivil" society:
personal relationships offer a shifting ground, and even the highly uncivil can
be helpful and sometimes work for good. Even within many single transactions, a certain degree of ambivalence prevails. The guy who cheated and
tricked you out to the Gulf on the promise of a job which did not exist may,
ten years later, be evaluated as somebody who did you a favor, because he was
the contact who first got you out of the village and enabled you to get a foot-
hold there and eventually to bring out relatives and friends.

The morality in the illicit economy may have an additional angle, in that it
can be seen as part of a pragmatism that sociology, following DeCerteau and
Bourdieu, recognizes as the short-term tactics (rather than longer-term strategy) available to the lower classes.[50] From this perspective, as Pardis Madhavi
notes in her paper, migrant networking practices and the moral frameworks
around them are born of a mix of people's desperation and their desire to
make a little money and do well, and are conditioned—as Andrew Gardner,
following Eric Wolf, explores with nuance—by wider "orchestrating" structures.[51] They correspond to what Asef Bayat has identified as the wider
imperative upon the marginalized and economically dispossessed to live an
"informal" life.[52]

The Gulf migrant's enmeshment in networks of the illicit, then, also
reminds us of similar ethnographic situations of economic disparity and hardship, in which the gap between aspiration and actuality, and the day-to-day

[50] Michael De Certeau, *The Practice of Everyday Life* (Berkeley: University of California Press, 1984); Bourdieu, *The Logic of Practice*.

[51] Gardner, *City of Strangers*.

[52] Bayat, "Radical Religion and the Habitus of the Dispossessed", pp. 579–90.

obviousness of extreme economic difference, actually encourage the expansion of informal economies and a realm of the illicit, where networks flourish and informal entrepreneurial skills can be put to use to work a system and make some small difference or advantage in life. We can mention here, from many potential examples, Wacquant's work on Paris and inner city USA,[53] and Hobbs' ethnography of London's East End. The latter is notable for exploring how a young working class British man may end up either going into the police force or becoming a petty criminal, with remarkably similar practices (and overlapping networks) around networking, favors, and making advantage for self and family via illicit economies.[54]

When it comes to evaluating this sort of skill, we can ask if this knowledge of how to work beneath the radar in a rigid system is not itself a form of social capital. Specifically, we can question the moral judgment and normativity inherent in Putnam-esque formations, which seek to draw clear lines between licit social capital and illicit networking, and a social science which could imagine and insist upon "pure" institutions. We note that the criteria of morality may not meet standardized or formal expectations, or conform to normative liberal ideas of "morality." One broker-hustler told us happily about having finally found a good sheikh who would offer phoney letters of employment to be sold on to would-be migrants for an honest price. From the point of view of those trapped in a system of structural violence and exploitation, the illegal labor broker who find a job or the *dalal* who sells fake SSLC certificates or phoney job contracts is often a godsend. In fact, such people often— with no irony at all intended or seen—name themselves, and are named within the Indian community, as *social workers*. There is morality here, in the illicit economy, make no mistake. It is a broader morality of fairness and lack of greed; and a morality of opportunity for the poor.

Outside of elite Indian circles, where top entrepreneurs play at very high levels, mingling with senior politicians from both the Indian nation and from Gulf states, and acting as hubs bringing major contracts and agreements between states, the majority of Indian networking is small scale and relatively hidden. Much of the networking and granting of favors is done fast and privately—as we have noted, often within the domestic sphere. A contractor may

---

[53] Loïc Wacquant, *Urban Outcasts: A Comparative Sociology of Advanced Marginality* (Cambridge: Polity Press, 2007).
[54] Dick Hobbs, *Doing the Business: Entrepreneurship, the Working Class, and Detectives in the East End of London* (Oxford University Press, 1988).

discreetly host a lavish and alcohol-fueled lunch for a public works department official in his own home; a broker may receive visitors seeking favors and help in the evenings sitting out on his veranda. If the elite—Kerala's Gulf entrepreneurs, British cabinet ministers and Indian politicians, Gulf sheikhs and North American industrialists—can all increase their share of renown, respect, advantage and profit through their energetic networking practices, then why should the subaltern be denied similar benefits?

Conclusion

If rich entrepreneurs and businessmen can obtain multi-dollar contracts, political honors, and so on through their elite networking practices, cutting bureaucratic corners when necessary in order to turn an advantage, then why should the subaltern be denied his or her portion of respect, reputation and material gain for also doing exactly that? Networks where friendship, support, and instrumental gain run alongside and reinforce each other run all the way through social life, and across every social stratum. To underline, we reiterate that in the end, the subaltern's—necessary, tactical, survival-oriented—resort to the illicit in the Gulf is given a kind of informal legitimacy, in that it is clearly part and parcel of the much wider and generalized system of networking; a system which then also encompasses *wasta* at its highest level, in domains such as big business and the smoothing of international entrepreneurship; or the way in which the state itself works, through practices such as *kafala* and the allocation to nationals of ministry employment. But these sorts of practices are by no means specific or confined to Gulf states. Rather, we see similar logics and practices operating in various societies, but they are always nuanced and inflected in a particular way in each specific ethnographic locale. *Dalal* is not *wasta* is not *guan xi* is not Wall Street is not the UK cabinet—but neither are any of these networking phenomena unique.

Clearly, more research is needed on the reasonings and logics of practices such as *wasta* and the *dalal*, on the processes through which they take place, on people's access to them and on their effectiveness and effects. We have observed in the Gulf some interesting articulations between Arab practices of *wasta* and Indian practices of middleman-ship, and we hope to see future empirical work on the chains and networks to be found around some of the many longstanding relationships between an Arab sponsor, a migrant broker, and the clients. A focus on both the host and the migrant and on the very connections between them, also thinking about such connections in wider comparative frameworks, will enable analysis to bring out, rather than take for granted, regional specificities.

We also need to remember here that there are, as Neha Vora has studied, wealthy Indian business families; and that there are, as Jane Bristol-Rhys tells us, plenty of lower-middle class nationals also struggling to keep up.[55] The issue is in no way a simple host-outsider story of simple relative advantage and disadvantage, and our proposed focus on the concrete relationships and connections between nationals and migrants at different socio-economic levels could be a very fruitful one. Wide-range study encompassing both high local elite articulations and smaller informal networks, and all the states in between, would eventually complexify and enrich our understandings. It would also enable us to think, as we have done here, about the networking for mutual advantage of Indian billionaire entrepreneurs, Gulf sheikhly families, and Indian politicians, as part of the same social processes that also inform the small-time broker-hustler selling fake SSLC certificates to Indian laborers hoping to get out of manual work and into retail, or the unemployed Gulf national selling bogus offers of work as a household servant via an Indian broker.

This, in turn, can lead toward reflection on the centrality of personalized connections and networks in the working of contemporary global capitalism. Migrants' informal networks, connecting south India and the Gulf—and often extending to include Europe, the United States and Southeast Asia—are neither marginal practices nor demotic alternatives to formal channels of migration and employment. The success of the Gulf economy, on the contrary, relies directly on these articulations between migrant and local informal networks in order to produce and maintain a cheap, docile and flexible workforce via the *kafala* system and widespread subcontracting.[56] These practices, which are as common in the Gulf as they are in the USA or the UK,[57] bring together multinational companies and a multitude of small employers who recruit labor through informal migrant networks, of which they themselves are often the center. From this perspective, notwithstanding recent shifts toward extending limited citizenship rights to certain categories of migrants, transnationalism here is as much an expression of migrant cross-border relationships and consciousness as it is a condition of life forced upon migrant labor.

Nor can suggestions of a split between the practices of labor and capital be sustained. As we have argued elsewhere, in the Gulf, as in the rest of the world,

---

[55] Jane Bristol-Rhys, *Emirati Women: Generations of Change* (London: Hurst, 2010).
[56] Gardner, *City of Strangers*.
[57] See Mollona, "Factory, Family and Neighbourhood", pp. 527–48.

modern technocratic "know-how" informing the discourse of contemporary business management remains indissoluble from longstanding social skills of "know-who."[58] The importance of social networks and social identities to business is by no means an unusual or imperfect moment in the wider sweep of the neoliberal project, but is a foundational feature of economic practice under global capitalism.[59] What differentiates the Gulf countries or India from northern Europe or the United States, then, is not the degree to which social networks inform business relations, but whether these networks and the practices of sociality and hospitality around them are readily named and acknowledged as a feature of economic life or not.[60]

We also return to Andrew Gardner's point that illicit practices in the Gulf stem from the deep rooted practice (harking back to maritime trade links) of offering carefully limited "hospitality towards strangers," who are not expected to become part of society and so should not expect rights on par with their hosts. The contemporary Gulf does indeed produce its own illicitness by means of its regulations, its control of institutions, its media, its anxieties about free movement, and its determination to hold on to ethnic privilege in such a way that non-citizens cannot hope for equal treatment in court or state. Living what Bayat calls the "informal life" is encouraged by the prevalence of poverty, inequality and debt bondage, with no hope of gain, redress or help through formal means. At the same time, Gulf economies, perhaps in a wider ideological sense, also sanction the flourishing of the illicit in as much as they promulgate and support (by means of very targeted and energetic structural and material incentives) a wider ethos of risk and entrepreneurship, normalized by wider social values of lavishness and glorification of wealth and an overwhelming stress upon the material. In this way much of Gulf life is indeed anti-Islamic, as Islamists strenuously point out.[61] Given the Gulf's claim to be

---

[58] Osella and Osella, "Muslim Entrepreneurs in Public Life between India and the Gulf", pp. 202–21.

[59] See for example Mark Granovetter, "Economic Action and Social Structure: The Problem of Embeddedness," *The American Journal of Sociology*, 91 (1985), pp. 481–510; David Harvey, *A Brief History of Neoliberalism* (Oxford University Press, 2007); Nigel Thrift, *Knowing Capitalism* (London: Sage, 2005).

[60] Joel Kahn and Francesco Formosa, "The Problem of 'Crony Capitalism': Modernity and the Encounter with the Perverse," *Thesis Eleven* (2002), pp. 47–66.

[61] To be sure, this is an ambivalent issue, which we have no space here to pursue. Some suggest that anxieties about walking the tight-rope between business and Islam are assuaged by periodic show-trials of foreigners for immorality.

Muslim space, attacks on the worst excesses of the system from Islamist quarters might eventually have more weight than critique from the perspective of liberal humanist values such as "civil society" or "transparency." The strong government control of Islamist organizations is telling.

Yang, analyzing *guang-xi*, follows feminist arguments such as that made by Gilligan to characterize this type of embedded, connected, personalized, horizontal integration via relationship as "feminine."[62] We can unpick this notion and instead of accepting the (common) gendering of connectedness, firstly take note of studies tracing the contours of connectedness as a value in many social arenas. We can then move on to ask ourselves how, in Western social and political theory, did disembeddedness, abstraction and disconnectedness, all come to be on the one hand gendered as masculine, on the other hand forced into a teleological progress narrative, and hence finally touted as necessarily superior on two counts: associated with the form of gendering deemed superior, and also evaluated as more socially "mature"? Turning around to avoid such judgments embedded in liberal Western theory, we could say that the problem here is not the system itself, but is the fact that in the Gulf not all have access to *wasta*, which continues to operate in strictly controlled and tight circles. The problem then is parallel to many others—citizenship, accommodation, healthcare, education—and is better framed as one of unequal access. Just as Neha Vora's informants claimed rights of belonging in Dubai, while drawing her attention to the recentness and unfairness of racial discrimination there, and to the gap between Gulf's rhetoric of a free open market and its restrictive hiring and working practices, the issue can be understood from a user's point of view as one of an unfair monopoly held by citizens over a form of capital that is a basic necessity. Starting not from neoliberal or even from classical liberal standpoints embedded in (imagined)[63] values, but from the more neu-

---

[62] Carol Gilligan, *In a Different Voice: Psychological Theory and Women's Development* (Cambridge University Press, 1982).

[63] We have no space here to explore more fully this aspect of our argument: that, as with other desirable goals of classical liberalism—modernity and secularism, for example—the projected image is far from the reality. For an overview of and critiques of classical modernity theory, see Dilip P. Gaonkar, "On Alternative Modernities," *Public Culture*, 11 (1999), pp. 1–18; Timothy Mitchell, "The Stage of Modernity," in Timothy Mitchell (ed.), *Questions of Modernity* (Minneapolis: University of Minnesota Press, 2000), pp. 1–34; Joel Kahn, *Modernity and Exclusion* (London: Sage, 2001); Osella and Osella, "Once upon a Time in the West," pp. 569–88. For a scrutinization of Western secularism, see Talal Asad, *Formations of the Secu-*

tral start point that *wasta* exists and is undoubtedly a resource in Gulf society, then more openness, more *wasta*-building opportunities, would be a good thing. To be able, as in India or China, to rely upon no more than a gift, or to be able to marshal endless connections, would give subalterns more access to the hub points which actually matter and can make things move for them.

But finally, this is where Yang's optimism cannot be imported into Gulf migrant society, nor into Indian society, where labor recruiters and brokers/go-betweens roam; and we cannot share Yang's optimism about the rise of a "second society," as we need to understand that the scale of gift required to forge a connection or get a situation moving will lead us immediately on to the issue of cash and resources. In Kerala, a Rs. 100 note to ward attendants will be enough for anybody to help make sure their loved one has a smooth and pleasant stay in hospital; but to secure admission to a top engineering college for one's child will cost tens of thousands of rupees. Even the widest and most open of networks, such as the Indian *dalal* system, will finally be always inflected by class inequality. *Dalal* is a relatively open system relying upon gifts, favor, tenuous connections, money; *wasta* is a relatively closed and hierarchical upward system relying heavily upon the cultural capital of lineage, name and substantial connection. And both are doing the work of channeling and restricting access to resources which is done, more obviously and starkly, by institutions such as the legal restrictions on citizenship and related benefits. Are we then, as Gardner and Meagher suggest, better off rethinking these networks in terms of their specific histories and operation, by which we are then better able to perceive that they are not separated from the state and its intent, nor are they actually subverting the state, but are acting as a form of "soft power" which eventually works toward the same goals as the state: maintenance and protection under a global capitalist regime of privilege for a minority?

lar: Christianity, Islam, Modernity (Stanford University Press, 2003); Saba Mahmood, "Secularism, Hermeneutics, and Empire: the Politics of Islamic Reformation," *Public Culture*, 18 (2006), pp. 323–47.

136

7

India-Persian Gulf Migration

Corruption and Capacity in Regulating Recruitment Agencies

Mary Breeding [1]

What are the processes for recruitment of low-skilled labor from India to the Persian Gulf? While a substantial body of research exists across different economic, political and cultural dimensions assessing India-Gulf migration, there has been little research to track the formal and informal processes of recruitment and the steps involved in migrating from India to the Persian Gulf. This research documents the process by which recruitment of low-skilled labor occurs in India. In doing so, I present an analytic narrative outlining the procedures of contract brokering between recruitment agencies, job candidates and Persian Gulf-based employers—including abuses and corrup-

[1] Grateful acknowledgment goes to the Center for International and Regional Studies and the Institute for the Study of International Migration, Georgetown University School of Foreign Service in Qatar, for generously providing research funding for this project. Particular thanks go to Lara Sukhtian for her research assistance in the project.

tion. This chapter is based on three months of fieldwork in India and Qatar, during which time I conducted in-depth interviews with recruitment agencies based in four cities of India, employers in Qatar, and government officials in both countries to better understand recent trends in India-Gulf migration. Findings highlight three informal practices common in contract brokering for India-Gulf Migration. These informal practices potentially undermine formal institutions and allow for abuses of contract brokering. They include: recruitment agencies working with subagents; fishing for candidates in rural areas; and information asymmetries between recruiters and job candidates regarding wages.

The recruitment of workers in India for construction and other low-skilled occupations in the Persian Gulf region has gained considerable attention in recent years. Thousands of Indians immigrate to Persian Gulf countries annually as contracted workers. In 2007 the number of low-skilled Indian migrants acquiring emigration clearance to work in the Persian Gulf was over 800,000 (809,453), well up from 466,456 in 2003.[2] These migrants were individually recruited by one of 1,835 licensed recruitment agencies in India and gained work clearance in Gulf countries. The overall number of Indian migrants currently residing in the Persian Gulf is unknown, but recent estimates suggest that 19 percent of all Non-resident Indians and Persons of Indian Origin living outside India are located in the Persian Gulf.[3]

Who are these migrants? Indian migrants first started going to Gulf Cooperation Council (GCC) countries in the 1970s after the oil boom in West Asia and the Persian Gulf. During the 1970s and 1980s the composition of migrants from India was largely restricted to south Indian migrants from Kerala.[4] During the 1990s the demand for labor in GCC countries increased and diversified across many sectors including construction, services, oil and manufacturing. As a result, the composition of Indian migrants emigrating also diversified. Indian migrants come from all states across India, but migrants from the southern states of Kerala, Andhra Pradesh, Karnataka, and

[2] Ministry of Overseas Indian Affairs, *2008 Annual Report* (Delhi: MOIA, 2008).
[3] Binod Khadira, "India: Skilled Migration to Developed Countries, Labour Migration to the Gulf." Paper presented at Asia Research Institute, National University of Singapore, 2006.
[4] Philippe Venier, "From Kerala to the UAE: Emerging Trends in a Mature Labour Migration System." Paper presented at Université de Poitiers, CNRS MIGRINTER, 2007.

Tamil Nadu have comprised more than fifty percent of emigration clearances over the past decade.[5]

To supplement the so far insufficient research on processes of recruitment and the steps involved in migrating from India to the Persian Gulf,[6] I seek to present an analytic narrative based on in-depth interviews with recruitment agencies based in four cities of India, employers in Doha, and government officials in both countries. Below, I present an overview of the research and some key findings from the fieldwork.

Narrative: cycle of migration and stakeholders

It is estimated that there are approximately five million low-skilled workers in GCC countries, but how did they get there? A recent document released by the Indian Council of Overseas Employment outlines three phases of a job candidate's India-Gulf migration process: pre-departure, the employment phase and the capacity building phase.[7] The first, the pre-departure phase, includes recruitment, obtaining a passport, the job search, insurance procurement, travel booking and emigration clearance from the Ministry of Overseas Indian Affairs (MOIA) to travel abroad. A recruitment agent facilitates these tasks. The second, the employment phase, is the period in which a migrant is working for an employer in the foreign country. The third and final phase is the return of the migrant to his/her home country. The Indian government positively refers to this period as the capacity building phase during which the migrant worker carries the skills learned abroad back to India.

To date, little is known about recruitment agencies. Current information comes largely from two sources: the Indian government and media coverage of recruitment abuses. In 2004 the Indian government created a new ministry to manage India-Gulf migration, the Ministry of Overseas Indian Affairs. Its duties include the formulation of policies for improving emigration management; proposing legislative changes; implementing emigration reforms

---

[5] Indian Council of Overseas Employment, "Impact Assessment of Global Recession on Indian Migrant Workers in Countries of the Gulf Cooperation Council and Malaysia" (New Delhi: ICOE, 2009).

[6] International Labor Organization, "Costs of Coercion" (Geneva: International Labor Organization, 2009).

[7] Indian Council of Overseas Employment, "Impact Assessment of Global Recession on Indian Migrant Workers in Countries of the Gulf Cooperation Council and Malaysia" (New Delhi: ICOE, 2009), p. 21.

(including institutional changes and e-Governance); formulation of welfare schemes for emigrants; and promoting bilateral and multilateral cooperation in international migration.[8]

In the context of low-skilled India-Gulf migration this translates into formulating policies to govern recruitment agencies and workers seeking employment abroad. It further entails implementing legislation, but there is no mention of regulation or oversight in the Ministry's formal duties and objectives. There is also no formally devised duty for regulation or oversight of recruitment agencies in the objectives of the Ministry of External Affairs, which manages diplomatic policy relations. The MOIA has worked to outline the process of India-Gulf migration (Figure 7.1).

Figure 7.1 depicts the process of recruitment as outlined by the Ministry of Overseas Indian Affairs. When an Indian citizen (laborer) wishes to work in the Persian Gulf, he or she must go through a recruitment agent. Recruitment agents are brokers, usually residing in India, who facilitate the process of emigration from India to the Persian Gulf. By law they are required to be registered with the Ministry, and so licensed. Employers based in the Persian Gulf

Figure 7.1.

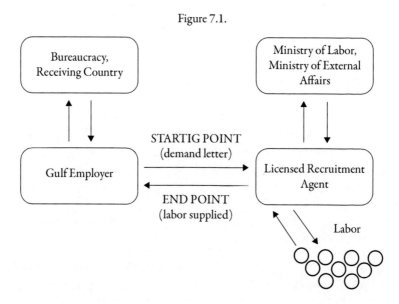

develop working relationships with recruitment agencies in India, and the agencies are responsible for matching qualified job candidates to the employers. When employers need labor, they must first send an official "demand letter" to the recruitment agency they will work with to hire Indian workers.

The recruitment agent finds qualified candidates to meet employers' needs. In addition the agent helps candidates with the required pre-departure activities, including obtaining approval from the Indian government for the candidate to migrate.[9] Recruitment agents are paid by employers, job candidates, or both for their services. The MOIA has set the maximum amount an agent can charge a job candidate at Rs. 10,000 (approximately US$200), but I found the average cost to migrants to be between Rs. 40,000 and Rs. 50,000 (US$800 and US$1000) among twenty two recruitment agencies I interviewed—a cost that can be the equivalent of one year's salary for many emigrants. On paper, the recruiter provides a service to both employers and job candidates, and this results in a win-win situation.

The real situation

Results from my research and fieldwork suggest, however, that in practice the outlined policy framework for India-Gulf recruitment presents many challenges. Information asymmetries between job candidates and recruitment agencies and unregulated recruitment provide opportunities for corruption.

Figure 7.2 more accurately depicts the kinds of scenarios I encountered in seeking to understand the process of India-Gulf Migration. What I quickly discovered is that there are multiple structures, institutions, and processes for labor migrants, recruitment agencies and employers to use in the process of emigrating to the Persian Gulf. There is a legal structure outlined by the Ministry (the Emigration Act, 1983, Section 10). There are also the institutions and processes described by the MOIA's website. The process in Figure 7.1 is the legal process of recruitment.

There are also several alternative ways operating openly, even advertised daily in newspapers. The most common alternative form of recruitment is through a subagent or "consultant" to a licensed recruitment agency. While there are a limited number of formally licensed recruitment agents (about 1,835), there are thousands of subagents. Through interviews with agencies

---

[9] MOIA, "Emigration Services", http://www.moia.gov.in/services.aspx?id1=66& idp=66&mainid=73 (last accessed August 15, 2010).

Figure 7.2.

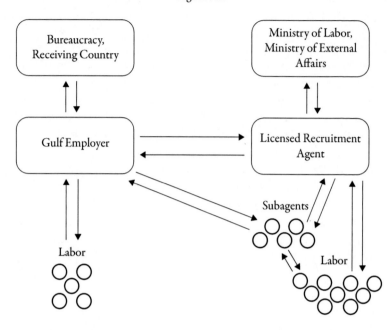

and informal conversations with return migrants I learned about a variety of scenarios of migrants' recruitment. In some cases – especially in the instances of domestic servants – migrants were recruited directly by their employers. I heard several stories of domestic servants who had emigrated with families they had worked for in India, and some domestic workers obtained contacts with Persian Gulf employers through friends who had emigrated and were working for families abroad. For example, in one case a household in Dubai was looking for a domestic worker. They asked a neighborhood household who had emigrated from Karnataka with their Konkani domestic worker, and the household asked the worker if she had any friends who would be interested. In other cases I heard stories of workers who bypassed the system of emigration entirely—particularly in Goa—by illegally taking work on ships. In these instances the processes and networks for recruitment fall outside the bounds of the legally defined structure of the Indian government. Given this framework, I am interested in two questions: What are the underlying processes involved in alternative forms of recruitment? And what are the regulatory failures in these processes?

Research design

The research design involves a mixed methods approach including both qualitative and quantitative components. Aside from the qualitative interview material presented, a second component of the research has involved the collection of Indian migration data from the Ministry of Overseas Indian Affairs in Delhi to obtain a better understanding of trends in Indian migration to GCC countries over time.

Interviews

The research design includes interviews with three kinds of stakeholders: licensed recruitment agencies, unlicensed recruitment agencies and government officials in India and Qatar. The objective was to develop a detailed understanding of the process of recruitment in four urban areas: Mumbai, Pune, Goa and Bangalore. In each of the cities, agencies were randomly selected from a list of licensed agencies obtained from the MOIA. At the time the interviews were conducted, the list of licensed agencies was not publicly available. Since December 2009 the list has been uploaded on the MOIA's website for public use.[10] In total twenty agencies were selected; of those, only fourteen were operational. Other agencies either did not exist or had closed since registering with the MOIA. Interviews with agents lasted between forty-five minutes and one and a half hours. In local agencies I interviewed the owners, and in corporate agencies I interviewed the managing director.

In addition to the licensed recruitment agencies interviewed, I visited several and interviewed eight unlicensed recruitment agencies, or "subagents." Agencies were selected through a method of snowball sampling and informal discussions with locals—usually with hotel staff, rickshaw drivers, or local restaurant employees. I would inquire about whether locals whom I encountered knew anyone working and living in the Persian Gulf and how they got there. From this question I would ask about recruitment agents in the area and where they were located. I would then proceed to make my way to find local agencies.

Interviews with both licensed and unlicensed agencies followed a standard format. I asked a series of questions covering five topics:

• Recruitment agency history—When did the agency begin its work? Are they registered with the MOIA and licensed? If so, under what name, and in what year did they register?

[10] http://www.moia.gov.in/services.aspx?id1=66&idp=66&mainid=73.

- Local scene—What kinds of job candidates does the agency recruit? What are their processes for selection? How do they operate—locally, regionally, or nationally?
- Gulf contacts—Who comprises their client-base in the Persian Gulf region? What countries do they send migrants to? Do they have preferences for working with employers in some Persian Gulf countries over others? Have they ever encountered difficult situations in working with Persian Gulf clients? Does the agency work directly with the employer or is there an intermediary? If there is an intermediary, who is it?
- Recruitment practice—How does the agent advertise? How does the agent select job candidates for the employer? Does the Gulf employer come and conduct interviews directly with the job candidates, or does the agent conduct interviews with job candidates on the employer's behalf? What fees does the agent charge to the candidate and what fees does the agent charge employers? What is the total cost charged to job candidates going to work in the Persian Gulf? How much do recruited candidates earn while working abroad? Does the agent process emigration clearance documents in-house, or are documents outsourced? Who conducts the medical examination of workers for the agent?
- Future aspirations—How is business currently? What has been the impact of the global economic crisis on the recruitment agent? What is in store for the agency's future? Does the agent see recruitment lucrative in the long run? Why or why not?

These questions provided a base to develop an analytic narrative about the agencies and their recruitment practices.

In addition to these interviews, I visited one migrant receiving country in the Persian Gulf, Qatar. I conducted ten in-depth interviews with managers in construction companies and hotels to better understand the recruitment practices of employers and to obtain a better understanding of the working and living conditions in a migrant-receiving state. Employers were selected using a list I obtained from the Indian Embassy. The Indian Embassy in Doha has a special department that works on behalf of labor migrants and works to mediate any disputes when they arise. It provided a list of employers with contacts for the HR personnel in the companies I contacted. During these interviews I met with HR personnel in construction companies and hotels. Both kinds of employers formally recruit workers from abroad and provide housing and benefits to their employees. The questions asked of these companies were targeted to understand: the country of origin and ethnic composition of their workers; the kind of contracts they offer; their recruitment practice—the firms with which they work in India; whether they were aware of illegal recruitment practices in India; their experiences with recruitment agencies; and working and living conditions of their employees in the Persian Gulf. Like interviews of recruitment agencies, interviews of employees provided another perspective from actors involved in recruitment and helped to build the narrative that follows.

The final type of interviews I conducted were interviews with government and various kinds of public officials in both India and Qatar. The purpose of these interviews and meetings was to understand the perspective of policymakers and officials in charge of recruitment and immigration in both countries—to have a more rounded perspective on the process as a whole. Included were interviews with officials in the MOIA, national Indian journalists, Indian embassy officials in Qatar, and the Qatar Foundation for Combating Human Trafficking (QFCHT). In March 2010, I attended a joint meeting hosted by the United Nations and the QFCHT. One agenda item for this meeting, which brought together public officials from throughout the region, was to discuss the definition of human trafficking as applied to labor migration. This further provided a comparative perspective into Qatar's position on labor migrants. The QFCHT at least acknowledges the potential for low-skilled labor migrants—other than domestic workers—to become victims of human trafficking, and offers a commitment to regulating employers and observing the practices of migration, as compared to countries like Oman and Kuwait which have no such commitments.

Profile of recruitment agencies and employers

Post-liberalization India sparks a number of images—of industrializing cities where remnants of traditional life meet the global pace of modernization, of cows wandering city streets and outsourced call centers—the face of cities such as Mumbai, Pune, Goa and Bangalore. Where do recruitment agencies fit within these modernizing urban spaces? What do they look like? As with the call center images made popular from movies and TV shows, the first image one might develop of a recruitment agency is the image outlined in Indian newspaper advertisements—of Corporate Indian environments with modern furniture, air-conditioning, and cubicle workspaces with computers. The reality I encountered, however, was different.

Recruitment agencies I interviewed were located in a variety of urban spaces: one in a government office, two in small suites in corporate high rises, and the rest in crowded streets among rows of shops. Most agencies were small, with a maximum of five to ten employees. The unlicensed agencies I encountered all operated alongside another kind of business, such as domestic labor market recruitment or travel agency. Goa was a popular spot for unlicensed recruitment agents posing as travel agents; I spoke with four such agencies there. Agencies were varied in their resources and the quality of trained staff they employed.

All agencies had at least one computer and usually a small waiting area for job candidates to sit. Most noted that they do their business in the evenings between five p.m. and nine p.m., after the regular workday is over. While I observed agencies during this time, my interviews usually took place in the morning and early afternoon. In Mumbai the agencies with which I met spoke of doing most of their business at a local market on Sundays, where job candidates would come with their papers if they were seeking employment abroad. Every Sunday the market acts as a jobs fair advertising jobs.

Several common themes arose during interviews with agencies, and some of the themes were reinforced during discussions with employers later. A first common theme to arise had to do with a modernizing pattern of recruitment within India. It became clear that trends first outlined in the work of social scientists such as Philippe Venier on migrant labor practices in Kerala seem to have changed in recent years. Recruitment agents, once local businesses that recruited only from within their localities and in a particular region, now have a far wider scope. While many agencies are located in modern urban spaces, their client base is not local. Large licensed recruitment agencies headquartered in Mumbai and Delhi discussed recruiting from rural areas in Tamil Nadu and Andhra Pradesh. For instance, one agent I interviewed in Pune said:

My office is in Maharashtra, but I never hire Marathis. The few times I have placed young Marathi men, they also cause some problem. This and that, their parents come in with concerns. It's a hassle, and they are lazy. They also know they get better jobs in cities like Bombay or Pune. Most of the construction men we take are from Tamil Nadu.... (Pune RA, December 29, 2009).

This was a common theme—agencies, especially licensed agencies, kept offices in large urban areas, but their candidate bases were elsewhere. Another agent noted: "You see it all depends on the job. You want masons, I contact my men in Rajasthan. You want cooks, I look in Goa. These regions have been specialized for hundreds of years" (Bangalore RA, January 7, 2010). When I inquired about who his "men" were, he did not hesitate to say he worked with consultants. He claimed that it was not feasible for him to operate for international clients without having access to a base of migrants across India.

The influence of the global financial crisis was a second striking theme to emerge from my interviews. Of the twenty licensed agencies randomly selected, six had closed in the previous two years. I was able to follow up with two former owners of these agencies. They both indicated that the fall of the market in the UAE in 2009 and the financial crisis in 2008 had destroyed their business. Their clients abroad no longer demanded new workers, and since the costs of keeping their licenses up to date with the MOIA had increased, they decided to shut their doors. Others discussed concerns about the future of their businesses. They noted that they were looking for clients outside of the UAE, namely in Oman, Kuwait and Qatar.

A General Manager of a large corporate recruitment agency I interviewed in Bombay made a strong case about changes in the Indian workforce relative to the Persian Gulf:

There has been no demand for workers, and even when there is demand we often struggle to find good workers. There is low supply. You see, with what is happening in India today, supply of workers to the Gulf has gone down. Slowly, slowly, earnings in India have been increasing. Workers don't want to go the Gulf unless they live in a remote village and don't know any better. In order to increase supply, Gulf companies are going to have to change their pay structures. If I'm a semi-skilled worker and I can earn $1000 per month here, and only $1200 there—why go? If I can make $2400 a month there, then I'll go. But now, Gulf firms cannot pay that. They cannot compete like they used to. (Interview with General Manager in Mumbai, January 4, 2010)

This Manager captured the essence of many interviews, noting the need to recruit in rural areas as a result of increases in wages of Indian workers in urban areas relative to wages of workers in the Persian Gulf.

A third theme has to do with the costs of recruitment charged to job candidates. The Indian government has set the maximum that recruitment agencies can charge employees at Rs. 10,000 (approximately US$200). Only one of the recruitment agencies I interviewed, a government based recruitment agent in Goa, said that was the fee workers are charged. All other recruiters with whom I spoke cited a figure between Rs. 40,000 and Rs. 50,000 (approximately US$800-US$1,000). This is the fee that job candidates must pay. There are several costs involved in the migration of one worker. These include costs of the candidate's passport, visa, emigration clearance fees, airline tickets and mandatory medical exam, and recruitment agent fees. If a subcontractor is involved, he will also charge an additional fee. The overall costs charged to a job candidate ultimately depend on who pays for what: the recruitment agent, the employer, or the job candidate. In the worst case scenario, the burden is entirely placed on the job candidate to cover all fees for traveling abroad. In most cases, however, the employer covers the cost of airfare. Conversely, the government recruitment agency I interviewed in Goa works only with employers who will cover mandatory costs of going abroad, and in most cases, the recruiter said the worker does not incur any costs. Other recruitment agents had different arrangements, and usually arrangements vary depending on the Persian Gulf employer for whom the recruitment agency is working. The government recruitment agency I interviewed was exceptional; job candidates applying to other agencies always end up paying between four and five times more than the maximum a recruitment agent can charge.

Interviews with firms in Doha reinforced these themes. For instance, many employers in the Persian Gulf prefer workers from specific regions in India. As one employer I interviewed noted:

When we first started recruiting workers from India, they all came from one state. We were not aware that workers in different parts of the country have different sets of skills. Over the past thirty years, there are more and more workers from other parts of India. In Rajasthan the masons are good. I like getting masons from there. Also, in Tamil Nadhu, the workers are used to the heat and long days. Their skin is darker and they are able to withstand the sun for many hours. We get our unskilled workers from there. (Interview in Doha, January 13, 2010)

This manager of a construction company in Doha makes a few important points. One, he highlights a historical change in India-Gulf migration trends. Two, he reflects several common stereotypes of Indian migrants from different regions that I encountered in other interviews with other employers.

Historically, the majority of India-Gulf migration consisted of workers from Kerala. Today, however, workers come from all states of India, and workers from other states far outnumber those from Kerala (Table 7.1).

In 2009 workers from Kerala comprised 19.7 percent of all emigration clearances to the Persian Gulf. Kerala is still a large migrant-sending state, but in 2009 there were more workers from Uttar Pradesh, which comprised 20.5 percent of all workers. As more workers have gone abroad from other regions and parts of India, employers have gained knowledge about the capabilities of workers, and it was evident in my interviews with ten employers that they shared common stereotypes about workers from different regions. One of these stereotypes with respect to workers from Kerala is that they are more

Table 7.1: Emigration Clearance Data, January—October 2009.

State	Males	Females	Total
Andaman Nicobar	59	7	66
Andhra Pradesh	47,363	11,162	58,525
Arunachal Pradesh	153	4	157
Assam	15,01	1	15,02
Bihar	42,075	4	42,079
Chandigarh	811	0	811
Chhattisgarh	39	2	41
Dadar and Nagar Have	2	0	2
Daman and Diu	8	0	8
Delhi	2122	36	2,158
Goa	1,333	63	1,396
Gujarat	7,921	43	7,964
Haryana	885	1	886
Himachal Pradesh	670	1	671
Jammu Kashmir	3,683	0	3,683
Jharkhand	2,955	5	2,960
Karnataka	15,619	330	15,949
Kerala	100,539	1,965	102,504
Lakshadeep	16	0	16
Madhya Pradesh	1,619	6	1,625
Maharashtra	16,229	338	16,567
Manipur	14	0	14
Meghalaya	17	0	17
Mizoram	2	0	2
Nagaland	5	0	5
Orissa	5,384	1	5,385
Pondicherry	280	7	287
Punjab	23,067	16	23,083
Rajasthan	37,866	13	37,879
Sikkim	11	0	11
Tamil Nadu	66,760	680	67,440
Tripura	272	1	273
Uttar Pradesh	106,607	22	106,629
Uttranchal	500	2	502
West Bengal	17,624	47	17,671
Total	504,011	14757	518,768

Source: Indian Council of Overseas Employment, "Impact Assessment of Global Recession on Indian Migrant Workers in Countries of the Gulf Cooperation Council and Malaysia." (New Delhi: ICOE, 2009).

skilled and better educated. The employers I interviewed said they did not usually try recruiting workers from Kerala in the area of construction, because most Keralites migrate to the Persian Gulf in more skilled capacities these days—as teachers, nurses, doctors, etc.

Doha employers reinforced another common theme I encountered in my interviews with recruitment agencies when I discussed the process of recruitment with them. Working with subagents is the reality for employers. Out of the ten employers I interviewed only three realized that working with subagents is illegal, and none of them were really versed in the legal framework for recruitment established by the Indian government. They all stated that their responsibility was sending an "offer letter" to the job candidate. Most said it was the responsibility of the recruitment agent to manage the legal framework in India. There was a general tendency to place blame on the recruiter for any illegal practices in India.

Lastly, with respect to the costs of recruitment, Doha employers stated an awareness that the costs to most migrants were more than one or two months of wages the migrant would earn working in Doha. All employers with whom I spoke said they pay for the airline tickets and room and boarding of workers while in Doha. Most managers I interviewed in Doha said it was the responsibility of the recruitment agent and the job candidate to agree upon a rate for the service, and employers tried to avoid being involved in this process. Doha employers highlighted the amenities and services they offer to their employees—good living conditions and dorms as well as work uniforms, medical and health benefits, and leisure facilities (TV, Internet, etc. in living areas).

Overall most employers avoided taking responsibility for their recruitment practices in India. The five hotel managers I interviewed took more responsibility than construction companies. In one instance, a manager said:

Our hotel is one in a chain of hotels in the Gulf and we all have one common pool of recruited workers from which we can hire. Since I came to this hotel one year ago, I have tried to work with our recruitment headquarters in Dubai to learn about the different agencies form where our workers are recruited. We have a very international staff, and Indians comprise about 15 percent of our employees. I know we were working with one agent, but I found that the agent was overcharging workers. Now headquarters had hired a new agent in Bombay. (Interview with Manager in Doha, January 24, 2010)

In this instance, the manager of this hotel was working very closely with her core staff to make sure they were both recruited fairly and earning a fair wage. The nightly hotel cleaning services, however, were contracted out to another company that recruits. She said she had no idea where the company gets its workers. She said she as one person could only do so much, and her job as a manager was to look after her direct employees.

Corruption and capacity in regulating recruitment agencies

Arising from these themes, I present three of the most prominent regulatory failures I encountered, based on my fieldwork and policy processes for addressing them. These cases include: unlicensed recruitment; incomplete information; and fishing for candidates.

Unlicensed recruitment

First, an obvious disconnect between the Indian government's recruitment framework and what I observed in my fieldwork is the use of unlicensed recruitment agents, or "subagents." The Ministry of Overseas Indian Affairs keeps a list of 1,835 licensed agents. In reality there are thousands of agencies, mostly illegal. Subagents operate out of travel agencies, teashops and their private homes. These agents illegally recruit job candidates on behalf of licensed agencies. Many licensed agencies I interviewed openly admitted to working with subagents. One subagent I interviewed, doubling as a travel agent in Goa, said he preferred to call himself a consultant to avoid hassle by the Ministry. When I asked him if he feared getting caught, his reply was: "My uncle, owning this travel agency, is with the Congress Party, and he is powerful. No one will touch us, but in the case that I am caught, I know that he will make sure my business stays alive" (Interview in Goa, December 21, 2009). Others were less worried because they perceive very little regulation on the part of the Ministry.

Subagents create an additional principal between the recruitment agency and job candidates. This is where many candidates end up facing fees exceeding the maximum charge set by the Indian government. Subagents result from the failure to regulate recruitment. While there is a fine for subagents who are caught, the reality is that very few agencies are caught. In March of 2009 the ministry had only six such agencies listed on its website.[11] Strengthening the capacity for regulation of subagents is needed to curtail corrupt practices and illegal contract brokering in India-Gulf migration.

[11] MOIA, "Emigration Services."

Information asymmetries and fishing for candidates

Two additional observations on the India-Gulf recruitment process are inter-connected and result from information asymmetries between agents and job candidates. Two practices observed in interviews include fishing for candidates and not disclosing full information to candidates. These are based on deception and call ethics of the recruitment process into question. Recruitment agents have an incentive to supply as much labor as they can to Persian Gulf employers. Fishing for candidates, for example, occurs when agents seek pockets of candidates in remote rural areas. This process often occurs with the help of subagents who work from villages to obtain qualified candidates who, in many cases, are illiterate. Agents create a picture of Persian Gulf countries as wealthy and often fail to provide full information about the working and living conditions migrants will be entering—working long hours outdoors in high temperatures and living in labor camps. To repeat what one recruiter I interviewed noted: "I only recruit in villages. You see, with what is happening in India today, supply of workers to the Gulf has gone down. Slowly, slowly, earnings in India have been increasing. Workers don't want to go the Gulf unless they live in a remote village and don't know any better." (Interview, General Manager, Mumbai Recruitment Agency, January 4, 2010).

This manager outlines why he has an incentive to recruit in villages and not to provide full information to potential candidates. If a candidate knows he is not going to earn more than he could earn by moving to the city, will he still have an interest to move? Likely not. His method of recruitment is luring workers through ignorance, which boils down to exploitation.

In the midst of the economic crisis, India's economy continues to grow while many countries in the Persian Gulf have made cuts, including cuts in wages to migrant labor. Nine out of ten employers I interviewed in the Qatar noted that they had either stopped hiring or let labor go. Three out of ten said they had lowered wages. At present recruitment agencies are not required to provide any information about workers' rights, their working and living conditions abroad, or return migration to job candidates. The idea of empowering job candidates about their rights and providing full information is non-existent.

In sum, there is a disconnect between the Indian government's documented policy framework on the recruitment process and the actual operations of recruitment. Notably as a result of failure to regulate recruitment agencies and information asymmetries between recruitment agencies and job candidates, several opportunities for corruption and abuse in the process of recruitment arise. Building capacity for regulation with the MOIA, and requiring information to be disseminated to migrants about their rights in India and in their destination country, are two potential steps toward limiting instances of corruption and abuse.

Conclusion

This chapter has documented formal and informal processes observed in the recruitment of Indian migrants to Qatar. I have sought to better understand the process of recruitment of low-skilled labor in India, using an analytic narrative compiled from three months of fieldwork in India and Qatar. I have presented findings from interviews with twenty-three recruitment agents and ten employers in the Persian Gulf. Three common issues observed in the process of recruitment were: a diversification of locations from which agencies recruit; a decline in the number of operating agencies after the 2008 financial crisis; and a realized awareness that the costs of migrating to the Persian Gulf are always four to five times the legal costs set by the Government of India. Regarding the first issue, as the flow of migrants from India to the Qatar has increased since the early 1970s, more employers are aware of different regions and different kinds of workers seeking emigration abroad; employers display regional preferences for Indian workers based on the kinds of jobs they seek to fill, and so recruiters have expanded beyond Kerala and urban areas to attract migrant labor abroad. Regarding the second issue noted, there was an observed impact of the financial crisis on recruitment of labor to the Persian Gulf; after 2008 many agencies lost business or closed their doors entirely, so that out of the twenty licensed agents randomly selected for initial interviews in this research project, only fourteen were open and had survived the crisis. Finally, regarding the third matter, the Indian government sets the maximum charge to job candidates applying to work abroad at Rs. 10,000 (approximately US$200), but all recruitment agencies I interviewed noted that candidates typically pay between Rs. 40,000 and Rs. 50,000 (US$800 to US$1,000).

Three informal processes emerged from these issues: working with subagents; fishing for candidates in rural areas; and information asymmetries on wages workers earn abroad. In the first process, as demand for workers from various regions of India has increased, so has the demand to recruit across India; several agencies interviewed discussed working with subagents, who are unlicensed illegal recruiters, to recruit job candidates. The second process, along with the rise in subagents, has been a rise in recruitment from rural areas. In the third process, recruiters have an incentive to recruit in rural areas where information asymmetries between the recruiter and job candidates over wages are potentially greater; after the 2008 financial crisis, urban wages in India have continued to rise while wages in the Persian Gulf have been sustained or have fallen, so that although many workers can potentially earn equal wages in urban India without migrating, job candidates in Indian rural areas may still find migration to the Persian Gulf more attractive because they have less information about urban wages. These informal processes, unregulated, potentially undermine the formal process of migration from India to the Persian Gulf, allowing for abuses and corruption in contract brokering between Persian Gulf employers, job candidates, and recruitment agents.

8

Nepali Migrants to the Gulf Cooperation Council Countries

Behaviors, Plans, and Values

Nathalie E. Williams, Arland Thornton, Dirgha J. Ghimire,
Linda C. Young-DeMarco and Mansoor Moaddel

The Gulf Cooperation Council (GCC) countries—Bahrain, Kuwait, Oman, Qatar, Saudi Arabia, and the United Arab Emirates (UAE)—have large migrant populations and their economies rely heavily on this population.[1] This reliance is unique in the world, as the United Nations Population Division estimates that over one-third of the combined populations of these six Persian Gulf countries are composed of migrants,[2] with the proportion

[1] This research was supported by the Center for International and Regional Studies (CIRS) of the Georgetown University School of Foreign Service in Qatar. We would like to thank Cathy Sun and Daniel Thompson for programming assistance, the staff of the Institute for Social and Environmental Research Nepal for data collection, and the respondents from Nepal for sharing their experiences of living in the Gulf Cooperation Council countries.
[2] United Nations Population Division, Department of Economic and Social Affairs,

reaching 78 percent in Qatar.[3] The percentage of migrants in the workforce is even higher, constituting at least 50 percent in every country[4] and reaching about 90 percent in Qatar and the UAE.[5]

This large number of migrants has significant implications for the host countries. Especially in countries of the GCC, which currently have huge, but not infinite, natural resources and relatively small native populations, migrants are essential for their thriving economies but raise an array of important issues as well. These issues may vary from infrastructure, recruitment and monitoring of migrants to turnover of the population, intermarriage, and the socialization and identities of the children of migrants.[6] Such large foreign populations also raise issues of security and the long-run composition of the populations of these countries. Similarly to migrants in other areas of the world, these foreign populations may also form transnational communities that have relationships with citizens of the host countries, with their countries of origin, and with immigrants from different places.[7] Furthermore, migrants influence

---

"International Migration in the Arab Region." Paper presented at the United Nations Expert Group Meeting on International Migration and Development in the Arab Region: Challenges and Opportunities, Beirut, Lebanon, May 15–17, 2006.

[3] United Nations Population Division, Department of Economic and Social Affairs, "International Migration in GCC countries." Paper presented at the Regional Symposium on Foreign Workers in the GCC: Towards a Common Strategy, Doha, Qatar, April 17–29, 2007.

[4] John Willoughby, "Foreign Matter. The Place of Strangers in Gulf Society," in John W. Fox, Nada Mourtada-Sabbah and Mohammed al-Mutawa (eds), *Globalization and the Gulf* (London: Routledge, 2006), pp. 222–43.

[5] Andrzej Kapiszewski, "Arab Versus Asian Migrant Workers in the GCC Countries." Paper presented at the United Nations Expert Group Meeting on International Migration and Development in the Arab Region, Beirut, Lebanon, May 15–17, 2006, pp. 1–21.

[6] Paul Dresch, "Foreign Matter: The Place of Strangers in Gulf Society" in *Globalization and the Gulf*, pp. 200–22; John W. Fox *et al.* (eds), *Globalization and the Gulf* (London: Routledge, 2006); Neha Vora, "Producing Diasporas and Globalization: Indian Middle-Class Migrants In Dubai," *Anthropological Quarterly*, 81, 2 (2008), pp. 377–406; John Willoughby, "Foreign Matter. The Place of Strangers in Gulf Society," pp. 222–43.

[7] Don Kalb, Marco van der Land, Richard Staring, Bart van Steenbergen, Nico Wilterdink (eds), *The Ends of Globalization: Bringing Society Back In* (Lanham, MD: Rowman & Littlefield, 2000); Alejandro Portes, "Globalization from Below: The Rise of Transnational Communities," in *The Ends of Globalization*, pp. 253–72.

the functioning of the economy, including the flow of remittances out of the Persian Gulf to other countries. The culture, behaviors, and values of migrants can also influence the native populations. These issues are relevant in the present day, and with changes in the global economy they may become even more pertinent in the future. Yet scholars and policy-makers know very little about these migrants and their behaviors, values, and future plans.

This chapter provides insight into some of these issues in an effort to address this knowledge gap. The broad aim is to establish ways in which the economic and social character of the GCC countries is influenced by their migrant populations. Specifically, this chapter focuses on Nepali migrants and four dimensions of their lives in the GCC countries: (1) key demographic characteristics of migrants; (2) work, income, remittances, and predictors of income and remittances; (3) plans of the migrants concerning return to Nepal or to migrate elsewhere; and (4) values and beliefs of the migrants. This chapter addresses these issues for the GCC region as a whole and provides comparisons of migrants and their impact across different countries in this region.

Our analysis is based on a unique data set collected from a sample of Nepali migrants in GCC countries. This sample is based on a large representative sample from the Chitwan Valley of south central Nepal. While collecting survey data from households in the Chitwan Valley, we also collected contact information on household members who were currently living in the GCC and then interviewed these migrants. Such a representative sample of migrants at destination is relatively rare in migration literature, which often relies on non-random sampling procedures, such as snowball and targeted sampling, which are widely acknowledged to provide unrepresentative samples. Because our sample of migrants is representative, we can have higher confidence that the results obtained from analysis of the sample reflect the larger population of Nepali migrants in the GCC countries.

Although Nepal is a small country of 26 million, a study of Nepali migrants to the Persian Gulf is important for examining the influence of migrants on GCC countries. First, South Asia is currently the dominant source of migrants into the GCC countries.[8] In the 1970s, the great majority of migrants to the Persian Gulf were from other Arab states.[9] This preponderance declined in later decades, and by the early 2000s less than one-third of these migrants were

---

[8] UN Population Division, "International Migration in the Arab Region."

[9] Kapiszewski, "Arab versus Asian Migrants in the Gulf States," pp. 1–21; John Willoughby, "Foreign Matter. The Place of Strangers in Gulf Society," pp. 222–43.

from other Arab countries. As the migration from those countries to the GCC countries declined, migration from Asia, especially South Asia, greatly expanded.[10] The largest Asian migration stream is now from South Asia, with South Asians comprising about 59 percent of migrants to the GCC countries.[11] Nepal has economic and social conditions that are similar in many ways to the other South Asian countries, including Bangladesh, India, Pakistan and Sri Lanka. Consequently, this analysis of migrants from Nepal to the GCC countries will provide many insights into the nature and impact of migrants from the South Asian subcontinent in general.

Nepal has substantial out-migration, with the GCC countries being an especially important destination. More than 100,000 and perhaps as many as 200,000 Nepali migrants, most of whom are legal, are living in these countries.[12] At the time of the 2001 Nepal census, Saudi Arabia was, with the exception of India, the most common destination country for Nepalis searching for work outside their country.[13] Qatar and the UAE held third and fourth positions, and sizeable numbers were reported for Bahrain and Kuwait.[14] Migrants are an important component of the Nepali economy, as one-quarter of all households in Nepal receive remittances from abroad.[15] The value of remittances has been estimated at between 15 and 25 percent of the Nepali GDP, accounting for more of the economy than tourism, exports,

[10] Douglas S. Massey, Joaquin Arango, Graeme Hugo, Ali Kouaouci, Adela Pellegrino, and J. Edward Taylor, "Labour Migration in the Gulf System," in *Worlds in Motion: Understanding International Migration at the End of the Millenium* (New York: Oxford University Press, 1998), pp. 134–59; John Willoughby, "Foreign Matter. The Place of Strangers in Gulf Society," pp. 222–43.

[11] Kapiszewski, "Arab versus Asian Migrants in the Gulf States," pp. 1–21.

[12] See Elvira Graner and Ganesh Gurung, "Arab Ko Lahure: Looking at Nepali Labour Migrants to Arabian Countries," *Contributions to Nepalese Studies*, 30, 2 (2003), pp. 295–325; David Seddon, Jagannath Adhikari, and Ganesh Gurung, "Foreign Labor Migration and the Remittance Economy of Nepal," *Critical Asian Studies*, 34, 1 (2002), pp. 19–40.

[13] Vidya B.S. Kansakar, "International Migration and Citizenship in Nepal" in *Population Monograph of Nepal* (Kathmandu: Central Bureau of Statistics, 2003), pp. 85–119.

[14] Ibid.

[15] Michael Kollmair, Siddhi Manandhar, Bhim Subedi and Susan Thieme, "New Figures for Old Stories: Migration and Remittances in Nepal," *Migration Letters*, 3, 2 (2006), pp. 151–60.

and foreign aid combined.[16] It is also estimated that the largest share of remittances to Nepal comes from the GCC countries, equaling 35 percent of all remittances.[17] It is likely that there have been recent increases in both the number of migrants and the value of remittances.[18] This substantial flow of remittances is an important link between the economies of the GCC countries and Nepal.

Study setting

The Chitwan Valley in rural Nepal provides an excellent setting to study individuals' migratory behavior, values, beliefs and their plans. Until the early 1950s this valley was completely covered with dense forest and populated only by sparsely settled groups of hunter-gatherers, mainly the Tharu people. Around the mid-1950s, the Nepalese government opened this valley for settlement by people from the neighboring hills and mountains.[19] Furthermore, since 1979, paved roads were built connecting Chitwan's largest town to Kathmandu in the north and to the east and west of the country.[20] As a result of these changes, primarily provision of land and transportation opportunities, large numbers of people from across Nepal moved into the Chitwan Valley. More than half of the migrants to the study area came from the hill districts

---

[16] See Graner and Gurung, "Arab Ko Lahure: Looking at Nepali Labour Migrants to Arabian Countries," pp. 295–325; Seddon, Adhikari and Gurung, "Foreign Labor Migration and the Remittance Economy of Nepal," pp. 19–40. Bal K. KC, "Migration, Poverty and Development in Nepal". Paper presented at the Economic and Social Commission for Asia and the Pacific, Ad Hoc Expert Group Meeting on Migration and Development, Bangkok, Thailand, August 27–29, 2003. Michael Lokshin, Mikhail Bontch-Osmolovski and Elena Glinskaya, "Work-Related Migration and Poverty Reduction in Nepal". Working Paper 4231, World Bank Policy Research, Washington DC, May 2007, pp. 1–59.

[17] Lokshin *et al.*, "Work-Related Migration and Poverty Reduction in Nepal," pp. 1–59.

[18] Ibid.

[19] Joseph W. Elder, Mahabir Ale, Mary A. Evans, David P. Gillespie, Rohit Kumar Nepali, Sitaram P. Poudyal and Bryce P. Smith, *Planned Resettlement in Nepal's Terai: A Social Analysis of the Khajura/Bardia Punarvas Projects* (Kathmandu: Tribhuvan Univeristy Press, 1976).

[20] Jennifer S. Barber, Ganesh P. Shivakoti, William G. Axinn and Kishor Gajurel, "Sampling Strategies for Rural Settings: A Detailed Example from Chitwan Valley Family Study, Nepal," *Nepal Population Journal*, 6, 5 (1997), pp. 193–203.

adjacent to Chitwan. However, significant and increasing proportions of immigrants come from other districts across Nepal and border areas of the Indian Terai. The Tharu are now a minority group in their native region. The immigrants since the 1950s have represented almost all ethnic groups in Nepal.

In addition to provision of land, paved roads, and a sharp increase in immigrants, over time schools, health services, markets, bus services and employment centers expanded considerably in Chitwan.[21] This massive expansion of services resulted in more young people going to school, working outside the family, living away from family, interacting with the mass media, and participating in youth clubs. For example, among those born between 1936 and 1945, only 31 percent ever attended school, whereas among those born between 1966 and 1975, fully 84 percent attended school. In the face of a rapidly growing young population with rising expectations for higher standards of living, a lack of economic opportunities at home, and an augmented labor demand both from the booming East Asian economies and from the GCC countries, which were undergoing a construction boom, the government of Nepal promulgated a Foreign Employment Act of 1985. The Act licensed non-governmental institutions to export Nepalese workers abroad and legitimized certain labor-contracting organizations. This ignited large streams of international migration, including to the GCC countries, to where immigration had been very much limited to people from India prior to this date.[22] By the early twenty-first century, it is estimated that up to 200,000 Nepali migrants were living in Gulf countries.[23]

At the same time as international migration to countries other than India was becoming more and more common, the internal armed conflict between the Communist Party of Nepal (Maoists) and the government, which began in 1996, became widespread over the whole country by 2000. This resulted in further increases in international migration. Although researchers claim the

---

[21] See William G. Axinn and Scott T. Yabiku, "Social Change, the Social Organization of Families, and Fertility Limitation," *American Journal of Sociology*, 106, 5 (2001), pp. 1219–61; Dirgha J. Ghimire and William G. Axinn, "Social Organization, Land Use and the Hazard of First Birth," *Rural Sociology*, 75, 3 (2010), pp. 478–513.

[22] See Kollmair *et al.*, "New Figures for Old Stories," pp. 151–60; Susan Thieme and Simone Wyss, "Migration Patterns and Remittance Transfer in Nepal: A Case Study of Sainik Basti in Western Nepal," *International Migration*, 43, 5 (2005), pp. 59–96.

[23] See Graner and Gurung, "Arab Ko Lahure: Looking at Nepali Labour Migrants to Arabian Countries," pp. 295–325; Seddon, Adhikari and Gurung, "Foreign Labor Migration and the Remittance Economy of Nepal," pp. 19–40.

official figures to be a gross underestimate, even these show a huge surge in migration, with the total number of migrant workers abroad (excluding those to India) increasing from 1,926 in 1992/93 to over a million by the end of 2007.[24] The decade-long armed conflict ended in a peace agreement between the Maoists and the government in 2006, but Nepal is currently undergoing a post-conflict socio-political transformation. Following the peace agreement Nepal experienced a series of major political transitions—the election of constitutional assembly, the formation of a new interim constitution, the abolition of the monarchy, the conversion of Nepal into a Federal Democratic Republic State with an elected head of state, and several ethnic movements. Even though great progress has been made in implementing the peace agreement, the ongoing bickering between political parties to form and run a coalition government, and various ethnic and minority movements, pushed the country into an uncertain political and economic situation, which has continued to lure young Nepali adults to international destinations including GCC countries.

Data

The data for this study come from the Nepali Migrants to the GCC Countries Study (NMGCCS) funded by the Center for International and Regional Studies (CIRS) of the Georgetown University School of Foreign Service in Qatar. NMGCCS directly builds on the Chitwan Valley Family Study (CVFS), a large scale longitudinal panel study of communities, households and individuals of the Western Chitwan Valley of Nepal. The CVFS selected a systematic probability sample of 151 neighborhoods in Western Chitwan (Barber *et al.*, 1997). The CVFS defined a neighborhood as a geographic cluster of five to fifteen households. Once a neighborhood was selected, all the households and individuals residing within those neighborhoods were included in the sample. If any of these study respondents had a spouse living

---

[24] See Pratikshya Bohra-Mishra and Douglas S. Massey, "Individual Decisions to Migrate During Civil Conflict," forthcoming in *Demography*; Sundar S. Shrestha and Prem Bhandari, "Environmental Security and Labor Migration in Nepal," *Population and Environment*, 29, 1 (2007), pp. 25–38. Nathalie E. Williams, Dirgha J. Ghimire, William G. Axinn, Elyse Jennings and Meeta S. Pradhan, "A Micro-Level Approach to Investigating Armed Conflict and Population Responses". Research Report No. 10–707, University of Michigan Population Studies Center, 2010, pp. 1–41.

elsewhere, that spouse was included in the study. The CVFS started in 1996 by collecting a wide array of information, including community histories, household censuses, household consumption and agriculture practices, individual baseline interviews, and life histories. The households living within Nepal were interviewed at regular intervals over the next fourteen years. In 2008 we launched a new data collection and repeated household censuses and relationship grids, individual baseline interviews, and life histories on those households and individuals who had been interviewed in 1996 and were currently living within Nepal, or else were currently residing in the sample neighborhoods. This data collection resulted in 2,091 household and 7,446 individual interviews, with 99 and 95 percent response rates respectively. Further details about the CVFS are available at the website of the Population and Ecology Research Laboratory, the organization that collected the data, at http://perl.psc.isr.umich.edu.[25]

Our household interviews identified all individuals considered to be a member of the household irrespective of their current location. For each of the household members living outside the household, we ascertained extensive information about their locations, contact information, and when they were expected for visits back home in Nepal. Our study population of Chitwan Valley migrants to GCC countries includes the members of the households residing in the CVFS sample neighborhoods who were living in one of the GCC countries during the period from July 2008 to January 2009. This study population definition resulted in 526 individuals from 508 households. As expected a vast majority of these migrants were young males, with about 3 percent female.

On the basis of migrant contact information collected during the household interviews, we administered the interview in two ways. First, those who had returned to Nepal for a vacation or a short visit were visited by our interviewer at their homes in Chitwan and interviewed face-to-face. As expected, a significant portion (34 percent) of migrants had returned to Nepal and they were interviewed face-to-face. Next, those who were still in the Persian Gulf

---

[25] Details can also be found in William G Axinn, Jennifer S. Barber and Dirgha J. Ghimire, "The Neighborhood History Calendar: A Data Collection Method Designed for Dynamic Multilevel Modeling," *Sociological Methodology*, 27, 1 (1997), pp. 355–92; William G. Axinn, Lisa D. Pearce and Dirgha Ghimire, "Innovations in Life History Calendar Applications," *Social Science Research*, 28 (1999), pp. 243–64; Barber *et al.*, "Sampling Strategies for Rural Settings," pp. 193–203.

and had no plans to return to Nepal within a year were interviewed by telephone while they were still residing in the GCC countries.

A few other studies have implemented this approach to the collection of data on migrants at destination, linking them to their home communities. The most prominent such study is the Mexican Migration Project which interviewed Mexican migrants who originated in select Mexican communities and were living in the United States.[26] However they used non-random sampling techniques, and so the representativeness of the sample is unclear. The Mexican Family Life Survey and the Migration Between Africa and Europe Survey implemented surveys on random samples of migrants from Mexico and Senegal respectively.[27] Demonstrating the difficulties of such an approach, the Mexican Family Life Survey was able to obtain contact information for 5 percent of its sample and the Migration Between Africa and Europe obtained contact information for 32 percent of its sample.

As one of the first few studies attempting to contact a representative sample of migrants from an origin community while they were still out of the country, our study faced some important challenges and also achieved some notable successes. On the one hand, we had no problem locating and contacting nearly all of the migrants who had returned to Nepal. On the other hand, we found it much more difficult than we anticipated to locate and contact migrants who were still in the GCC countries. A number of factors were working against us. At the household level, our attempts to collect migrant residential addresses in the Gulf were not very effective because a vast majority of migrants and their families back in Chitwan did not know their addresses. Next, we were unable to get email or work mailing addresses for most migrants. In cases where we were able to get work addresses, we were not able to contact migrants at those addresses. Consequently, the only feasible way to contact these migrants was via telephone. This was complicated by the fact that most of the migrants did not have land lines at their places of resi-

[26] Douglas S. Massey, "Measuring International Migration: Theory and Practice," *International Migration Review*, Special Issue 21, 4 (1987), pp. 1498–522.

[27] See C. Beauchemin and A.G. Ferrer, "Multi-Country Surveys on International Migration: An Assessment of Selection Biases in Destination Countries." Paper presented at the annual meeting for the Population Association of America, Detroit, Michigan, 2009. L. Rubalcava, G. Teruel, E. Arenas and C. Herrera, "Tracking Beyond Borders: Mexican Family Life Survey Experience." Paper presented at the annual meeting for the Population Association of America, Detroit, Michigan, 2009.

dence and we were unable to contact them at their work contact numbers. Finding contacts was particularly difficult for migrants who were domestic workers, most of whom were women.

Thus we concluded that the most feasible way to contact the migrants in GCC countries was by mobile telephone. Even this presented challenges as many of the migrants did not have stable jobs and were not able to afford mobile phones. For those who did have mobile phones, obtaining the phone number from those family members in Chitwan was a long and tedious job requiring our interviewers to make multiple visits to their households. The most difficult migrants to contact were women working as domestic helpers, as most often they were not allowed to have either a mobile phone or access to a land line.

Once we obtained contact telephone numbers and production interviewing began, we again faced a number of challenges and noted a number of successes. Because Nepali migrants are in the GCC to work and make as much money as possible, they usually work as many hours as they possibly can. It was thus difficult to contact them and schedule an interview time. To add to this, inadequate communication technology (poor telephone connections) on the Nepal side and dependence on mobile phones with limited battery power were other major hurdles. These limitations required most interviews to be completed via multiple phone contacts rather than during just one call. Together, all of these disadvantages increased the possibility of encountering respondent refusal or just partial interviews. Yet, the respondents were very excited to speak to a person from Nepal and were happy to participate in the study.

Therefore, despite the challenges both in Nepal and in the GCC countries, we were able to achieve an 87 percent response rate because of the extraordinary level of respondent cooperation, the persistence of our well-trained interviewers, and our multiple-method approach. Out of 526 eligible respondents, 459 interviews were completed. The average interview length was 110 minutes, which included an individual base line interview, a life history calendar, and a questionnaire on migration.

Measurements

Previous research from Nepal and elsewhere suggests that such individual demographic characteristics as ethnicity, gender, age and religion are important predictors of migration.[28]

---

[28] See Prem Bhandari, "Relative Deprivation and Migration in an Agricultural Setting

Ethnicity

Nepali society consists of diverse ethnic and linguistic groups.[29] These groups differ in many respects that have important consequences for their migratory behavior. Although ethnicity in Nepal is complex, in this study we use five major ethnic categories that are also used by other scholars in previous studies: Brahmin and Chhetry (High Caste Hindus), Dalit (Low Caste Hindus), Newar, Hill Indigenous (mostly Hill Tibeto-Burmese) and Terai Indigenous (mostly Terai Tibeto-Burmese).[30] Our analyses use a series of dichotomous measures for each ethnic group. For example *Brahmin/Chhetry* is coded '1' if

of Nepal," *Population and Environment*, 25, 5 (2004), pp. 475–99; Piatikshya Bohra and Douglas S. Massey, "Processes of Internal and International Migration from Chitwan, Nepal," *International Migration Review*, 43, 3 (2009), pp. 621–51; Douglas S. Massey, William G. Axinn and Dirgha J. Ghimire, "Environmental Change and Out-Migration: Evidence from Nepal," *Population and Environment*, 32, 2 (2010), pp. 109–136; Douglas S. Massey, Nathalie Williams, William G. Axinn and Dirgha J. Ghimire, "Community Services and Out-Migration," *International Migration*, 48, 3 (2010), pp. 1–41; Martin Piotrowski, "Mass Media and Rural Out-Migration in the Context of Social Change," forthcoming in *International Migration*; Shrestha and Bhandari, "Environmental Security and Labor Migration in Nepal," pp. 25–38; Nathalie Williams, "Education, Gender, and Migration in the Context of Social Change," *Social Science Research*, 38 (2009), pp. 883–96, Williams, "Betting on Life and Livelihoods: The Role of Employment and Assets in the Decision to Migrate During Armed Conflict". Research Report No. 09–679, University of Michigan Population Studies Center, 2009), pp. 1–30.

[29] See Lynn Bennet, Dilli Ram Dahal and Pav Govindasamy, *Caste, Ethnic and Regional Identity in Nepal: Further Analysis of the 2006 Nepal Demographic and Health* Survey (Calverton, MD: Macro International Inc., DFID and World Bank, 2008); Dor Bahadur Bista, *People of Nepal* (Kathmandu, Nepal: Ratna Pustak Bhandar, 1972); Dilli Ram Dahal, "Rethinking Fertility Transition: Some Observation from Nepal," in *Population Dynamics in Nepal* (Kathmandu: Tribhuvan University, Central Department of Population Studies, 1993), pp. 49–58; Harka B. Gurung, *Vignettes of Nepal* (Kathmandu: Sajha Prakashan, 1980); Harka B. Gurung, *Nepal Social Demography and Expressions* (Kathmandu: New Era, 1998).

[30] See William G. Axinn and Jennifer S. Barber, "Mass Education and Fertility Transition," *American Sociological Review*, 66, 4 (2001), pp. 481–505; Axinn and Yabiku, "The Neighborhood History Calendar," pp. 1219–61; Dirgha J. Ghimire, William G. Axinn, Scott T. Yabiku and Arland Thornton, "Social Change, Premarital Nonfamily Experience, and Spouse Choice in an Arranged Marriage Society," *American Journal of Sociology*, 111, 4 (2006), pp. 1181–1218.

a respondent reported that they were a member of this ethnic group, and '0' if they reported being a member of another ethnic group.

Gender

As elsewhere, gender inequality in various aspects of social life is deeply rooted in Nepali society.[31] Compared to men, women have lower social status in South Asian societies in general.[32] Most women, regardless of their ethnic group, wealth, and age, are discouraged from participation in education, the labor market, politics, and business. Furthermore, their personal autonomy and decision-making power are limited. This disadvantaged position of women has substantially reduced their ability to freely move around or migrate abroad. Gender is coded '1' for female respondents and '0' for males.

Age

Previous research around the world has shown that an inverted U-shaped function generally summarizes the relationship between age and migration, where there is a low rate of migration in childhood, a peak of migration during the twenties, and then a progressive decline through middle and older ages.[33]

[31] See Meena Acharya and Lynn Bennett, *The Rural Women of Nepal: An Aggregate Analysis and Summary of Eight Village Studies* (Kathmandu: Centre for Economic Development and Administration, 1981); Lynn Bennett, *Dangerous Wives and Sacred Sisters: Social and Symbolic Roles of High-Caste Women in Nepal* (New York: Columbia University Press, 1983); S. Philip Morgan and Bhanu B. Niraula, "Gender Inequality and Fertility in Two Nepali Villages," *Population and Development Review*, 21, 3 (1995): pp. 541–61; UNICEF, *Children and Women in Nepal: A Situation Analysis* (Kathmandu, UNICEF, 1998).

[32] John C. Caldwell, P.H. Reddy and Pat Caldwell, "The Causes of Marriage Change in South India," *Population Studies*, 37, 3 (1983), pp. 343–61; Tim Dyson and Mick Moore, "On Kinship Structure, Female Autonomy, and Demographic Behavior in India," *Population and Development Review*, 9, 1 (1983), pp. 35–60.

[33] Douglas S. Massey and Kristin E. Espinosa, "What's Driving Mexico-U.S. Migration? A Theoretical, Empirical, and Policy Analysis," *The American Journal of Sociology*, 102, 4 (1997), p. 939–99; L.K. Vanwey, "Land Ownership as a Determinant of International and Internal Migration in Mexico and Internal Migration in Thailand," *International Migration Review*, 39 (2005), pp. 141–72; Williams, "Education, Gender, and Migration," pp. 883–96; Yaohui Zhao, "Leaving the Countryside: Rural-To-Urban Migration Decisions in China," *American Economic Review*, 89 (1999), pp. 281–6.

We asked respondents how old they were at the time of the interview and recorded their answers in years.

Religion. Religion is another important factor that can influences migrants' behavior, contact with host country nationals, and assimilation. Respondents were asked about their religion and we coded answers into three dichotomous measures for the primary religious identities in Nepal—Hindu, Buddhist and Other.

Work. The type of jobs that migrants do in host countries has important consequences both for the host's economy and for migrants' earnings and remittances. In order to ascertain the type of job the migrants had, the migration questionnaire asked respondents, "Now let's talk about your main job in [COUNTRY]. Which one of these categories best describes your main job— working in a salaried job with government or private company; working as a domestic laborer; working as some other type of laborer; owning your own business; or going to school?" Next, in order to determine whether the respondent had a professional job or not, we asked a follow up question, "Is that job as per your educational qualification?" This question was put only to those respondents who had bachelor's degrees or higher qualifications.

Next to learn about how migrants got their jobs we asked, "How did you get your main job in [COUNTRY]? Was it through a relative or friend, through an employment agency, through the newspaper, on the internet, or did you find it yourself?" As finding a job may involve more than one step, respondents were allowed to make multiple choices. Respondents' answers were coded into categorical measures for "relative/friend", "employment agency", "newspaper or internet", "oneself", and "other".

Income. To ascertain migrants' incomes and benefits, we began with asking whether or not they got any other kind of benefits besides salary. If the respondent answered yes, then we asked about those benefits. We asked the respondent, "I am going to read you a list of benefits you might get from your job. Please tell me which ones you get: food, housing, health benefits or life insurance, or something else." Again, as there could be more than one type of benefit received by each respondent, they were encouraged to choose multiple choices. The responses were then coded into separate measures for "food", "housing", "medical benefits and/or life insurance", "transportation", or "other". We created a measure for transportation benefits because many respondents indicated that they received this; in most cases this involved transportation from their housing unit to the work site by bus. Next we asked about wages or salary with the question, "Thinking about this job, and any other jobs you might have right now, altogether how much do you earn in wages or salary each month?" Here respondents were allowed to give the amount they earned in any currency per hour, week, or month. We then converted it to US dollars per month.

Remittances. Remittances are a key reason for and consequence of international labor migration and are of great importance to both host and sending countries. Host countries might be interested to know how much money is being sent out of the country through remittances and how much is being recycled through spending in the country. On the other hand, remittances are an interest for sending countries, many of which receive large proportions of their GDP through remittances from overseas. To ascertain the amount of remittances we began with a question about migrants' savings. We asked, "About how much money do you save each month after your personal expenses?" Again the respondent was allowed to report in any currency but we later converted the answers into US dollars.

Next we asked the worth of all goods, gifts, or money that the respondent sent to Nepal. The respondent was asked, "Have you sent or brought any money, goods, or gifts to your household in Nepal (in the past twelve months or while in [COUNTRY])?" We also asked the amount of money, goods, or gifts that respondents had sent to or brought for anyone else in Nepal besides their households. Respondents were also asked whether they received any money, goods or gifts from their households or anyone else in Nepal. These questions were worded similarly to the previous questions.

Intentions for future migration destinations. Previous research on intention and behavior has shown a positive relationship between an individual's intentions and their behavior, but this relationship is not completely correlated.[34] An understanding of migrants' intentions could have important implications for both host and sending countries. In order to learn about the intentions of Nepali migrants to the GCC countries, the respondents were asked, "Ignoring vacations or visits to Nepal or any other country, do you plan to leave [COUNTRY] at any time in the future?" Note that the Nepali language

---

[34] See Gordon F. de Jong, "Expectations, Gender, and Norms in Migration Decision-Making," *Population Studies*, 54, 3 (2000), pp. 307–319; Gordon F. de Jong, Kerry Richter and Pimonpan Isarabhakdi, "Gender, Values, and Intentions to Move in Rural Thailand," *International Migration Review*, 30, 3 (1996), pp. 748–70.

version of this question used a word that approximately translates as 'definite plans'. Thus while the vast majority of respondents likely know they must leave, this question aimed to record if they had made plans already, such as deciding on a date of departure or next destination. If the response to this question was 'yes', then respondents were asked where and when they plan to move next.

Values and beliefs concerning 'modern' or 'traditional' society. We ascertained information about the values and beliefs of Nepali migrants by presenting respondents with a set of choices between things commonly seen as "modern" and things commonly seen as "traditional." We asked respondents to select which of the attributes was better for most people in Nepal today—the "modern" attribute or the "traditional" attribute. For example, with regard to spousal choice, we asked respondents, "Overall, which do you think is better for most people in Nepal today—young people choosing their own spouses, or parents choosing their spouses for them?" A similar question format was used for a variety of values and beliefs. We accepted a response of "no difference" or "about the same" only if respondents spontaneously replied. Questions of this type have been asked successfully in several different countries around the world.[35]

Results: Demographic characteristics

Demographic characteristics of the NMGCCS sample are shown in Table 8.1. The first column presents the characteristics of the total sample and the next three columns disaggregate the sample of Nepali migrants by their country of residence in the GCC. The fifth column in Table 8.1 is presented for comparison and shows characteristics of a sample of non-migrants living in the Chitwan Valley from the CVFS. To create a relevant comparative group, this sample includes men only of the same age range that we find in the NMGCCS sample, aged 17 through to 55.

As shown in Table 1, of the total 459 Nepali migrants interviewed, the vast majority live in three countries—38 percent live in Qatar, 30 percent in Saudi Arabia, and 26 percent in the United Arab Emirates (UAE). Among the

[35] Arland Thornton *et al.*, "Creating Questions and Protocols for an International Study of Ideas About Development and Family Life," in Janet Harkness *et al.* (eds), *Survey Methods in Multinational, Multiregional and Multicultural Contexts* (Hoboken, NJ: John Wiley and Sons, 2010), pp. 59–74.

Table 8.1: Demographic Characteristics of Nepali Migrants to GCC Countries.

	All GCC countries	Qatar	Saudi Arabia	United Arab Emirates	Nepal sample[1]
Total no. of people	459	38%	30%	26%	2,487
Interviewed in GCC country	64	63	64	62	0
Living in GCC country[2]	80	76	83	83	0
Sex (% male)	97	100	93	99	100
Age (mean years)	32	31	33	32	35
Married	89	90	91	87	79
no. of children (mean)	1.30	1.37	1.26	1.20	1.21
Education (mean years)	8.00	7.57	7.42	9.18	7.39
Ethnicity					
Brahmin and Chhetry	46	46	45	51	45
Dalit	11	16	9	7	11
Hill Indigenous	21	17	22	23	15
Terai Indigenous	14	12	18	14	20
Newar	7	8	4	6	6
Other	1	1	1	0	3
Religion					
Hindu	83	85	79	86	84
Buddhist	14	13	17	14	11
Other	2	3	4	0	5

Notes: Unless otherwise indicated, all numbers are percentages. Professionals are included in this analysis.

[1] For comparative purposes, this column shows similar statistics for a representative sample of men ages 17–55 in the Chitwan Valley Family Study who are currently living in Nepal.

[2] This includes those who were interviewed in a GCC country and those who were interviewed Nepal while on a visit. This is in contrast to those who were interviewed in Nepal while living there, after a final return from a GCC country.

remaining 4 percent of the sample, a few people live in Kuwait, Oman and Bahrain. The heavy concentration of Nepali migrants in these three Persian Gulf countries could partially reflect a difference in labor demand in each country. However, it is more likely a consequence of the importance of social networks in migration[36] and employment agencies in recruitment and hiring

[36] Douglas S. Massey, "Social Structure, Household Strategies, and the Cumulative Causation of Migration," *Population Index*, 56, 1 (1990), pp. 3–26; Douglas S. Mas-

in Nepal. For example, the first Nepali migrants to work in the GCC went to Qatar. The migrant social networks that ensued, as well as the institutionalization of employment agencies associated with Qatar, likely affected the later preponderance of Nepalis going to that country. Thus, despite the fact that Qatar is not a large country, even by GCC standards, the majority of Nepali migrants in this study were working there.

The vast majority of Nepali migrants in this sample, 97 percent, were male. This differed little by country, with only Saudi Arabia having slightly more females, who made up 7 percent of the Saudi migrant sample. This is consistent with previous research showing that most migrants leaving Nepal for any country are male and that the vast majority of jobs in the GCC are in the construction or oil sector and are primarily open to men.[37] Amongst the few women in our sample, the vast majority were working as domestic servants in the households of nationals of the host country.

The average age of migrants is 32. This is slightly higher than the median age of the first adult migration from the Chitwan Valley sample, 26 years old.[38] We expect that this age difference between Nepali migrants in GCC countries and first time Nepali migrants to any destination reflects a changing pattern of migration destinations with each migration experience. As described by Ravenstein in one of the earliest studies of human mobility, in some cases migration might involve multiple moves, whereby an individual might first move to somewhere relatively nearby their origin, and then in subsequent migrations move progressively further away.[39] While stepwise migration is clearly not a universal phenomenon, there is evidence of this process in other settings.[40] The data in this study indicate that this might also be a process through which many Nepali migrants reach the Persian Gulf. This

---

sey, Rafael Alarcon, Jorge Durand, and Humberto Gonzalez, *Return to Aztlan: The Social Process of International Migration from Western Mexico* (Berkeley: University of California Press, 1987).

[37] See Bohra and Massey, "Process of Internal and International Migration," pp. 621–51; Williams, "Education, Gender, and Migration," pp. 883–96.

[38] This median age of first migration is calculated from a sample of adults who were at least 15 years old. If all ages had been included in the sample, the median age of first migration would be even lower.

[39] E.G. Ravenstein, "The Laws of Migration," *Journal of the Statistical Society of London*, 48, 2 (1885), pp. 167–235.

[40] Dennis Conway, "Step-Wise Migration: Toward a Clarification of the Mechanism," *International Migration Review*, 14, 1 (1980), pp. 3–14.

not only serves as a possible explanation for the comparatively older age of GCC migrants, but also indicates that many of the Nepali migrants currently in the GCC countries likely have previous migration experience and this is not their first move away from home. In addition, our age estimation is current age rather than age at first migration. Since these migrants have been in the GCC for some time, we would expect their current age to be higher than their age at first migration.

An average of about 89 percent of Nepali migrants in this sample were married. This is consistent across countries in the GCC.[41] It is consistent with the pattern of almost universal marriage in Nepal, but notably somewhat higher than the 79 percent of non-migrant men in the CVFS who were married. Migrants had an average of 1.30 children between the ages of 0 and 15 years. This is also similar to, and slightly higher than, the average 1.21 children born to male non-migrants in Chitwan. These statistics indicate that in regard to family, Nepali migrants in the GCC are not wholly different from their non-migrant counterparts.

In terms of educational attainment, the average number of years of schooling completed in this sample is 8.00. This is somewhat higher than the average of 7.39 years of schooling completed by non-migrant men in Chitwan. Furthermore, migrants in the UAE stand out, with a higher 9.18 years of schooling. It is likely that this higher educational attainment of migrants in the GCC countries is a result of migrants in general having higher education.[42] It is also likely that migrants to GCC countries in particular have higher educational attainment than migrants to such other countries as India, for example.

The largest ethnic group amongst migrants is Brahmin/Chhetri, which comprises 46 percent of the migrant sample. A further 11 percent are Dalit, 21 percent Hill Indigenous, 14 percent Terai Indigenous, 7 percent Newar and 1 percent of other ethnicities. These statistics are similar across countries in the GCC and in the non-migrant sample in the Chitwan Valley.

Similar to Nepal and the non-migrant sample shown here, the majority (83 percent) of migrants in the GCC ascribe to the Hindu religion. A further 14

---

[41] See Fred Arnold and Nasra M. Shah, "Asian Labor Migration to the Middle East," *International Migration Review*, 18, 2 (1984), pp. 294–318; Y. Gaudel, "Remittance Income in Nepal: Need for Economic Development," *The Journal of Nepalese Business Studies*, III, 1 (2006), pp. 9–17; Graner and Gurung, "Arab Ko Lahure," pp. 295–325; Thieme and Wyss, "Migration Patterns and Remittance Transfer in Nepal," pp. 59–96.

[42] Williams, "Education, Gender, and Migration," pp. 883–96.

percent are Buddhist and only 2 percent ascribe to any other religion, including Hindu-Buddhism, Islam, or Christianity. This pattern of religious association of Nepali migrants is similar across individual GCC countries.

Results: Work, income, and remittances

As shown in Table 8.2, the vast majority of Nepali migrants (90 percent) reported that their main job was some form of labor. In light of previous research and government statistics, this is not surprising.[43] Amongst other types of work, 6 percent of respondents were doing domestic labor, and 2 percent were professionals. Less than 1 percent were engaged in another type of work. A total of twenty men (5 percent of the sample) were working as domestic laborers. Of the fourteen women in the sample, nine were in domestic labor and five reported working in other types of labor jobs. The 2 percent of the sample that were working as professionals include eleven men, seven of whom were in Qatar, with a further three in the UAE and one in Saudi Arabia. Because of the small number of professionals and the vastly different circumstances in which they live and work, the remainder of the analyses in this paper includes only non-professionals.

Employment agencies were the most common way in which respondents found their current jobs. 58 percent of the sample reported that they found their jobs through employment agencies, although this is slightly higher in Saudi Arabia and lower in the UAE. Amongst other routes, jobs were commonly found through recommendations by friends and seldom through newspapers or the internet.[44] While it is not surprising that many people used employment agencies to secure their jobs, the surprising result is that 42 percent of the sample did not use employment agencies. Without the assistance of an employment agency, it would be very difficult for a Nepali in Nepal to find employment in the Persian Gulf and arrange for a visa and other logistics.

[43] See Gaudel, "Remittance Income in Nepal," pp. 9–17; Graner and Gurung, "Arab Ko Lahure," pp. 295–325; Thieme and Wyss, "Migration Patterns and Remittance Transfer in Nepal," pp. 59–96.

[44] For this question, respondents were allowed to report all routes that they used to find their jobs. For example, if friends recommended that they apply to an employment agency, they could report that they found their job through both of these sources. If respondents only reported the primary method, we expect that the percentages would decrease for each of the routes other than through an employment agency.

Table 8.2: Work, Income, and Remittances of Nepali Migrants to GCC Countries.[1]

	All GCC countries	Qatar	Saudi Arabia	United Arab Emirates
Type of job (%)				
Labor	90	91	88	94
Domestic Labor	6	3	11	3
Professional	2	4	1	3
Other	0	1	0	0
How R got this job (%)[2]				
Employment agency	58	53	68	53
Relative/friend	34	42	25	33
Found it oneself	17	15	15	24
Newspaper or internet	5	5	2	7
Monthly wages/salary (US$)				
Wages/salary (mean)	358	341	314	443
Benefits (%)[2]				
Housing	83	83	80	84
Food	57	52	60	59
Medical and/or life insurance	66	58	68	72
Transportation	81	80	80	81
Monthly savings (US$, mean)	279	264	251	337
Yearly remittances (US$)				
Net remittances to Nepal (median)	2,225	2,049	1,540	2,678
% salary remitted to Nepal (median)	58	60	56	57

Notes: Unless otherwise indicated, all numbers are percentages.

[1] Except for 'Type of job', professionals are excluded from this analysis.

[2] These categories are not mutually exclusive. Respondents were allowed to select as many categories as fitted their situation.

Thus we suspect that many of the 42 percent of respondents who did not report using an employment agency found their jobs while already in the Persian Gulf. This likely indicates a significant amount of job changing, or that many Nepali migrants might use employment agencies to secure a first job in a GCC country but then, after arrival, take new jobs that they find through other sources. We believe that this is the most logical interpretation of these data, but we are not able to test these hypotheses given the data currently available from this study.

The average monthly base salary or wage (not including overtime) is US$358.[45] The average salary in the UAE is higher, at US$443 per month. This salary difference between the UAE and the rest of the sample is statistically significant.

Amongst the benefits that migrants receive from their employers, housing, food, medical treatment or insurance, and transportation are all common. About 83 percent of migrants received housing, 57 percent food, and 66 percent medical care. This varied little across countries. A few respondents reported receiving clothing or other benefits.

The average amount of savings per month was US$279. The amount was higher in the UAE, surely reflecting the higher average wages. Across all countries, the average monthly savings was over 75 percent of the salary. This large percentage might be surprising in other countries. However, in the context of GCC countries where most migrants receive housing, food, and medical benefits, and where many migrants go for the specific purpose of earning money to remit, the large amount of savings is not at all surprising.

Turning to remittances, net remittances from Nepali migrants in this sample were about US$2,225 in the past year.[46] This is a net calculation that includes the amount each individual sent to Nepal in the form of cash or gifts, from which the amount in cash or gifts they received from Nepal is subtracted. Not surprisingly, remittances sent to Nepal vastly exceed the amount of money or gifts received from Nepal. Only 47 percent of migrants received any money or gifts from Nepal, and 53 percent received none. Net remittances sent to Nepal are somewhat lower in Saudi Arabia with a median of US$1,540, and significantly higher in the UAE at $2,678 per year. Compared to yearly salaries, Nepali migrants across the GCC countries annually remit about 58 percent of what they make. This is fairly consistent across countries. In evaluating the magnitude of the remittances, it is useful to note that our estimates

---

[45] Based on a conversion rate of 75 Nepali rupees to the US dollar.

[46] Remittances vary drastically by year. Informal discussions with Nepali migrants in GCC countries indicate that many migrants save money for more than one year and then bring all their savings when they return to Nepal to live or visit. Furthermore, many migrants who are not able to return home at a given time, give money to another Nepali who is returning. Thus the amount of remittances sent in the last year is exceptionally high for some respondents, to the extent that a few report remitting four times more than they actually made in the last year. As a result, we report the medians instead of means for remittance calculations.

do not take into account the expenses that the migrants and their families accumulated in making the transition from Nepal to the Gulf.

Influences on work, income, and remittances

We next turn to multivariate analyses to examine influences behind variances in yearly wages or salaries and remittances. We used ordinary least squares (OLS) regression to predict these outcomes, based on demographic characteristics, country of residence in the GCC, and ethnicity. Again, we include only non-professionals in these analyses. Results are presented in Table 8.3. As shown in Model 1, which tests the influences on yearly wages, the only statistically significant predictors of the amount of salary that migrants received were education and residence in the UAE. The coefficient for education is positive, at 16.25, meaning that for each extra year of education an individual had, they received about US$16 more in salary per year. This means that compared to someone with five years of education, another migrant with ten years of education would be expected to make about US$81 more per year. Considering that average yearly salaries are about US$4,296, this increase of US$81 is not a substantial amount. Furthermore, working in the UAE had positive effects, increasing salary by US$75 per year. Again, considering average yearly salaries, this difference is not large.

Turning to remittances, results are shown in Model 2. Notably, only one measure had statistically significant effects on the amount remitted per year. We find no significant effects on remittances due to age, gender, marital status, children, length of stay, education, ethnicity, and country or residence; yearly wages was the only significant predictor. With a coefficient of 0.45, this means that with every extra dollar a migrant earns in salary, we can expect that they will remit 45 more cents back to Nepal.

Results: Intentions for future migration destinations

Results concerning migration experience and future intentions of Nepali migrants in GCC countries are shown in Table 8.4. On average, at the time of interview, migrants had been in the GCC country for 47 months, almost four years, with a large standard deviation of 40 months. As shown in Figure 8.1, the majority of migrants were in the GCC less than this amount of time. The large standard deviation highlights that the mean length of stay is heavily impacted by a few migrants who have been in the Persian Gulf for over 15

Table 8.3: OLS Regressions predicting Income and Remittances.

	Model 1 Yearly wages	Model 2 Remittances[1]
Age	− 0.53	− 3.42
	(0.31)	(0.05)
Gender (female)	− 64.47	757.71
	(1.05)	(0.28)
Married	30.30	322.02
	(0.79)	(0.19)
no. of children	− 14.25	− 207.33
	(1.30)	(0.43)
Length of stay in GCC	− 2.37	− 131.80
	(1.20)	(1.50)
Education	16.25***	149.20
	(4.61)	(0.94)
Yearly wages	−	0.45**
	−	(2.56)
Country in GCC		
Reference	*Reference*	Qatar
Saudi Arabia	− 21.39	529.46
	(0.83)	(0.49)
UAE	75.46**	1739.93
	(2.93)	(1.52)
Other	− 29.40	38.79
	(0.64)	(0.02)
Ethnicity		
Brahmin and Chhetry	*Reference*	*Reference*
Dalit Hindu	54.59	633.34
	(1.64)	(0.43)
Hill Indigenous	50.16	1652.28
	(1.91)	(1.42)
Terai Indigenous	8.78	938.93
	(0.28)	(0.68)
Newar	45.70	854.96
	(1.15)	(0.48)
R^2	0.1424	0.0477
Adj R^2	0.1165	0.0167
No. of people	447	447

Note: Professionals are excluded from these analyses.
[1] Amount reported here might include remittances from several years of savings.
* p < 0.05 ** p < 0.01 *** p < 0.001 (two-tailed tests).

years. The median length of stay was substantially smaller, at 39 months. Thus 50 percent of the migrants had been in the GCC for at least 39 months, 75 percent for at least 16 months and 25 percent for at least 63 months, or just over five years. Length of stay was slightly longer in Saudi Arabia, with a mean of 55 months, and slightly shorter in the UAE with a mean of 39 months. As for previous experience in the GCC, about 28 percent of migrants had lived in the same GCC country before this time, while a further 15 percent had lived in another GCC country before moving to their current residence. Notably, the percentage of migrants living in the UAE who had lived there before was much higher, 36 percent.

About 22 percent of the total sample of migrants (or 77 people) who were living in GCC countries had definite plans to leave. The majority of Nepali people living in GCC countries had no definite plans to leave in the future. To repeat the word "plan" translated in Nepali refers to definite plans, including deciding on a date to leave, applying for a release from work, buying airline tickets, or arranging for the next destination. Of those 77 people who did have plans, their intended next destinations vary widely. Only 12 percent planned to return to Nepal. Thus a full 83 percent intended to continue living outside

Figure 8.1.

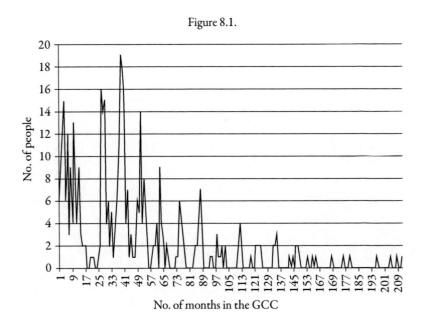

No. of months in the GCC

Table 8.4: Intentions for Future Migration Destinations.

	All GCC countries	Qatar	Saudi Arabia	United Arab Emirates
Length of stay in GCC country this time (months)	47	46	55	39
Have lived in this country before this time (%)	28	24	25	36
Have lived in other GCC country before (%)	15	13	13	21
For those living in GCC country[1]				
Definite plans to leave GCC country (%)	22	24	19	23
Definite plans to leave GCC country (No. of people)	77	31	22	22
For those living in GCC country who have definite plans to leave				
Intended next destination				
Any GCC country	33	45	45	5
UAE[2]	23	29	36	n/a
Other Middle East/North Africa	4	10	0	0
Nepal	12	6	9	25
Other Asia	17	6	18	30
Europe/Australia/North America	15	16	9	15
Don't know	19	16	18	25
For those living in Nepal				
Plans to leave Nepal again (%)	58	49	57	84
Plans to leave Nepal again (No. of people)	52	20	13	16
For those living in Nepal who have plans to leave again				
Intended next destination				
Any GCC country	63	65	54	67
UAE[2]	35	40	8	40
Other Middle East/North Africa	8	15	8	0
Other Asia	12	0	15	27
Europe/Australia/North America	4	0	8	7
Don't know	13	20	15	0

Notes: Unless otherwise indicated, all numbers are percentages. Professionals are excluded from this analysis.

[1] These people were either interviewed in a GCC country, or interviewed in Nepal while they were on vacation.

[2] Note, the UAE is also included in 'Any GCC country'. A separate line for the UAE is included in this table to show that the vast majority of people who want to return to GCC countries are aiming for the UAE.

Nepal. 33 percent of migrants already living in the GCC planned to go to another GCC country; the table shows that the UAE is the favored country of destination. This is not a surprising result, given the significantly higher salaries in the UAE. Amongst other intended destinations are Europe (Belgium and the United Kingdom), Australia, North American, Asia (Malaysia, Singapore, Japan, Macau), and Israel. 19 percent of migrants who had plans to leave the Persian Gulf did not know where they would go next.

Results also show that a significant proportion (58 percent) of migrants who had recently returned to the Chitwan Valley in Nepal after living in GCC countries also planned to migrate again in the future. Of the 52 people who planned to leave Nepal, 63 percent intended to return to the Gulf. Again, the UAE is the favored destination; 35 percent of those with migration plans intended to go to the UAE. Amongst other intended destinations are the United Kingdom, Japan, Afghanistan, Libya, Iraq and Israel. 13 percent of respondents in the Chitwan Valley who planned to leave again did not know where they would go next.

This evidence that a majority of migrants who were living or had lived in the GCC planned to migrate provides some notable insights into classical migration theory. The new economics of migration theory, which has received strong empirical support in migration literature,[47] proposes that migration is not only a strategy for people to increase their earnings: importantly, migration of an individual can be a family-based strategy to manage risk in imperfect local markets and gain access to capital to finance consumer purchases and production activities in the migrant's place of origin. In terms of the latter explanation—that a migrant may be seeking to gain access to capital— migrants are sometimes described as target earners, migrating to earn enough to purchase specific items such as land, tractors, livestock, or a house; once a

---

[47] See Massey and Espinosa, "What's Driving Mexico-U.S. Migration?," pp. 939–99; Oded Stark and David E. Bloom, "The New Economics of Labor Migration," *American Economic Review*, 75 (1985), pp. 173–8; Oded Stark and J. Edward Taylor, "Relative Deprivation and International Migration," *Demography*, 26 (1989), pp. 1–14; Stark and Taylor, "Migration Incentives, Migration Types: The Role of Relative Deprivation," *Economic Journal*, 101 (1991), pp. 1163–78; J. Edward Taylor, "Differential Migration, Networks, Information, and Risk" in Oded Stark (ed.), *Research in Human Capital and Development Vol. 4, Migration, Human Capital, and Development* (Greenwich, CT: JAI Press, 1986), pp. 141–71; Taylor, "Undocumented Mexico-U.S. Migration and the Returns to Households in Rural Mexico," *American Journal of Agricultural Economics*, 69 (1987), pp. 616–38.

migrant earns the desired amount of money, it is often believed that he or she will return home. Evidence from our sample in the GCC countries suggests that this might not always be the case. Although on average they had earned and remitted significant amounts of money over an average of almost four years in the GCC, the majority of migrants intended to migrate again, instead of returning to live in Nepal. It is possible that some migrants had not yet met their target earnings, but given the high average remittances, it is most likely that many did. Instead, the relatively long stays and intentions to migrate again suggest that these migrants might be seeking to manage risk in the imperfect markets in Nepal, particularly given the political and economic instability resulting from the armed conflict and reorganization of the government. Thus this evidence supports the new economics of migration theory in terms of the management of risk in imperfect markets, but is contrary to the proposition that many migrants are target earners who will return to their origins upon reaching a monetary savings target.

Results: Values and beliefs

We now turn to the values and beliefs of Nepali migrants in the GCC countries concerning the best societal and family arrangements for most Nepali people. We are particularly interested in whether Nepali migrants value things that are commonly believed to be part of a "modern" or a "traditional" aspect of society and family life. The degree of people's support for the ideas of modernity and development has been found to be an important element in decision making and behavior.[48]

Table 8.5 shows the percentage of respondents choosing the "modern" attribute for each item. The furthermost left column lists each individual measure, with the "modern" choice shown in italics. The distributions are displayed in the remaining columns for both the GCC countries combined as well as for each individual country.

We draw two general conclusions from these distributions. First, there is little variation either within or across the individual countries regarding which attributes migrants think are better. That is, for nearly all societal and family

---

[48] See Arland Thornton, "The Developmental Paradigm, Reading History Sideways, and Family Change," *Demography*, 38, 4 (2001), pp. 449–65; Arland Thornton, *Reading History Sideways: The Fallacy and Enduring Impact of the Developmental Paradigm on Family* Life (University of Chicago Press, 2005).

characteristics, migrants firmly endorse either the "modern" or the "traditional" attribute at least eight out of ten times. 87 percent of all migrants believe it is better for a woman to give birth in a hospital (ranging from 86 to 89 percent across individual countries), 89 percent believe it is better for married children to live with their parents (ranging from 80 to 90 percent across individual countries), more than nine out of ten migrants believe it is better to have a TV in the home than not (96 to 97 percent ranges across individual countries), and so on.

Table 8.5: Migrant Values—Percentage of migrants agreeing that certain "modern" societal attributes are better for most people in Nepal today. 'Modern' response choice is in italics.

	All GCC countries	Qatar	Saudi Arabia	United Arab Emirates
Women giving birth in a *hospital*/at home	87	89	86	86
Culture in *America*/in Nepal	9	8	11	8
Visiting a *medical doctor*/local healer	100	100	99	100
Having/not having a TV in one's home	96	97	96	97
Working *outside the home*/at home	92	92	92	92
Having *great*/little personal freedom	89	89	92	90
Married children living *separately*/with parents	11	10	12	12
Choosing own spouse/parents choosing	82	80	81	86
Unmarried cohabitation *acceptable*/unacceptable	11	13	12	9
For women—*sex*/no sex before marriage	4	3	5	5
Divorce/unhappy marriage	59	61	60	56
Putting *individual needs*/family needs first	9	9	5	13
Marrying *outside*/within own caste	31	26	34	33
Not to get married/get married	1	1	1	2

Notes: All numbers are pecentages. Professionals are included in this analysis.

The only measures with substantial variation regarding which is considered better are those relating to divorce and inter-caste marriage. Although both measures concern marriage and both show considerable ambivalence, it is possible to apply separate interpretations to each anomaly. When asked about marital dissolution, Nepali migrants appear to be conflicted about whether a divorce is better (60 percent) or an unhappy marriage is better (40 percent). While on the surface this might be attributed to a growing acceptance of divorce, this variation may in fact be due to the composition of the migrant sample. Historically, divorce in Nepal has been taboo mostly for members of high-caste groups; more variation is seen amongst other ethnic groups. Indeed, we see that approximately 46 percent of our migrant sample consists of high-caste Hindus (Table 8.1). On the other hand, inter-caste marriage is generally unacceptable to most Nepali people regardless of caste, although its acceptability has recently become a topic of growing debate. Therefore, the ambivalence seen in Table 8.5 relative to this measure (30 percent believing marriage outside of one's caste is better versus 70 percent believing the opposite) may indeed reflect growing differences of opinion amongst our Nepali migrant respondents.

The second conclusion we draw from these distributions is that a very clear pattern emerges relative to the type of attribute respondents choose as being better for most people in Nepal today. Television ownership, use of medical facilities and personnel, having a job outside the home, and having great personal freedom are all attributes generally associated with material wealth and with "development." Nepali migrants in this sample overwhelmingly endorse these material aspects of "development" as being better than their "less developed" alternatives. Premarital sex, non-marital cohabitation, choosing not to marry, and married children living away from parents are family-related attributes that are often viewed as being related to "development." Yet, most Nepali migrants reject these familial attributes by saying that they are not better than what has been "traditionally" acceptable. This way of thinking would appear to be confirmed by the measure asking, "Which is better for most people in Nepal today—culture in America or culture in Nepal?": 91 percent of all migrant respondents say that Nepali culture is better than American culture.

An exception to the emergent pattern of endorsing "modern" material things and "traditional" family or cultural attributes is found in the spousal choice item. 82 percent of migrant respondents believe that spousal choice is better left to the individual rather than to the parents, thereby endorsing the family behavior commonly associated with "modernity." We note however that in Nepal, spousal choice has long been a joint venture involving children and parents alike. When viewed within this context, the distributions for this measure are more consistent with the overall pattern.

Conclusion

This chapter provides some important insights into the lives, work, values, behaviors, and intentions of Nepali migrants from the Chitwan Valley who were living in the GCC Countries of Qatar, Saudi Arabia, the UAE, Kuwait, Bahrain, and Oman. Furthermore, as Nepal is similar in many ways to other migrant-sending South Asian countries, including India, Pakistan, and Bangladesh, the information in this study is likely relevant to understanding the lives of South Asian migrants, the largest group of foreign workers in the GCC countries. This study is unique in that it is based on data collected from a representative sample of migrants from one area of Nepal, the Chitwan Valley. The logistic and financial difficulties of collecting data from a representative sample of migrants at a destination inhibit most migration research from doing so.

Data for this study were collected using innovative procedures that included sampling in the Chitwan Valley (the origin), collecting contact information for any household members who were migrants, and finally interviewing these migrants via telephone while they were in the GCC or face-to-face when they returned to Nepal. With these methods, we were able to achieve an exceptional 87 percent response rate. Thus, we argue that while there were difficulties encountered in data collection, this method of sampling and contacting migrants can be effective and efficient and should be considered for future studies of migration; and for addressing selectivity in origin-based samples of other topics in areas with high out-migration.

Results from this study show that Nepali migrants in the GCC countries were relatively similar to their non-migrant counterparts in the Chitwan Valley in terms of age, marital status, childbearing, education, religion, and ethnicity. Furthermore, there was very little variation in social and economic characteristics of migrants living in the different GCC countries. Not surprisingly, most migrants in the sample were male and working as laborers. There were very few professionals and very few women. We find that remittances to Nepal were common and large, averaging about 58 percent of each person's yearly pay. Perhaps the only major difference we find between GCC countries is that salaries, savings, and remittances are considerably higher in the UAE.

Overall, yearly remittances from this sample of migrants totaled over one million US dollars. This of course is only calculated on the basis of the 459 migrants in this sample. The amount of money moving from the GCC to Nepal, or to South Asia in general, is much higher if all Nepali or South Asian migrants are considered. Migrant origin countries, and families, likely depend on these remittances. Unfortunately, this income source is contingent on labor demand in the GCC, as well as oil prices and the health of the global capitalist economy. These processes, and the large amounts of money that annually cross borders through remittances, must be considered by policy makers in both origin countries in South Asia and destination countries in the GCC.

This study also addressed migrants' future intentions. Far from the classical perception of migrants as target earners who will immediately return to their countries of origin, results show that amongst this group of Nepali migrants, most intended to migrate again. GCC countries were high on the list of intended future destinations, with the UAE being the most sought after destination. These results highlight the need for further enhancements to migration theory that consider the likelihood of second, third, and higher order migrations, and the possibility of migrant intentions changing with time and experience. Because much of migration research considers single migration trips, we might be missing key dynamics of intrapersonal change as well as patterns of the development of transnational relationships and a peripatetic international labor force.

Our measures of the values of Nepali migrants to the GCC countries indicate that most migrants endorse the various material aspects of "modernity" in that they believe that such things as hospitals, doctors, television, and working outside the home are good. These attributes probably help to fuel the desires of these migrants to seek employment in the Persian Gulf. At the same time, the great bulk of migrants retain most of their historical Nepali values centered on marriage, family, and the restriction of sex and cohabitation with regards to marriage.

This study provides valuable insights into the lives, work, values, behaviors, and intentions of Nepali migrants living in the GCC. However, it is limited to the extent that it is based on a cross-sectional survey. Many of the results in this study draw attention to the possibility of change over time in all these dimensions of migrants' lives and behaviors in the GCC. These changes, due to individual migrant experience, family circumstances at home, and global economic, social, communication, and transportation changes, likely play a large role in the well-being of migrants and the host populations and governments in the GCC. Further research based on longitudinal data collection could provide immense contributions toward understanding these processes over time.

9

The Legal Regulation of Migrant Workers, Politics and Identity in Qatar and the United Arab Emirates

*David Mednicoff**

How do the unusual extent and nature of the labor force in contemporary Persian Gulf societies shape governmental postures and policies toward rights and benefits for the non-citizen population? This chapter addresses this broad and important question with particular reference to the cities of Doha, Qatar and Dubai, the United Arab Emirates (UAE). These cities are critical examples of the uniqueness of the GCC, where small national populations and large economic resources have created natural incentives for an enormous foreign labor market. Indeed, Qatar and the United Arab Emirates share the demographic feature of indigenous citizens representing less than 20 percent of the resident population.[1] The two countries also have in com-

* Grateful acknowledgment goes to the Center for International and Regional Studies, Georgetown University School of Foreign Service in Qatar, for providing research funding for this project.
[1] Foreigners represent 85 percent of the population and 90 percent of the labor force

mon high scores on the composite measure of the rule of law used by the World Bank, especially in comparison with other Arab states.[2] I theorize connections between these two commonalities. In brief, I aim to address the following questions: how has the unusual level of migrant labor in Persian Gulf countries with small populations influenced legal reforms in these societies? What strategies for legal regulation are suggested by a globalized labor force that far outnumbers the native population?

The small, rapidly globalized states of Qatar and the UAE are similar in their levels of wealth and dependence on a demographically dominant foreign labor population. Their main cities, Doha and Dubai, also share patterns of enormous growth and increasing global influence. Yet, the cities also differ, most obviously in Doha's development as a regional center of education, sports and media along conservative social lines, as compared with Dubai's status as a more cosmopolitan center of finance, entertainment and tourism. They also diverge in their recent short-term economic performance, where Dubai's bust and construction over-extension stand in contrast to Qatar's ongoing, if somewhat slowed, pattern of growth.[3]

At the same time, both cities' similar basic choice to invest in long-term, globally-oriented development entails large-scale permeation by transnational forces, such as international law and great power politics. This makes the city and national officials sensitive to conforming their economies to the expectations of international law,[4] which in turn may help to explain their high performance on comparative measures of legalism, like the World Bank's.[5]

---

in Qatar, and 80 to 85 percent of the population according to recent data at http://www.state.gov/r/pa/ei/bgn (last accessed 20 January 2009).

[2] Qatar and the UAE are in the 81st and 65th percentile among all countries, and 1st and 4th among Arab ones, respectively. Computed from data (2009) available at the World Bank website, http://info.worldbank.org/governance/wgi/mc_countries.asp.

[3] The cities also differ in that Doha is the capital of a single country, while Dubai must deal with its own internal government, along with the broader federal UAE structure. While this is important, I minimize these governmental differences in this paper for the purposes of augmenting the central comparison.

[4] One of many examples that could be cited of this is Dubai's 2009 investigation of major fraud and bribery at the Dubai Waterfront. See for example Simeon Kerr, "Three held in Dubai corruption probe" *Financial Times* (February 11, 2009), p. 4.

[5] I focus mostly on the two cities to sharpen comparisons between Qatar, a country dominated by its large, growing city, and the UAE, a federation with diverse city-states, some of which would not compare as obviously with Doha. However, I am

My basic research question—whether and how the large migrant labor population of two leading cities of the Arab world has framed legal change and regulation—links three important areas of socio-legal studies and social science, namely, the politics of development in the Persian Gulf; how law is understood and connects to politics in Arab countries generally; and how globalized law and labor markets link to local identity and politics in particular non-Western societies. My basic argument is that the varied pressures and high stakes involved in places like Doha and Dubai with respect to regulating non-citizen workers favor *ad hoc* accommodations and informal regulation over more general legal policies. Nonetheless, the presence of significant recent legal reform, especially in Dubai, suggests a need to look closely at the comparative politics of law and development across my two cases, and across the GCC more generally.

The context: a clash not of civilizations,[6] but of globalizing narratives

The regulation of non-citizen workers in Doha and Dubai involves a wide array of actors, including native Arabs, foreign residents of diverse generational, national and class backgrounds, local and global corporations, transnational and domestic rights activists and foreign governments. Yet these diverse actors, which will be unpacked and elucidated in the next section, operate within two significant symbolic narratives of progress that color and push the politics of regulating non-citizen workers. I describe these narratives as at odds, explicitly without endorsing or commenting on the legitimacy of either one. It is precisely the point and poignancy of the narrative clash that each can be highly compelling in its own terms.

The first narrative comes from within countries like Qatar and the UAE, which may be the most rapidly growing in global history, at least in terms of urbanization, citizen wealth, and integration into the global economy. The nationalist narrative in contemporary Persian Gulf societies therefore builds

---

aware of the possible concerns in comparing the dominant city of one country with one of several urban models of another one, and, indeed, address this issue more directly in the concluding section below.

[6] This is a reference to Samuel Huntington's famous assertion that global politics in recent years has developed into a civilizational conflict between "the West and the rest." Huntington, *The Clash of Civilizations and the Remaking of World Order* (New York: Simon and Schuster, 1998).

on planks of fast success in creating diverse developmental markers of global pride, and successful practices of reconciling tradition and development. For the hereditary Islamist monarchies of the UAE and Qatar, this nationalist narrative is important. After all, these countries are among the youngest in the world, gaining formal independence as late as 1971. Moreover, the sheer scale of urban growth, founded as it is on massive quantities of non-citizen workers, creates tremendous potential for socio-political conflict and disruption.

That the creation of national pride in the context of young, highly dynamic countries is important can be seen by the amount of effort Emirati and Qatari leaders put in spending their considerable wealth on symbols of global prominence, such as the world's tallest building, now complete in Dubai, and the first Middle Eastern hosting of the World Cup, awarded for 2022 to Doha. Yet alongside these global superlatives are multifarious other projects with likely deeper social impacts based on this first plank of nationalism: such as the proliferation of outstanding higher education outlets in Doha's centrally-planned Education City and the development of the financial and tourist sectors of Dubai.

If the new, quickly-grown global prominence of Qatar and the UAE is likely to engender citizen pride, the more subtle dynamics of a social developmental model that is true to local history form the essential second plank of contemporary Persian Gulf nationalism. Before the commercial exploitation of oil and natural gas, these societies were small relative backwaters, united by strong extended family and tribal ties, and relative conformity around Islamic communal involvement. Rapid urban and social change have only solidified the need for concrete sources of cultural cohesion, so that religious, familial and tribal identity remain as important as ever in Emirati and Qatari life. Islam is important in a variety of ways, including its role both as a general signifier of social cohesion and as a reference point, in the *shari'a* (Islamic law), to a strong source of indigenous legitimacy for making law, however limited its actual contemporary sway may be in particular laws.

Yet the above requires a critical qualifier and amplifier. To underscore the importance of Islamic and familial identity in Doha and Dubai is not to suggest that such identity sources are static, backward, or inevitably at odds with the hyper-modern developmentalism that punctuates these new urban spaces so strikingly. While an important part of the clash of broad developmental narratives relevant to the regulation of non-citizen workers is around balances between traditionalism and change, Gulf nationals have no reason to see Islam and rapid growth as fundamentally at odds. Indeed, part of the interest of living in and studying the contemporary Gulf lies in the imagination and reinterpretation of traditional social tropes in the self-conscious context of hyper-globalized growth, such as the subtly modern *souq*s of Doha and Deira, Dubai, which are larger, contemporary, air-conditioned interpretations of traditional markets that were of only minor actual historical significance.

The point here is that the clash of developmental discourses between Gulf nationals and some global actors is not a trade-off between modernization and tradition *per se*. Instead, it is about what norms and models are appropriate or necessary in the wake of hyper-globalized development in the contemporary Persian Gulf, with differences of emphasis that shade, often subtly, pressures and discourse around the legal regulation of non-nationals in places like Doha and Dubai. The nationalist narrative holds that the contemporary Gulf represents a new, internally legitimate template for the successful linkage of Islamic and social tradition with increasing global integration and influence.

The countervailing developmental narrative, espoused generally by Western governments and activists outside of the region itself, is of progress through global harmonization around common economic, socio-cultural, and—especially, for the purposes of this chapter—legal norms. This story tends to cast doubt, at least indirectly, on the success of the internal cultural legitimacy of Gulf nationalism. Instead, it highlights the imperative for Qatar, the UAE and their neighbors to learn from and accept Western-grown syntheses of formal legal equality and secularism, as opposed to *shari'a*, and with particular emphasis on universal rights. This is a complex narrative, in that Western human rights and foreign aid workers generally preach and often practice learning from, and adapting their methods to, local realities.

Nonetheless, in the field of law, the influence and success of the American model of judicial review and the Constitution have led to their application elsewhere,[7] and to a possible presumption that non-Western, less democratic systems should conform to Anglo-American models in more particular ways. This can take a variety of forms, one of which is the emphasis on contractual regularity and procedural predictability of global economic actors, such as the World Bank, as evinced in their rule-of-law governance indicators. More political understandings of law, involving a judiciary independent of the government, or civil rights, are another form of Western legal developmentalism,[8]

---

[7] See, for example, R. Daniel Keleman and Eric C. Sibbett, "The Globalization of American Law," *International Organization*, 58 (2004), pp. 103–36.

[8] For example, Ran Hirschl uses the term "juristocracy" to denote a global trend

as are assumptions around the modern secular disconnection of law from a dominant religious tradition. If the internal Gulf society narrative of progress centers around rapid growth and nationalist development, the Western legalist global narrative as applied to the Gulf highlights deficits in individual liberties and rights. Such perceived deficits apply to issues like religious identity and social mores, which are among the most significant within Gulf societies.

I contend that the legal status and regulation of non-citizens in the Persian Gulf form an important flashpoint for the divergence and contestation of the above internal and transnational developmental narratives. This is because the unusual demographic non-citizen majority within these countries creates particular tensions around symbols of national solidarity, such as restricting citizenship, bolstering religious identity and trumpeting developmental success. Yet these precise features are called into question by the Western/globalist legalist narrative, because the majority population of non-national workers suffers from at least some, and often a great deal of, lower legal status than that of nationals. And this triggers strong legalist reactions against inequality, implicating local culture and asserting a sense of Gulf socio-legal underdevelopment that questions the salience of the local developmental success story.[9]

Thus, legal reform is a central piece of the tension between Gulf and Western ideas of development and globalization. Gulf hyper-globalization, and the cosmopolitan exposures among Gulf citizens and non-citizen workers that this produces, mean that this tension is not simple, bipolar, or unresolvable. Yet it is important to underscore the ease with which Persian Gulf citizens can see foreign workers as guests, analogously, for example, to an Islamic tradition in which sub-populations could be separate but not entirely equal.[10] In con-

---

toward transferring power in diverse elected governments from representative institutions to judiciaries, so that American adversarial legal discourse becomes a "dominant form of political discourse." *Towards Justistocracy* (Cambridge, Mass.: Harvard University Press, 2004), p. 1. See also Tom Ginsburg, "The Global Spread of Judicial Review," in Keith Wittington and Daniel Keleman (eds), *The Oxford Handbook of Law and Politics* (Oxford University Press, 2007).

[9] A typical example of this clash of narratives is the reaction of an American undergraduate upon my return from Dubai, which implies the backwardness of the UAE: seeing me laden with purchases from the world's tallest building, he responded, "Oh yes, the place that they have mass slavery."

[10] In Islam, *dhimmi* denoted non-Muslims who could be protected and largely self-

trast, non-citizens, particularly those coming to fill professional positions in the Gulf from Western backgrounds, are wont to frame differential practices toward citizen and non-citizen workers as deviating from a universalizing legal discourse of substantive civil and political rights.

Globally, the challenges of the economic recession at the end of the first decade of the current millennium have only added to this already charged environment around non-citizen workers, because of the increasing extent to which governments frame the inflow and management of people from other countries as a security issue.[11] The relative roles of citizens and governments in the securitization of non-citizen worker status may be hard to determine and vary across countries. As a broad trend, though, states see the control and the potential threat of non-citizens as a core, paramount domain of their authority. This can be used to justify unnecessarily coercive tactics or even official flirtations with racism, as some might characterize the tenor of policies toward non-natives in Western countries, such as the US and France, in recent years.

In other words, given the Persian Gulf's extraordinary amount of capital and imported labor, hyper-globalization exposes in particularly acute ways tensions between national development/control and universalizing international legal norms. One way in which this plays out with respect to the status of non-native workers is a general tendency for Western-based lawyers to assume the need and possibility for bringing their own or more global human rights law to Qatar and the UAE, based on the relative underdevelopment of formal legal institutions in these countries.

This, on the local side, can lead both to sensitivity around perceived Western condescension and neo-imperialism, or—more likely, from Gulf governments—official efforts to highlight the compliance, and even leadership, of

---

regulated under an Islamic government, which led to relatively beneficial status for many Christian and Jewish minorities during many periods of Islamic rule. That *dhimmi* status was generally accorded along religious lines to non-Muslim Western monotheists, or *ahl ul-kitab* ("people of the Book"), naturally limits the specific relevance of the idea to contemporary Persian Gulf states, where a mosaic of legal sources legislates the status of foreign workers who are often non-Western and/or Muslims. My point is rather that an historical, indigenous model exists in the Persian Gulf to legitimate the idea that guest workers can be fairly accorded different legal status from that of core communal citizens.

[11] For an early example of some key analytical issues that are affected by this shift, see Myron Weiner, "Security, Stability and International Migration," *International Security*, 17, 3 (1993), pp. 91–126.

the Gulf in the fealty to international law. This helps make sense, for example, of Qatar's role in hosting perhaps the largest gathering of global judges, scholars and other legal luminaries in contemporary history, at the Qatar Law Forum in May, 2009.[12] The event was meant to signal that Qatar was a global player in the arena of law, and hardly the backwater center of weak legal institutions and protections for non-natives that Western rights and other lawyers might assume it to be.

Yet national identity is a key, ongoing concern for Arab governments. The task of the dynastic monarchs who rule over contemporary Persian Gulf societies has been to retain historic patterns of native elite loyalty while expanding to integrate a more technocratic base in line with rapid growth and infrastructural expansion.[13] This general pattern of updating a traditional pattern of authoritarian rule with mechanisms of elite consensus has allowed for distinct variations in terms of articulating a concept of modern national identity for countries that have generally been independent for only four decades. Indeed, the logic of internal rivalry and distinctiveness among member states of the Gulf Cooperation Council suggests that different sheikhs would articulate their societies' emerging nationhood in rather distinct ways.[14]

In sum, in a general world context of economic challenge and state securitization of policies toward non-citizens, the Persian Gulf's minority native population and hyper-globalization highlight the issue of regulating foreign workers, against a background of likely divergences in local and global discourses around development and law. All of this, I conclude, steers officials in Doha and Dubai to prefer *ad hoc*, less public regulatory strategies for non-native residents, and to do their utmost to keep the question of migrant worker citizenship off the table.

[12] Coverage of this can be found at: http://www.qatarlawforum.com/.
[13] See for example Fatiha Dazi-Héni, *Monarchies et sociétés d'Arabie* (Paris: Presses de la FNSP, 2006), especially pp. 28–35.
[14] Thus Dubai, as a city of the UAE, has stressed economic and touristic importance, and succeeded in building for itself a worldwide reputation as a marvel of constructed wonders and commerce. Qatar, for its part, has preferred to develop a national image as a center for sports, media and education. The governments of both societies nonetheless stress a careful balance between the new and the traditional. Yet, the relative newness of national identity, juxtaposed with the reality of constant growth and rapid change, makes the meaning of citizenship and nationhood fragile and particularly contestable in places like Doha and Dubai.

Legal policy actors, the basic legal framework and a 'torturous' example

With this background in mind, I return to the question of the nature and substance of government approaches to regulating non-citizens in Doha and Dubai. Regarding pressures to regulate foreign workers, the background above sets up three intersecting and internally diverse sources of pressure for legal action in Qatar and the UAE, as Figure 9.1 suggests. These sources are the native citizen population, foreign governments and international organizations, and the non-citizen foreign workers themselves.[15] A simple reading of these three broad pressure points suggests diverging interests. Native citizens want to ensure their status within their own countries, including the considerable benefits of national citizenship, and the continued ability to hire and manage foreign workers. For a combination of economic, personal comfort and national identity issues, they might be expected to want to minimize non-citizen worker rights. On the other hand, Western, Arab and Asian governments (from which workers come) and international rights organizations have incentives to press Gulf countries for the provision of improved legal protection for foreign workers, as long as this does not undermine seriously the benefits of Gulf workers' remittances or the two cities' broader ties to the global economy. The workers themselves are large enough in number to be of possible concern and a source of instability for Gulf governments, and are under even stronger incentive to press for economic benefits and civil rights, although they have more to lose as individuals in doing so.

Yet, the reality of these basic interests is much more complex. At the very least, each point in this triangular set of pressures needs to be broken down into its own internally diverse facets. A basic way of doing this is shown in Figure 9.2. With respect to the citizen population, there may be simple incentives for many to frame the non-citizen worker population as a combination of guests who can reasonably be accorded differential status from themselves and a potential national identity or security challenge. Nonetheless, Gulf hyperglobalization's exposure to global rights issues and Arab Islamic indigenous social justice ideals can create real awareness of foreign workers' prob-

[15] My analysis, including the categories here, does not preclude the possibility that non-natives can become national citizens, or that non-citizen descendants of non-citizens may be natives, both of which are possible, albeit unusual. Nonetheless, I generally refer to native citizens and foreign non-citizen workers both for simplicity, and to underscore the perceived tension that broadly exists between indigenous citizens and imported workers.

Figure 9.1. General possibilities for legal regulation of foreign workers.

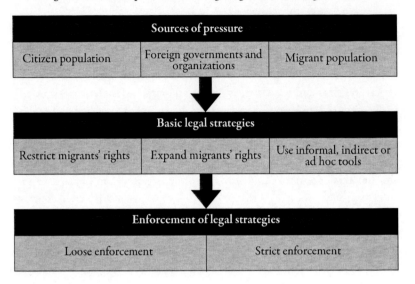

lems, particularly among well-educated and/or younger Emiratis and Qataris who are themselves well-connected to diverse legal and other norms. Thus, the impetus for reforms exists purely within elements of the native population.

As for foreign governments, economic interests may generally be a pressure against pushing for improvement with respect to non-citizen workers' rights. Yet this is also likely to differ according to government. Generally, Western governments can feel staked in the political stability and overall economic prosperity of places like Doha and Dubai, but can often also afford to put more specific pressure with respect to rights issues, as illustrated by the US government's recent scrutiny of the UAE on human trafficking issues.[16] One way this plays out is an emphasis from Western governments, and the many advocacy groups headquartered within them, on broad international human rights frameworks, but inconsistent overall policy attention to the problem.

The governments of countries that send large numbers of workers to the Persian Gulf, mostly in South or Southeast Asia, on the other hand face a possibly even more acute trade-off. They are dependent on the very high level

---

[16] See Pardis Mahdavi's contribution in this volume on US human trafficking designations in the UAE for a detailed examination of how this issue has played out.

of economic remittances and employment options that the Gulf labor market represents; yet the particular need to redress the often acute rights issues facing a large number of their citizens is also quite salient. Given this trade-off, Asian mass labor-supplying countries have tended to seek specific bilateral arrangements between themselves and Qatar or the UAE that provide redress in cases of particular egregious treatment, while maintaining the likelihood that workers will enjoy continued labor contract possibilities.[17] In short, depending on their exported citizen worker populations, foreign governments and related NGOs push generally more for universal legal reforms or for limited bilateral reforms, or often none at all. And this reflects both the influence of the Western legalist developmental discourse in the West and the appeal of less universal, focused approaches in the Gulf countries and elsewhere outside of the West.

A similar set of divergences occurs with respect to foreign workers themselves. Resident workers in Doha and Dubai from the West, and the most privileged professionals from other societies, enjoy an enviable level of status and wealth, albeit clearly lower than those of native citizens. The contrast with the poor, low-skilled non-Western population could hardly be more stark, with the result that privileged professionals have more leeway, but less real incentive, to advocate persistently on behalf of the larger underprivileged foreign population. This latter group often divides by area of origin, as well as type of work. Generally, though, the diverse, large lower-class worker subpopulations lack economic, cultural or political capital to press for improvements, and face major potential negative consequences if they do so. Yet, because of the real hardship that many of these workers face, and the vague cultural, moral, national identity and security challenges that this hardship can raise for the citizens directly or indirectly responsible for their presence, a need to "do something" about low-skilled workers is voiced frequently by Emirati and Qatari officials and citizens alike. Of course, the varied possible meanings of "doing something" are precisely what makes the question of regulating workers' status so complex in the GCC.

Thus, the migrant workers' country of origin may affect how local law and law enforcement deal with them, although the actual dynamics of this are complex.[18] On the one hand, contract workers of Western origin are both

[17] See discussions of how the government of the Philippines has used bilateral treaties of this nature in Susan Martin's contribution to this volume.
[18] If the country of origin of migrant workers is likely to play a role in their relationship to the legal system in Doha and Dubai, this is also true with respect to whether they

197

Figure 9.2. Breakdown of major sources of pressure for worker regulation.

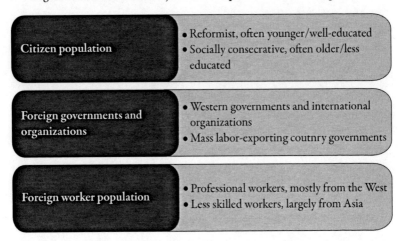

Citizen population	• Reformist, often younger/well-educated • Socially consecrative, often older/less educated
Foreign governments and organizations	• Western governments and international organizations • Mass labor-exporting coutnry governments
Foreign worker population	• Professional workers, mostly from the West • Less skilled workers, largely from Asia

more likely to connect with transnational networks to object to particular local practices, and to have their concerns taken seriously by local officials, partly as a result. Yet, in the broader context of contemporary Western-Arab global politics, workers from Western countries may seem to embody a greater challenge to identity and social cohesion than other foreign labor.[19] This may help explain high-profile prosecutions of Western visitors in Dubai for drunkenness or public fornication.[20]

As for non-Western migrant workers, whether employed in unskilled or skilled positions, they come in very large numbers to enjoy the perceived economic advantages of working in the Gulf. This suggests that, individually, their concerns are unlikely to be salient to Gulf officials. At the same time, the very large numbers of these workers has made Qatar and the UAE dependent on them, and, therefore, sensitive to legal policy that affects them. Moreover,

---

entered the Gulf lawfully or unlawfully. However, for analytical clarity, I limit my focus to workers who arrive in Qatar and the UAE with legal sponsorship.

[19] For example, interview with Paul Dyer, Dubai School of Government, October 2009.

[20] A particularly prominent example of this was a feature of global news reports in the summer of 2008. See for example http://articles.latimes.com/2008/oct/17/world/fg-sexonbeach17 (last accessed 8 February 2009).

unrest among non-Western migrant workers in Gulf cities has grown in recent years, and may be linked to the global economic downturn.[21]

While socio-political tensions around foreign workers in the Persian Gulf are not new, what has changed in recent years is the extensiveness of globalization generally,[22] and the scope of Persian Gulf developmental ambitions, as Dubai in particular has embodied. Moreover, the global ambitions of places like Doha and Dubai have entailed an extremely broad range of nationalities and professions among the expatriate worker population. Thus, the numbers and even national origins of non-natives in Gulf societies are less telling in themselves than the diverse sub-populations and their vocational and educational profile.

While it is tempting to think of British or Egyptian workers in the Gulf as mostly a single demographic element, the sectoral diversification of the labor force in places like Doha and Dubai means that British and Egyptian educators, for example, may have more in common with each other than with their co-citizens in the construction sector. Even more specifically, workplaces with people of diverse citizenship but similar vocational training, such as contemporary universities or media outlets like Al Jazeera International, may well forge particular postures or interests among non-citizens with respect to issues of workers' status and rights. Another possibility is for relatively privileged non-native workers to take out their own status concerns on workers of other nationalities beholden to them.[23]

In addition to nationality and class, generational status is another source of difference within both non-native and native communities with respect to political positions on workers' rights issues. Perhaps the best known way in which this issue appears with respect to non-natives is the question of the status of residents of Dubai from varied Asian and Arab backgrounds who have spent most or all of their lives in the Gulf city and raised families there; such families may well think of themselves as Dubai natives. As for native Gulf residents, the educational and vocational backgrounds of younger citizens,

[21] See for example "Migrants demand labour rights in Gulf," a recent BBC report that notes growing foreign labor unrest and suggests ties to recent economic pressures at http://news.bbc.co.uk/1/hi/world/middle_east/7266610.stm (last accessed 10 February 2009).

[22] See David Held's work on globalization, in particular *Global Transformations* (Stanford University Press, 1999).

[23] For an anecdotal account of a non-Qatari Arab that illustrates this phenomenon, see: http://www.qatarvisitor.com/index.php?cID=448&pID=1603.

which have been formed in the context of increasing global exposure, often lead to expectations of good, challenging work, and perhaps fears of the future. Additionally, it is easy for natives to see in their demographic minority status within their own societies a security threat from some or all of the non-nationals among them, even if this is generally unjustified.

Indeed, for natives, such a sense of threat comes up frequently precisely around issues that might demand or carry an expectation of legal regulation. One knowledgeable Qatari professor recounted several incidents as flashpoints for widespread native discussion and concern around native rights. These included a Qatari man's alleged harassment while driving by another driver of American origin; a second driving incident involving a Qatari and Westerner, that led to a fight; and a dispute between a Qatari women and a Filipina worker wearing a short skirt during Ramadan. The latter was discussed during a daily morning national radio program, "My Beloved Nation" (*Watani Habib*). In Dubai, of course, it is common enough to hear natives complain about the impact of rapid development and cosmopolitanism on their identity; reports about natives' flight to other parts of the UAE are rampant. A prominent native progressive social science professor, for example, empathized with foreign workers' problems, while suggesting that addressing national identity and demographic imbalance concerns was more pressing. She also decried Dubai's speed of development, which has left little sense of history.[24]

The point of the above comments is twofold. First, they suggest that perceptions of feeling estranged and underprivileged are common both to diverse sub-populations of the non-citizen labor force and citizens, owing to the demographic peculiarity and rapidity of change. A second, more subtle point here is that even natives who are well aware of the complexities of the regulation of the majority non-citizen population, such as the two indigenous professors above, have reason to appreciate the national existential issues that arise for citizens, as opposed to foreigners. Because cities like Dubai and Doha tend to create housing communities for non-natives so that natives and foreigners live apart, it is tempting for members of different national sub-communities, including natives, to accentuate the problems they face with respect to other groups. For this reason, the pressures on local officials to balance citizen and non-citizen concerns are especially high.

[24] Interview with Dr Suaad Al Oraimi, Professor of Sociology, the United Arab Emirates University, October 2010.

Figure 9.2 breaks down each major population group into subcategories that are relevant to workers' status. The column on the left shows each of the three broad relevant population groups. The column on the right breaks down each group into its two most significant population subcategories. These subcategories may well be at odds with one another with respect to workers' status (indeed there are more subcategories). This hints at the complexity of possible pressures that interact around workers' status. Indeed, the Figure's arrangement of the two subcategory rows within each population group suggests possible affinities that cut across the three basic groups. Each first subcategory in every population group may share common ground around improving workers' status, while each second subcategory might be less predisposed toward or able to foster such reform.

In short, there are at least three successively detailed pictures of actors relevant to the legal status of foreign workers in Doha and Dubai. At the broadest level, the different narratives around development described above frame broad views around law, progress and identity that tend to distinguish international actors from natives. At a more intermediate level citizens, foreign actors and workers carry their own perspectives, and break down within each group around tendencies towards or against improving foreign workers' status. At an even more specific level, there are many possibilities for coalitions among particular subgroups and individuals with respect to the legal regulation of foreign workers in Dubai and Doha.[25]

Because of the range of actors and pressures, and the central importance of foreign workers, officials in Doha and Dubai prefer to enact as little legislation as possible that deviates from the basic existing framework. That framework, the *kafala*, or sponsorship system, stresses the connection between local employer (*kafeel*) and foreign employee as a patron-client relationship brokered and managed only to a limited extent by the government. Thus, the number of workers in Qatar and the UAE does not reflect a numerical quota predetermined by the national governments, but corresponds instead to the articulated needs of particular corporate, civic and citizen employers. With hyperglobalization in Dubai and Doha, these needs have been tremendous.

---

[25] For an example of intersections between international pressures and domestic challenges surrounding internal reform that augments the rights of foreign workers, see the report summarizing the regional conference "The Situation of Migrant Workers in Asia and the Arab Region" that took place in Doha in June 2007, under the auspices of Bahrain's and Qatar's national human rights groups, at http://www.fidh. org/IMG/pdf/MigrationDohaasiearab497ang2008.pdf.

In the *kafala* system, Gulf authorities centralize the paperwork that allows workers to live in their countries for fixed terms based on the needs of individual and collective local employers. This has the effect of privatizing the policy process somewhat around who and how many can be non-citizen residents. At the same time, the system also serves to distance the state somewhat from direct responsibility for the large numbers, social challenges and inhumane treatment of some foreign workers. As there is no fixed number of work visas in a system that is driven by the dictates of companies and citizens, the regime has grounds to assert that unscrupulous labor recruiters and brokers, particular corporate entities or an isolated minority of local citizens, are to blame for workers' problems; and these assertions are not only frequent but often accurate, at least in part. The *kafala* system also roots the non-native worker to the employer, rather than the state, so that the presumption from the start is that residence is based on a fixed contract, rather than a more potentially general right. With national citizenship off the table as a possibility for non-native workers because of the nature of the residence procedures, the state can articulate for itself a relatively minimal role in providing social and political help to non-natives.

This is not at all to say that officials in Doha or Dubai are insensitive to the rights violations or suffering of foreign workers. Indeed, nearly every person among the group of local officials, lawyers, journalists and policy experts I interviewed[26] indicated that Gulf national and city governments take quite seriously the human rights, and broader, problems faced by many workers, and not merely as a result of the negative light shone on this issue by rights activists. While the *kafala* system allows some degree of government disavowal of responsibility for the patterns of employee exploitation that some employers undertake, it still creates a need and ample opportunity for legal and other forms of amelioration of major problems. At the same time, the limited state role implied by the *kafala* system, coupled with the assumption that foreign workers are transient, rather than being potential citizens, creates incentives for officials to seek less formal, selective mechanisms to ameliorate the worst abuses.

This is because non-native workers are not regarded as future citizens, but rather as individuals seeking chances for temporary enrichment in a favorable

---

[26] My research included approximately twenty-five detailed interviews with labor officials, policy experts, journalists, academics and other Emirati and Qatari natives. Many of my interviewees asked for their specific comments to remain confidential, although the general points they made have found their way into my analysis.

market climate. The paradigm for many Gulf citizens and officials is that workers come because they are paid better than they could in their home countries, making them willing market-driven partners in the arrangements. This makes their dependence on the relevant Gulf government one of temporary socio-economic protection to protect or redress their relationship with their employers, rather than enforcement of general civil and political rights. With the acute tensions between the ongoing developmental ambitions of the rulers of Doha and Dubai and the large-scale presence of change and foreign workers this has created, the *kafala* system has allowed local officials to avoid somewhat comprehensive legal involvement that could hurt their credibility in terms of either of the two broad narratives discussed above.

In short, given the *kafala* system, and the Persian Gulf's ability to absorb millions of workers from abroad, it is not surprising that, as one experienced official in Dubai suggested off the record, the government strongly prefers to "do nothing at all" with respect to the legal status of non-citizens.[27] Yet, in the wake of such powerful forces as described above, bureaucrats in Doha and Dubai have had at least to react to concerns raised by their citizens, outside governments and NGOs, or by non-citizen workers themselves. Most often, such reaction is hard to demonstrate. The political and policy processes of Qatar and the UAE are not transparent, and Emirati federalism adds an additional dimension of complexity to these processes. Yet the advantage to officials in Dubai and Doha of mostly indirect or unpublicized legal action with respect to balancing citizens' and non-citizens' privileges is that it does not suggest overall policy coherence or a clear overall philosophy on the relevant issues.

If doing nothing or resolving workers' problems informally may be the preference of local officials, legislative reform and enhanced legal enforcement have nonetheless occurred in recent years. It is important from the outset to be clear that such measures can as easily support natives and exacerbate conditions for foreigners as they can improve non-citizens' conditions. Thus, increasingly legal responses to the presence and problems of non-citizen workers are not clear evidence of the progressive triumph of the globalist legal development narrative.

Such responses do represent, however, an interesting puzzle. If the intensity of the contrasting developmental discourses of globalization in the Persian Gulf creates incentives for officials to avoid clear-cut responses, the actors associated with these discourses demand such responses nonetheless. Analysis of the complex arrays and possible alliances among actors described in Fig-

[27] Interview with senior economic official (not for named attribution), October 2009.

ure 2 might indeed account for legislation or legal enforcement in particular cases. At the same time, when such legislation or enforcement occurs, the end result still does not necessarily represent a clear-cut outcome with respect to foreign workers' status.

A graphic example of this is the recent Sheikh Issa case. In 2009, a Lebanese-American businessman released a graphic and damning two-hour video of Sheikh Issa bin Zayed al-Nahyan, a prominent member of the Emirates' ruling family, repeatedly beating an Afghan grain merchant. The initial reaction of the Emirates government, as expected from my argument, was a statement by the Ministry of Interior that the incident was a private matter to be settled between the parties. This is in line with a tendency for officials in Persian Gulf contexts to prefer individual, informal accommodation to broader legal policy, as well as to consider foreign workers' issues as economic and contract matters, rather than of civil and political rights.

In line with this, Sheikh Issa indeed settled for an undisclosed sum with the grain merchant. Yet the video's widespread availability on the internet, its clear showing of the Emirati royal's violence toward the foreign merchant, and the underlying Western tropes of presumed Persian Gulf rights backwardness that this inflamed, led to blistering international criticism, which empowered local rights activists in Dubai and elsewhere.[28] Coverage on American news media ABC and CNN, pressure from the US government on Abu Dhabi, and diverse other calls to hold the Sheikh accountable, provoked the unusual step of a criminal trial for torture of a member of the Emirati royal family in al-'Ayn.

The Sheikh Issa case thus shows the sort of scrutiny that can lead to collations around legal enforcement in the service of protecting foreign workers, which was quite strong in this case to bring to trial a central member of the royal family. The trial also illustrates the general point that officials tend to seek *status quo* solutions that do not reflect a clear stand between foreigners' rights and natives' protection. This is not only because of the Interior Ministry's initial reaction, but because of the actual verdict in the case. The verdict held that Sheikh Issa had been drugged by the Lebanese-American business-

---

[28] For a summary of the Sheikh Issa case, see: http://www.thenational.ae/apps/pbcs. dll/article?AID=/20100113/NATIONAL/701129852/1010, http://www.hrw. org/en/news/2010/01/24/world-report-2010-abusers-target-human-rights-messengers, and http://www.hrw.org/en/news/2010/01/10/uae-sheikh-s-trial-insufficient-stop-torture. For a general analysis that suggests many of my points here, see Christopher Davison, "Rule of Law in the United Arab Emirates: 2010 Review," (10 January 2011) at http://www.currentintelligence.net/gulfstream.

man who smuggled the video of the beating, and the businessman and his brother, who live in the US, were sentenced to five years of jail.[29]

Thus, the verdict in no way seemed to endorse the right of Emiratis to mistreat foreign contract workers, while it also portrayed the prominent local citizen in question as a partial victim. In addition, the case shows that media globalization, a major feature of both Dubai and Doha, can be an important impetus for government legal action, or at least the appearance of legal action. US media outlets, prone to reinforce the legal underdevelopment trope common in the West vis-à-vis the Arab world, made a big deal of the case. Nonetheless, Doha's international television giant Al-Jazeera, and the UAE's increasingly influential newspaper *The National*, both covered the Sheikh Issa verdict and its aftermath extensively.

In addition to confluences among diverse actors energized by a particular issue related to workers' rights or national identity, particularly when the issue gets picked up by media, the regional Persian Gulf competitive context is likely to encourage officials in Doha and Dubai to take some action with respect to non-citizen workers' legal status. Both for general socio-political reasons and in light of the similar developmental trajectories that require comparable types and numbers of workers, Persian Gulf leaders often look over each other's shoulders in an evident, if under-analyzed, inter-regional competitive fashion. With respect to the status of foreign workers, the slightly less wealthy and somewhat more politically accountable Persian Gulf country of Bahrain redesigned its legal regimes for workers by highly-touted new provisions to eliminate *kefala*. Kuwait has claimed it will also do so by early 2011.[30] If, in practice, Bahrain's and Kuwait's new laws still privilege employers and base their systems on employers contracting initially with foreign employees,[31] the global public-

---

[29] In accordance with Islamic legal precedent that a drunk person unaware that he was drinking cannot be held responsible for crimes of which he was mentally unaware, the Sheikh was acquitted in the beating, but paid the merchant in a private settlement. See http://www.timesonline.co.uk/tol/news/world/middle_east/article 6982820.ece http://www.ft.com/cms/s/0/7ab2c522-fe20–11de-9340–00144 feab49a.html#axzz1AjurwuUe and http://www.thenational.ae/news/uae-news/ sheikh-issa-verdict-will-stand.

[30] See Human Rights Watch's positive assessment of Bahrain's 2009 reform at: http:// www.hrw.org/en/news/2009/05/13/bahrain-labor-reforms-major-advance. Kuwait's legal revisions are underway at the time this chapter is nearing completion.

[31] See the discussion of the disagreements around reform in Kuwait and the references to Bahrain's implementation of the 2009 law in Jamie Etheridge, "Kuwait Sparks confusion with labour U-turn," *Financial Times* (October 18, 2010) at http://www.

ity and the attractiveness of the new reforms to key potential sending states or workers have raised the incentives for Qatar and the UAE to introduce comparable legislation.

To sum up this section, then, the strong counteracting pressures in favor of foreign workers' rights and natives' privileges make direct legislation or consistent legal enforcement unappealing to officials in the UAE and Qatar, while, at the same time, requiring some sort of public response in either direction, based on particular combinations of domestic and global actors in a specific situation. An official public response is especially likely in the face of global media involvement or action on the issue elsewhere in the Persian Gulf. Yet, even such a response tends to reinforce the basic economic contractual basis of the *kafala* system, and leave intact and unresolved the contending discourses around development and law that often separate Western rule-of-law advocates and advisors from Gulf citizens.

Examples of legal regulation in Doha and Dubai

With the above in mind, I turn to a discussion of major examples of legal reforms and legal enforcement relevant to non-citizen workers in Doha and Dubai in recent years. Official responses can fall under the categories of direct legislation, legal enforcement, and, thirdly, legislation that relates to the relative status of foreign workers and citizens more indirectly, such as regulations concerning whether, how and where non-citizens can buy property.

I have already suggested that legal moves relating more to economic and contractual benefits than to civil rights are likely, given the prevalence of the *kafala* model and the determination of Emirati and Qatari officials to avoid looking as though they are giving in to the global legal underdevelopment discourse in front of their citizens. This third possibility is the amplification of benefits to citizens or foreigners through laws or other regulation that connect only indirectly to labor relations. It allows another way of addressing natives' concerns about national identity without imperiling global legal credibility. Since officials avoid direct legal action, regulation of this third indirect sort can be important, particularly when it benefits Gulf citizens.[32]

---

ft.com/cms/s/0/063fe278-dad5-11df-a5bb-00144feabdc0.html#axzz1ArLM c1Qv.

[32] A recent legislative example of this is the UAE law that creates a unified limit throughout the Emirates on the grant of residency permits to foreign property-

Thus, direct legislative reform relevant to workers' rights and status occurs, but somewhat infrequently. The regional imitation effect noted earlier may play into the fact that legal reform directly related to workers' rights has taken place in Qatar and the UAE, and a more particular contrast in the nature of this reform. Qatar's Law Number 4 of 2009, which came out in the wake of increasing global reporting on foreign workers' status but before Bahrain's and Kuwait's fairly sweeping changes in the *kafala* system, illustrates my general argument that direct legislation on foreign workers' rights aims to maintain the *status quo* of the *kafala* system.

The recent law amplifies the state's ability to enforce *kafala* arrangements, while providing some concessions to lessening some of the more egregious concerns of workers and advocacy organizations.[33] Most notably, sponsors of foreign workers cannot legally hold these workers' passports, the Ministry of Interior can waive customary two-year limits on re-entry for workers who have been dismissed or have quit, and women can sponsor husbands on a work visa. Domestic employees, who are not generally covered by Qatar's Labor law, can have a transfer of sponsorship approved under the Ministry as well.

As of 2011, the UAE has put into place more sweeping labor law changes, most notably allowing workers to obtain work permits with new employers without leaving the country, reducing labor contracts to two years, and removing the requirement for employees to obtain a no-objection certificate from their employers before gaining new employment. An analysis of this legal shift in the UAE's national daily English language newspaper—increasingly influential politically—discusses the impetus for change that comes from post-economic crisis competitiveness, as well as the fact of reform in Bahrain and Kuwait.[34] Indeed, these changes, which the government claims will help

---

holders. Although the law is not aimed at workers' rights directly, a government official of the UAE noted that automatic residency rights conveyed through property purchases "endangered national interest and the identity of the UAE as Emiratis were increasingly outnumbered by expatriates, and that some residents had begun demanding rights." See http://www.khaleejtimes.com/DisplayArticle08.asp?xfile=data/theuae/2008/December/theuae_December366.xml&section=theuae.

[33] An unofficial English translation of the law can be found at: http://www.brasemb-doha.com.qa/files/Law_No%204–2009_%20Lawyer_translation.pdf.

[34] For details, see "UAE leads on path to worker sponsorship reform," *The National* (January 11, 2011) at http://www.thenational.ae/news/uae-news/uae-leads-on-path-to-worker-sponsorship-reform.

ensure that workers receive their end-of-contract benefits and enjoy increased rights in the marketplace, have led to a certain level of self-congratulatory rhetoric in the UAE press.[35]

While the new legal measures should indeed make it easier for some employees to change jobs and depend less on *kafeel* employers, it nonetheless conforms to the notion that legislative reform seeks to avoid taking a clear stand on the discourses of global rights and local privileges. For one thing, the two-year period keeps employees in their jobs, and therefore, in legal residence in the UAE, for a shorter time. Other new regulations have created a three-tiered categorization of workers based on their degree of educational attainment, with more liberal expectations for labor mobility for the best-educated workers.

Here it becomes clear that the government's trumpeting of its hopes to retain professional workers through the new law has an unstated underside: that less-skilled workers will be subject to increased state scrutiny and face shorter periods of residency. The government's role in protecting workers remains limited; whether or not it enforces protections is an open issue,[36] and the new measures themselves actually increase the idea of differential treatment by category of worker and likely national origin. Thus, the new regulations, important though they may turn out to be, amplify a paradigm of class-differentiated treatment at odds with universal rights at least as much as they move towards it.

The new Emirati regulations also address another issue clearly associated with native rights, rather than those of foreigners, namely workforce nationalization.[37] A frequent government response to citizens' concerns about their work and society, and even national security, is to look to restrict proportions of the labor force and specific segments of the labor market to nationals. Public sector jobs have been party to this process, but Gulf governmental initiatives in this area have also included sectors like travel (Saudi Arabia)[38] and corporate

---

[35] See, notably, "A good couple of years for labour reform in the UAE," *The National* (January 10, 2011) at http://www.thenational.ae/thenationalconversation/editorial/a-good-couple-of-years-for-labour-reform-in-the-uae.

[36] Ibid.

[37] See "New Emiratisation Scheme targets 15% of Private Jobs," *The National* (December6,2010)athttp://www.thenational.ae/news/uae-news/new-emiratisation-scheme-targets-15-of-private-jobs.

[38] Nasra Shah, "Restrictive Labour Immigration Policies in the Oil-Rich Gulf: Implications for Sending Asian Countries," prepared for United Nations Expert Group Meeting on International Migration and Development in the Arab Region, Beirut

human resources workers (the UAE). The new UAE regulations target 15 percent of private skilled work positions for Emiratis.

Workforce nationalization as a legislated strategy generally fails, and the reasons for this failure are well chronicled, at least in terms of indigenizing entirely the relevant labor sector or resolving native concerns around labor.[39] Lack of consistent training in the case of higher-skilled positions, and lack of consistent interest in the case of low-skilled jobs, remain important given the generous citizen benefits of oil-rich governments. As several of my informants in official positions in Dubai or the UAE noted off the record, efforts at keeping fixed quotas for Emirati workers in the past have often led private employers to change job titles or add positions to ensure that needed work is completed.

At the same time, the very success of societies like Qatar and the UAE mostly precludes a largely native solution to labor, because of the globalized dynamism that turning oil money into developmental diversity entails. In other words, if cities like Doha and Dubai wish to continue their recent multifaceted growth patterns, there is no realistic way that labor force nativization can vastly reduce the proportion of foreign workers. Thus, the issue of legal measures for nationalization of the workforce should be looked at in the UAE and Qatar in largely symbolic terms, as a reflection of the pressures that government officials juggle.

The above examples of actual legislation with respect to foreign and native workers in Qatar and the UAE relate to the second legal tool available to these Gulf countries, that of enforcement. In the area of judicial and other enforcement of law related to foreign workers, again a picture emerges of officials taking a mixture of stands that keeps the government somewhat insulated from charges of either supporting major rights violations or undermining the

---

2006, pp. 10–11; available at: http://www.un.org/esa/population/meetings/EGM_Ittmig_Arab/P03_Shah.pdf.

[39] See for example Jasim Al-Ali, Himanshu Kumar Shee and Patrick Foley, *Structural Barriers to Emiratisation: Analysis and Policy Recommendations* (2005), a report carried out by a member of the Dubai Municipal government and other specialists on the problems in this area in the UAE. The report is discussed on the Dubai Municipality's website at: http://login.dm.gov.ae/wps/portal/switch_en?TARGET=en&WCM_GLOBAL_CONTEXT=/wps/wcm/connect/dmegov/dm+internet+en/home-en/internet+news-en/news080409–02. The report is available at: http://www.wbiconpro.com/230-Al-Ali,J%20&%20Others.pdf.

identity and privileges of national citizens. Whatever their commitments both to guest workers' rights and citizens' status, officials in Persian Gulf countries are inconsistent about enforcing labor rules for a variety of reasons. These include the diversity of sources of law mentioned earlier in this chapter, the relatively weak nature of courts, the framing of non-native workers as a security issue, the securitization of global politics generally in the post-9/11 Western and Arab worlds, and the lack of transparency of the policy process.[40]

This said, the UAE, consistent with its recent broad shift in legislation around the *kafala* system generally, has recently improved its enforcement mechanisms to help foreign workers' severe problems. The improvements include the possibility of heightened scrutiny from the 2011 legislative reforms, as well as a new court panel to oversee charges of human trafficking.[41] Although a senior Emirati official pledged in 2006 to allow for labor unions in the construction sector, a major strike in 2007, along with citizens' general insecurities around foreign workers, help explain the lack of actual follow-through on this promise.[42]

As the unfulfilled pledge of trade unions in the UAE suggests, statements around enforcement mechanisms for non-citizen workers' rights have a strong symbolic content, especially given the difficulty of external data collection regarding their enforcement. The Sheikh Issa case, discussed above, gave a prominent example of the ability for officials to claim somewhat credibly that a fair enforcement process favoring foreign workers' rights even against natives

[40] I do not mean to imply here these factors only affect Arab policy-makers, or that the unpredictability of the legal enforcement process is qualitatively different in Persian Gulf states than elsewhere in the world. Rather, my point is simply that there are indeed many features of law and policy in these countries that allow for differential enforcement, without detailed treatment of specific cross-regional comparisons in legal policy enforcement.

[41] See *Khaleej Times* (November 10, 2010) at http://www.khaleejtimes.com/displayarticle.asp?xfile=data/theuae/2010/November/theuae_November286.xml&section=theuae&col=. See also *Gulf News* (November 10, 2010) at http://gulfnews.com/news/gulf/uae/crime/special-court-panel-to-try-human-trafficking-cases-1.709582.

[42] See for example the advocacy website mafiwasta (although it has not been updated since 2008) at http://www.mafiwasta.com/. The strike was covered in Western media, although covered less publicly within Dubai and the UAE themselves. See for example Barbara Surk, "Foreign Construction Workers go on strike in Dubai," *New York Times* (October 28, 2007) at http://www.nytimes.com/2007/10/28/business/worldbusiness/28iht-labor.4.8084022.html.

took place, since the process and even evidence in the case remain protected. Thus, announcing or setting up mechanisms to enforce foreign workers' rights appeals to officials, as long as they are not then deemed so ineffective or unfair to backfire politically. This latter calculus may help make sense of why Qatar, in contrast to the UAE, has been overall subject to less recent economic turbulence than its larger, more populous federal neighbor, has announced fewer specific enforcement mechanisms for workers' rights. Instead, Qatar has hosted major global symbolic conferences on the rule of law and human trafficking, trying to assert leadership in a more general manner.

As with the promulgation of legislation, legal enforcement with respect to non-citizens can also be used to appeal to elements of national culture. This, too, has been more evident in Dubai than in Doha. Prosecutions and harsh judicial punishment by Dubai courts of instances of public lewdness, sexual behavior or drinking, despite the city's cosmopolitanism, are clear cases of legal enforcement triggered by strong symbolic native concerns about the threats to traditional culture represented by contemporary hyper-globalized development.[43] Such legal enforcement confirms the delicacy of the tightrope with respect to foreign workers and citizens that Gulf Arab officials walk.

A similar pattern of mixed measures that benefit non-citizen workers but also citizens characterizes the third type of legal measure: laws or law enforcement that do not address issues of foreign versus citizen rights directly. In the UAE, officials have implemented regulations that require employers to pay their employees through government-monitored bank accounts, as well as minimum wage requirements. Such provisions do not ostensibly take a stand on possible trade-offs between foreign workers' and citizens' legal status. Yet, these measures are most likely to matter to low-status workers who could otherwise be subject to employers' withholding of wages. Emirati officials can undertake such indirect measures without excessive fears of triggering citizen

---

[43] See the highly publicized "sex on the beach case" (2008) that led to jail sentences, later suspended, for two unmarried British citizens in Dubai, at http://news.bbc. co.uk/2/hi/7673046.stm. Another example is the "finger will get you the boot" case, in which a Pakistani resident in Dubai was ordered to be deported by a Dubai court for raising his middle finger to another driver while on the road, see http:// www.washingtonpost.com/wp-dyn/content/article/2011/01/09/AR2011010 901263.html. On the other hand, the case of a married Pakistani couple caught and convicted for public indecency after having sex in their car was overturned on an appeal, perhaps because they were married and their car was closed, see http://news. bbc.co.uk/2/hi/middle_east/8660305.stm.

resentment, and with the ability to cite such policies as signs of concern for workers' rights within the overall paradigm of fulfilling private socio-economic contracts to temporary foreign guests.

A less obvious, yet interesting, example of legal enforcement that connects indirectly to the politics of regulating non-citizen workers is the gradual efforts to boost traffic safety in Doha. Because of the frequently observed high speeds and fast cars of citizen drivers in Qatar, as in the UAE, locals probably account for the largest proportion of traffic fatalities in the country. Thus, government publicity campaigns for traffic safety and heightened enforcement can be said to be primarily in the interest of citizens' well-being. Yet, traffic safety is a particular topic of agitation and pressure from non-native drivers, particularly those from Western countries with lower rates of high speed violations and more intrusive safety regulations. Thus, the combination of Qatari general support for reducing traffic accidents and the strong feelings of foreign residents on this subject can appear to satisfy simultaneously the interests of citizens and the needs of foreign worker residents, this being beneficial from both sides to the government.

Comparisons and conclusions

My core argument has been as follows. The strong tensions between the basic development narratives of the Persian Gulf likely to inform foreign legal reformers and native citizens, coupled with the diverse array of transnational and national actors with respect to the legal regulation of non-citizen workers, produces a situation in which officials in Qatar and the UAE prefer to address this issue through informal or, less often, formal policies that avoid manifesting a clear philosophical policy choice. In partial response to the strong scrutiny they receive in the crucible of rapid globalization from both global actors and citizens, government officials in Doha and Dubai go to great lengths to host events that highlight both their embrace of international legal standards and their sensitivity to local culture. This explains phenomena that can be puzzling to outside observers, such as government professions to acknowledge the importance of international human rights for workers, alongside prosecutions of Westerners for public morals violations.

At the same time, there is interesting variation in the Gulf, specifically between my two cases of Doha and Dubai. The latter in recent years has undertaken more clear legislation with respect to workers' rights, while the former can be said to have gone to greater lengths to show its symbolic loyalty to global law on the world stage, as well as to improve civil and political freedoms more generally. Dubai may be emerging as a new standard in foreign workers' potential to change jobs without a letter from their *kafeel*, yet it is also a much more likely site than Doha for public prosecution for a morals offense. In a nutshell, Doha's management of the balance between citizens and non-citizens appears relatively constant, while Dubai's evinces more recent measures that address concerns related both to foreign workers and Emiratis.

What accounts for this difference? One issue is likely to be economic. Dubai's economy suffered considerably during the 2008 global economic downtown, in large part because of its prior breakneck growth and its success at establishing itself as a center of global finance, both of which left it very exposed to international market losses, with many ambitious projects having to be scrapped or put on hold. Additionally, Dubai lacks natural resources of its own, which puts in context its developmental strategy of diversification through construction, tourism and financial services.[44] Doha, on the other hand, not only is the hub of a small country rich in oil reserves, but also benefits from natural gas revenues. Qatar's estimated GDP growth of 9 percent in 2009,[45] as compared with contractions in economies such as Dubai, facilitated a more steady, less openly reformist path towards non-citizen workers' rights than in Dubai, which had to worry more about retaining its best workers.

At the same time, Dubai's stalled growth plays into a larger context of Emirati federalism, which raises issues around national identity that differ from Qatar. Dubai's pain during the financial crisis, and well-known bailout by the oil-rich federal capital, Abu Dhabi,[46] heightened pre-existing tensions among Emiratis as to the role of the cosmopolitan dynamo in the country generally.[47] Unlike Doha, Dubai is one among several urban developmental models available to national citizens, which include more traditional Abu Dhabi and less expansive Sharjah. Native and other governmental workers whom I inter-

---

[44] For more on this, see Christopher M. Davidson, *Dubai: The Vulnerability of Success* (New York: Columbia University Press, 2009).

[45] Estimated by the International Monetary Fund (February 17, 2010), http://www.imf.org/external/np/sec/pn/2010/pn1022.htm.

[46] See for example http://news.bbc.co.uk/2/hi/8411215.stm.

[47] See the interesting recent paper by a prominent Emirati political scientist, Abdulkhaleq Abdulla, "Contemporary Socio-Political Issues of the Arab Gulf Moment," Kuwait Programme, London School of Economics (2010), especially pp. 27–30, at http://www.lse.ac.uk/collections/LSEKP/documents/PaperAbdulla.pdf.

viewed in both Qatar and the UAE agreed that perceived concerns about national identity are much greater in Dubai than in Doha.[48] Corresponding with the faster pace and scale of Dubai's growth, this has meant a variety of strategies of voice and exit (to use Albert Hirschman's well-known formulation) for Dubai natives, such as local TV programs like *Freej* that examine Dubai's cultural conflicts in a light manner, or Dubai citizens who move to less bustling members of the loose Emirati federation.

These starker identity issues for Dubai natives help explain the periodic symbolic legal enforcement measures for perceived affronts to traditional public moral norms, even though widespread vice is a well-known concomitant of Dubai's cosmopolitan success. As one expert on Dubai policy suggested to me,[49] the relatively small number of migrants from Western countries is more significant as a perceived threat to Emirati identity than the much larger Asian worker population, which is culturally less visible. This would suggest the symbolic utility for officials of clamping down legally on occasion on some of the most flagrant symbols of encroaching Western moral laxness. Certainly, the confusion and somewhat amorphous national identity anomie created by Dubai's hyper-globalization are more marked than Doha's, and probably have heightened the pressures on municipal and federal officials to respond to foreign workers' problems and natives' insecurities in the more public way that has occurred with recent legislation and prosecutions.

Thus, the recent, more evident changes concerning non-native workers' status in Dubai underscore the utility of engaging in comparative work across time and space to highlight the diversity of experiences in the contemporary Persian Gulf. Nonetheless, officials in Doha and Dubai have shown a generally similar approach in handling the legal regulation of their huge non-native worker resident majorities. This has seen a preference to avoid legislation or consistent legal enforcement that would actually undermine the basic contractual assumptions and nature of the regional *kafala* model or endorse a clear universal civil rights frame.

---

[48] One knowledgeable journalist in Dubai, off the record, noted that the UAE's ruler, Sheikh Khalifa, declared 2008 to be the country's "year of national identity," but then forbade the Emirates' quasi-elected quasi-legislative body, the Federal National Council, from discussing the issue, likely out of concern that it would exacerbate bad feelings among citizens regarding the demographic imbalance. For a general discussionseehttp://gulfnews.com/news/gulf/uae/general/the-debate-on-uae-national-identity-1.106921.

[49] Interview with Paul Dyer, Dubai School of Government, October 2009.

If Persian Gulf governments have sought to avoid major legal change with respect to non-citizen workers' rights, these more recent features of global economic downturn and media scrutiny have made such a posture harder to sustain.[50] Doha, Dubai, and other major cities of the Persian Gulf may represent intriguing models of record-breaking rapid development and global integration. But will they also stand for innovative ways to balance the labor needs of rapid growth, the concerns of a citizen population that is a tiny minority within its own country, and the demands of global and local rights advocates? With Dubai's considerable achievements as a new cosmopolitan Titan and Doha's ensured ongoing growth in the lead up to its hosting of the 2022 World Cup, the central importance for officials to master legal tools to manage citizen and non-citizen populations will not diminish anytime soon.

[50] For a study that affirms the general likelihood of Gulf governments to deal with the challenges of migrant workers in a non-explicit way, and also suggests the importance of forming policy alternatives, predominantly in economic terms, see Peter Cappelli, "Labor Markets in the Gulf States: Prospects for Reform" in the *World Economic Forum Arab Report* (2005), especially pp. 78–80.

10

Protecting Migrants' Rights in the Gulf Cooperation Council

Susan F. Martin *

Promoting the rights of migrants and improved working and living conditions is a development issue, as well as a fundamental human rights issue. As the United Nations (UN) Development Program explains, "Human development and human rights are mutually reinforcing, helping to secure the well-being and dignity of all people, building self-respect and the respect of others."[1] Limitations on basic human rights constrain choice, prompting migration of those who are unable to develop their full potential and lead productive lives at home. Denying migrants the ability to exercise their rights constrains their contribution to the development of their home countries and their countries of destination.

During the past four years, governments have gathered at the Global Forum on Migration and Development (GFMD) to discuss how best to reinforce the

* Grateful acknowledgment goes to the Center for International and Regional Studies, Georgetown University School of Foreign Service in Qatar, for providing research funding for this project.
[1] UN Development Program, *The Human Development Concept*, available at http://hdr.undp.org/en/humandev/.

217

benefits of migration for the development of source countries, destination countries and the migrants themselves. Prominent on the agenda has been examination of best practices in promoting the rights of migrants and increasing the payoffs they receive from the migration experience. The United Arab Emirates (UAE) has been particularly influential in setting the agenda and tone of the discussions, both through the UAE's assumption of the chair of several working groups within the Global Forum context, and through its leadership in establishing the related Abu Dhabi process for consultation between the Gulf Cooperation Council (GCC) countries and the principal source countries of migration to the Gulf.

These processes are new and as yet untested. This paper reviews progress made to date in addressing the situation of migrant workers in the Gulf countries and suggests some ways forward in using the GFMD and Abu Dhabi processes to enhance migrants' rights. The paper begins with a discussion of the international migrants' rights framework and discusses some recent initiatives at the national level to improve migrants' rights. It then describes the GFMD and Abu Dhabi processes. The paper concludes with recommendations for the future.

International legal framework

While international legal norms by themselves will not prevent abuses, they can serve as a basis for advocating implementation of policies and programs to achieve these goals. In emphasizing the importance of a strong normative framework, this article follows Martha Finnemore's understanding of the interplay between international norms and state behavior: "State interests are defined in the context of internationally held norms and understandings about what is good and appropriate. That normative context influences the behavior of decisionmakers and of mass publics who may choose and constrain those decisionmakers."[2]

While states possess broad authority to regulate the movement of foreign nationals across their borders, this authority is limited by the unalienable rights all non-nationals enjoy under international law, irrespective of state ratification of the more specific instrument. The Universal Declaration of Human Rights, the International Covenant on Civil and Political Rights and the International Covenant on Economic and Social Rights define the basic

[2] Martha Finnemore, *National Interests in International Society* (Ithaca, NY: Cornell University Press, 1996), p. 2.

rights of all persons. They include: the right to life, liberty and security; the right not to be held in slavery or servitude; the right not to be subjected to torture or to cruel, inhuman or degrading treatment or punishment; the right not to be subjected to arbitrary arrest, detention or exile; freedom of movement and residence within the borders of each state; the right to marry and to found a family; and the right to work, free choice of employment and just and favorable conditions of work.

A number of countries have ratified more migrant-specific conventions established by the International Labor Organization (ILO). Forty-two countries have ratified the Convention concerning Migration for Employment. Eighteen countries have ratified the Convention concerning Migrations in Abusive Conditions and the Promotion of Equality of Opportunity and Treatment of Migrant Workers (No. 143). Other relevant ILO conventions are the Convention concerning Forced or Compulsory Labor (No. 29), the Convention Concerning Abolition of Forced Labor (No. 105), the Equal Remuneration Convention (No. 100), and the Discrimination (Employment and Occupation) Convention (No. 100).

The Convention on the Rights of All Migrant Workers and Members of their Families, ratified by more than forty states, reaffirms basic human rights norms and embodies them in an instrument applicable to migrant workers and their families. The convention builds on the ILO's conventions. The underlying goal of the Convention is to guarantee minimum rights for migrant workers and members of their families who are in a legal or undocumented/irregular situation. Its implementation could significantly encourage basic humane treatment of all migrant workers. However, the number of states ratifying the Convention is still disappointingly small.[3] No major destination country of migrants has yet signed the Convention, which raises further questions about its effectiveness.[4]

The Convention defines the rights of migrant workers under two main headings: "The human rights of migrants workers and members of their fami-

---

[3] States party to the Convention are Albania, Algeria, Argentina, Azerbaijan, Belize, Bolivia, Bosnia and Herzegovina, Burkina Faso, Cape Verde, Chile, Colombia, Ecuador, Egypt, El Salvador, Ghana, Guatemala, Guinea, Guyana, Honduras, Jamaica, Kyrgyzstan, Lesotho, Libya, Mali, Mauritania, Mexico, Morocco, Nicaragua, Niger, Nigeria, Paraguay, Peru, Philippines, Rwanda, Senegal, Seychelles, Sri Lanka, St. Vincent and the Grenadines, Syria, Tajikistan, Timor Leste, Turkey, Uganda and Uruguay.

[4] Several regional destinations for migrants, such as Argentina, Chile and Libya, have ratified the Convention.

lies" (Part III), which reaffirms the human rights of all migrants regardless of their legal status, and "Other rights of migrant workers" (Part IV), which sets out additional rights applicable only to migrant workers in a regular, documented situation. Documented migrants are defined as those "authorized to enter, to stay and engage in a remunerated activity in the State of employment pursuant to the law of that State and to international agreements to which that State is a party" (Article 5).

A number of provisions focus on the right of migrants, regardless of documented status, to protection from violence and attacks. Article 10 prohibits torture or cruel, inhuman or degrading treatment or punishment. Article 11 prohibits slavery or servitude and forced or compulsory labor. Article 14 prohibits arbitrary or unlawful interference with privacy or attacks on honor and reputation. Article 16 entitles migrants "to effective protection by the State against violence, physical injury, threats, and intimidation, whether by public officials or by private individuals, groups or institutions."

A number of other articles focus on the social and economic status of migrants. Article 64 (2) states that "due regard shall be paid not only to labor needs and resources, but also to the social, economic, cultural and other needs of migrant workers and members of their families involved, as well as to the consequences of such migration for the communities concerned." Article 70 guarantees "working conditions ... in keeping with the standards of fitness, safety, health, and principles of human dignity" of those of the native population. Article 43 provides equal treatment of documented migrants with nationals with respect to access to education, vocational training, housing, and health services (Article 45 confers the same rights for members of families). Article 50 provides that in case of death or dissolution of marriage, the state shall favorably consider granting authorization to stay to the families of documented migrants.

Although the rights provided by the Convention apply to both men and women migrants and Article 45 specifically addresses the equality of the rights, the Convention fails to address expressly many needs that are particular to women. Many migrant women work in non-regulated sectors of the economy, including domestic work, which leaves them vulnerable to exploitation and abuse. Guaranteeing equal treatment with nationals will not help migrant workers in such situations because the regulatory structure is weak for both populations.[5]

---

[5] See S. Hune, "Migrant Women in the Context of the International Convention on the Protection of the Rights of All Migrant Workers and Members of Their Families,"

The Protocol to Prevent, Suppress and Punish Trafficking in Persons, Especially Women and Children, and the Protocol against the Smuggling of Migrants by Land, Sea and Air, both of which supplement the United Nations Convention against Transnational Organized Crime, have garnished considerable support, with more than 100 signatories and 67 and 59 parties respectively. The Trafficking Protocol requires states to adopt measures criminalizing trafficking, to prevent and combat trafficking, and to provide assistance and protection to trafficking victims, including the provision of repatriation assistance. The Smuggling Protocol requires states to adopt measures criminalizing smuggling, to prevent smuggling, to protect the rights of migrants who have been smuggled and to facilitate their return.

Promotion of migrants' rights at the national level

Over-reliance on international law has many flaws, especially when governments fail to ratify conventions or, even if they ratify them, fail to implement them. It is particularly problematic in the Gulf countries since they are not signatories to some of the basic instruments outlining the rights of migrants, although most of the GCC countries have ratified important ILO Conventions and the Trafficking Protocol.[6] By contrast, the principal source countries of migrants to the GCC have ratified a number of the migration-related instruments. Without acceptance of the standards by destination countries, however, the source country signatories can do little to ensure implementation of the standards in line with international accords.

Hence, national law and practice become far more important in setting out the rights of migrants. Policies and programs at the national level by both source and destination countries can be effective ways to protect the rights of migrants. Better informed migrants are better able to assert their rights. This

---

International Migration Review, 25, 4 (1991) and R. Cholewinski, *Migrant Workers in International Human Rights Law: Their Protection in Countries of Employment* (Oxford: Clarendon Press, 1997).

[6] For example, most have ratified ILO Conventions related to forced labor and child labor (C29 Forced Labor Convention, 1930; C81 Labor Inspection Convention, 1947; C105 Abolition of Forced Labor Convention, 1957; C111 Discrimination (Employment and Occupation) Convention, 1958; C138 Minimum Age Convention, 1973; and C182 Worst Forms of Child Labor Convention, 1999), but not those related specifically to migrant workers.

is particularly the case for contract laborers who may have little idea of the wages or working conditions to which they are entitled. Similarly, workers migrating to join family members need to know and understand their rights, both in relation to their spouses or children (particularly regarding domestic violence) and regarding their immigration status.

Monitoring recruitment agencies and employers is essential to the protection of migrant workers. Both source and destination countries can play a role in providing migrants with an outlet to report abuse and in training government officials, employers and others as to the rights of migrant workers and their obligations under international and national law. Embassies of the Philippines and Indonesia maintain hotlines, which can also receive SMS messages. Singapore requires first-time employers of foreign domestic workers to go through a three-hour orientation program covering their responsibilities as employers, as well as educating them on how to create a positive working relationship with their employees.

When abuses occur, legal representation of migrant workers can help them fight against discrimination, sexual harassment, lost wages and other violations of their labor rights. Consulates can intervene on the behalf of migrants, covering the costs of such representation. The Philippines embassies, for example, will pay legal costs if a case alleging abuse goes to court. Destination countries also pay costs of representation. In Bahrain, if a contract dispute involving a domestic worker cannot be resolved and goes to court, the court will appoint a lawyer for the migrant worker.

Programs that provide shelter and social services to migrant workers who have experienced abuse are essential to protecting their rights. Embassies can facilitate workers' access to services and documentation by opening on weekends and/or by traveling to areas where migrants live and work. In locations with high concentrations of Filipino workers, the Philippines embassy opens on weekends to allow workers to attend community activities and skills training programs and to access consular services. Migrant workers who decide to return home after escaping abusive conditions may also need assistance in repatriation and reintegration.

Trade unions can be an important source of advocacy and support to migrant workers in the destination country. Coverage of migrant workers under collective bargaining ensures their equal treatment in terms of wage and employment standards. Migrant workers in Bahrain are free to join, vote and run for office in local trade unions.[7] Furthermore, Bahraini unions have taken a strong stance

[7] Interview with Daniel Cork, Solidarity Center , June 18, 2008.

in relation to protecting migrant workers' rights, viewing this as a necessary part of efforts to improve the working situations of national workers.[8]

Many of these initiatives are ones in which source countries are more proactive in providing the framework for advancing the rights of migrants (their citizens) than are the destination countries. Many of the programs are pre-migration ones, generally based on the concept that information is a powerful weapon against abuse. Programs that take place in the country of destination are often aimed at removing vulnerable migrants from abusive situations. There is a limit to how much the source countries can do, however, in the absence of active collaboration by the host government. After all, many abuses take place on the territory of the destination country. Other abuses are transnational in nature. Effectively regulating recruitment agencies, for example, requires cooperation in order to ensure that abusers are unable to circumvent the law by claiming to be operating in the other country. In the absence of cooperation between source and destination countries, little progress will be made in instituting reforms that cover all phases of the migration process— from pre-migration recruitment though employment to either return or resettlement.

The global forum on migration and development

The international community is slowly coming to the realization that effective management of international migration and its impacts defies unilateral action. By definition, movements of people across borders involve at least two states, and often three or more as migrants transit countries in order to move from source to destination countries. Bilateral and regional consultation mechanisms have proliferated to help states address the need for cooperation in managing flows of people. But negotiating bilateral and regional agreements to manage movements of people is an inefficient, time-consuming way to address what are increasingly global problems and global opportunities.

To date, most governments appear willing to talk with each other about international migration, and even to consult in identifying effective policies and practices, but they have not shown the desire or even capacity to coordinate migration policies or to establish an institutional locus of responsibility for helping states manage movements of people. The only recent effort to bring the United Nations explicitly into the process of inter-state cooperation

[8] Ibid.

in this matter—the UN High Level Dialogue (HLD) on Migration and Development, held in September 2006—resulted in a broad consensus that the dialogue should continue, though there was also a similarly broad view that moving beyond talk to mutual action was premature. The Special Representative proposed the establishment of a Global Consultation mechanism that would permit states to meet regularly to discuss migration issues. Most states agreed, but a majority preferred the consultations to occur outside of the United Nations.

The result was establishment of the Global Forum on GFMD, which has proceeded as a state-owned process, relying primarily on governments to plan and execute the forum. Forums have been held in Belgium (2007), the Philippines (2008) and Greece (2009). The most recent forum was in Mexico in November 2010. Switzerland will host the GFMD in 2011. The past, present and future countries that host the GFMD form a troika in preparing for the annual meeting. The host country assumes responsibility for the preparatory process and the implementation of each Forum, chairing all preparatory meetings and the Forum itself. The host is assisted by co-Chairs from the country that organized the previous Forum and, once a decision is made about the next Forum, from the country that has agreed to host it in the following year.

A Steering Group is composed of governments that are actively engaged in the preparations. It is balanced between developed and developing countries and includes representatives from all regions. It meets at regular intervals to provide advice on the upcoming meetings and activities of the Forum.[9] The Steering Group provides substantive input into the agenda of the Forum, the various roundtables, and the materials disseminated to participants. The Special Representative of the UN Secretary General on International Migration and Development is invited to participate in Steering Committee meetings but is not a member of the group.

The Friends of the Forum is open to all state members and observers of the United Nations. Specialized agencies of the UN and other international organizations participate as observers. The Friends of the Forum provide an opportunity to keep potential participants in the Forum up to date on preparations and to receive input on the substance of the deliberations.

An increasingly important part of the GFMD is the role of civil society. The GFMD is now defined to include two components: the Civil Society

[9] For further information on the Steering Group see http://www.gfmd.org/en/supporting-framework/steering-group.html.

Days (CSDs) that precede the government meetings and the government meetings themselves, with an interface between the two sessions in which the civil society delegates can communicate the recommendations of their meeting. The interface has been growing in time and seriousness: from a brief report on the CSDs in Brussels, to half-day meetings in Manila and Athens, to a full day of exchange in Puerto Vallarta in Mexico.

Much of the work of the Forum is organized around roundtables, organized by government teams headed by co-Chairs, generally one each from a destination and source country. The host of the GFMD sets out an agenda that is discussed and then adopted by the Steering Committee. While each host has attempted to put its own imprint on the proceedings, certain core issues have received attention at each forum: identifying and reinforcing the contributions of migrants to development; strengthening the capacity of migrant and diaspora organizations; protecting the rights of migrants; addressing specific issues faced by migrant women; defining options for labor migration, with a particular focus on circular movements; and improving data, research and policy coherence.[10]

At each of the previous forums, countries in the GCC have played an important role in the discussions. Qatar and the United Arab Emirates (UAE) are members of the Steering Group. After the Manila GFMD, the UAE funded "A Market-based Approach to Reduce the Cost of Migration: A Bangladeshi Feasibility Study" to determine the best ways to lower the recruitment, travel and other transaction costs faced by very poor Bangladeshis seeking to migrate to the GCC countries. The study determined that "many Bangladeshi migrants pay interest of 10 percent a month on loans incurred to migrate, so that a $2,000 debt can more than double in a year."[11] The study determined that efforts to reduce the costs through regulation had failed, largely because of the entrenched interests of those (particularly recruiters) who benefit from the fees. Although the Bangladeshi government has set maximum charges for each migrant, "key informants report that the actual cost of migrating from Bangladesh was at least twice the official maximum charge of 84,000 taka ($1,220) in 2009, including $500 to $700 for the 5–6 hour flight

---

[10] This conclusion is based on the author's participation and observation during the GFMDs held in Brussels, Manila, Athens and Puerto Vallarta.

[11] Philip Martin, "Reducing the Cost Burden for Migrant Workers: A Market-based Approach," Geneva: Global Forum on Migration and Development (2009), p. 2 Available at http://www.gfmdathens2009.org/fileadmin/material/docs/roundtables/martin_bangla_report.pdf.

to most Gulf states ...."[12] In the same manner, such destination countries as the UAE mandate that employers pay recruitment fees and not pass these on to the workers.

Even when recruiters and employers comply with regulations regarding recruitment fees, there can be additional costs to migrants including: health checks, pre-departure orientation and training, visa application fees, and travel costs not covered by the employer. The report proposed an alternative to the failed regulatory approach: providing an opportunity for Bangladeshi migrants to obtain low-cost loans to repay the costs of migration. The idea was to build on Bangladesh's success in microfinance by tapping the resources and expertise of such institutions as the Grameen Bank and BRAC in designing low interest loans for would-be migrants. With such low-interest loans, migrants could recoup the cost of migration more quickly and, if they wished, return home at an earlier date with sufficient resources to support their families.

In Athens, the UAE joined with Argentina as co-Chair of the Roundtable on "migrant integration, reintegration and circulation for development." Other countries and international organizations that helped prepare the discussions included Australia, Brazil, Ecuador, Egypt, Greece, Israel, Mexico, the Philippines, Portugal, Spain, the ILO, the UNOHCHR, and the World Bank. The Roundtable proceeded from the assumption that the more migrants are included, protected and accepted in their host societies, the better they are able to secure the well-being of their families and contribute to development in the host and origin countries. There is some evidence that these efforts at migrant "integration" are critical for the integrity of regular migration programs, the public perception of migrants, and the added value of migration for development.[13]

The Roundtable concluded that more research and pilot programs are needed in order to identify best practices, recommending that governments:

• Compile best integration practices and publish these on the GFMD website;
• Undertake further research on how to evaluate impacts of integration policies on development (including cost-benefit analyses);

[12] Ibid., p. 34. Martin also reports that domestic workers' charges are supposed to be no higher than US$145 and employers are to pay transport costs to the Gulf.
[13] Background paper prepared for the Roundtable by B. Lindsay Lowell, Director of Policy Studies, Institute for the Study of International Migration (ISIM), in consultation with the co-Chairs.

- Conduct a comparative study on social protection policies for migrants; and,
- Give consideration to strengthening the networks between Migrant Resource Centers in origin and host countries, and evaluate their effectiveness from the migrants' perspective.

The most concrete recommendation was to commence a "pilot project on a bank/non-governmental program for low cost pre-departure loans to migrants as a follow-up to the Bangladesh study for Roundtable session 2.1, and to offer lessons for other governments"—an idea drawn from the UAE-funded study.

In formal comments in Manila, Ghobash Saqr, the UAE Minister of Labor, spoke of the importance of protecting the rights and improving the quality of life of contractual workers employed in the Gulf States. In the plenary session in Athens, he reiterated these views and also "underlined the need to weigh the costs and benefits of migration from the standpoint of all stakeholders." On behalf of his government, the Minister of Labor cited the value of the GFMD as a platform for "sharing views, ideas and policy experimentation in a climate of trust and respect."[14]

In less formal comments about the interest of the UAE in the integration of migrants, another representative noted that there must be a middle ground between permanent migration eventually leading to citizenship – as practised by such countries as Canada, Australia and the United States – and temporary worker programs that afford few rights to migrants while they are in the host country.[15] In keeping with this perspective, the governments at the Roundtable came to a "general consensus about the *inalienability of fundamental human rights* of migrants, both in society and in the workplace, where many temporary migrants suffer from discrimination and xenophobia. Regarding other social services and entitlements, there was a need to examine more closely how to tailor policies for the different contexts or types of migration, short-term temporary, longer-term, permanent etc."[16]

The UAE once again co-Chaired a Roundtable at the GFMD in Mexico in November 2010, along with Sweden and Sri Lanka. The theme was specifically "reducing the costs of migration and maximizing human development." The Roundtable addressed three key issues:

---

[14] Notes taken during the speech; quotes taken from the Proceedings of the GFMDs.
[15] Personal conversation, the Athens GFMD.
[16] The Athens GFMD report, p. 25.

- Reducing up-front expenses and other costs, which affect opportunities to migrate "regularly" and safely;
- How to best regulate private intermediaries; and,
- Access to and provision of social services to migrants in the country of destination and the provision of social services to migrants abroad by origin countries.[17]

The Roundtable participants agreed that "High up-front costs of migration can jeopardize the rest of the migration life cycle if they are not addressed by countries of origin and destination in cooperation with the private sector and other stakeholders." They also determined that lowering the costs of migration is a "joint responsibility of origin and destination countries; national efforts alone are rarely sufficient."[18] Among the new practices discussed at the Roundtable was the establishment of an Expatriate Welfare Bank in Bangladesh to provide collateral-free loans to migrants and loans to returnees. The bank was the direct outcome of the UAE-funded study. The UAE also announced that it would be funding further pilot programs for reducing the costs of migration for temporary contract workers; this was during the Abu Dhabi Dialogue, as discussed below.

As follow-up, the UAE sponsored a workshop in January 2011 to promote further discussion and to examine issues around recruitment and to engage recruitment agencies in better preparing and protecting overseas contract workers. Based on the outcomes of the Dubai meeting, the UAE committed to work with Bangladesh, India and the Philippines on a generic architecture of protection and empowerment, which would include: developing a contract validation system to combat contract substitution; testing a low cost loans scheme for temporary contract workers abroad; and developing a draft framework of regional cooperation on recruitment practices to be submitted for consideration by the Abu Dhabi Dialogue process.[19]

---

[17] Report of the Rapporteur to Roundtable 2 at the Puerto Vallarta Global Forum on Migration and Development, available at http://gfmd.org/en/gfmd-documents-library/mexico-gfmd-2010/cat_view/989-mexico-gfmd-2010/1021-report-of-the-proceedings.html.

[18] Ibid.

[19] These outcomes are outlined at http://gfmd.org/en/adhoc-wg/protecting-and-empowering.html.

Abu Dhabi Dialogue

The GCC and the source countries of migration have picked up on a number of these issues in the context of the Ministerial Consultations on Overseas Employment and Contractual Labour for Countries of Origin and Destination in Asia, also known as the Abu Dhabi Dialogue. Begun in 2008, the Abu Dhabi Dialogue has brought together eleven source countries (Afghanistan, Bangladesh, China, India, Indonesia, Nepal, Pakistan, Philippines, Sri Lanka, Thailand and Vietnam) and nine countries of destination (Bahrain, Kuwait, Malaysia, Oman, Qatar, Saudi Arabia, Singapore, the UAE and Yemen). Joint Secretariat services are provided by the Ministry of Labor of the UAE and the International Organization for Migration (IOM), which provides technical support to a number of consultative processes. Several governments outside of the region participate as observers, including the United States, France, Germany, Japan, Mauritius, the Republic of Korea, Poland and the European Commission.

The principal goal of the Abu Dhabi Dialogue is to promote properly managed temporary contractual labor mobility. A ministerial level meeting, held in January 2008, set out four areas in which partnerships between source and destination countries could improve policy and practice. Framed as partnerships, these areas include:

Partnership 1: Enhancing knowledge in the areas of: labor market trends, skills profiles, temporary contractual workers and remittances policies and flows and their interplay with development in the region.

Partnership 2: Building capacity for effective matching of labor demand and supply.

Partnership 3: Preventing illegal recruitment practices and promoting welfare and protection measures for contractual workers, supportive of their well-being and preventing their exploitation at origin and destination.

Partnership 4: Developing a framework for a comprehensive approach to managing the entire cycle of temporary contractual mobility that fosters the mutual interests of countries of origin and destination.

The governments agreed to meet again at the ministerial level in 2010 while working on these partnerships in the interim.[20]

---

[20] The meeting did not take place in 2010 but is scheduled for 2011.

An assessment of the Abu Dhabi Dialogue pointed out that it is one of the few initiatives in which governments with different perspectives on migration are meeting to discuss possible areas of collaboration. The assessment pointed out that "In the GCC states, the Abu Dhabi Dialogue helped formulate a particular understanding of temporary and circular migration as the predominant form of movement to the region: participants came to conceive of it as a migration cycle with distinct phases—preparation, arrival, incorporation into the labor market, and return and reintegration."[21] The results can be seen in new initiatives to address the rights of migrants. The Abu Dhabi Dialogue has placed the human rights of migrant workers on the policy agenda of the GCC states. The long-term impact of this gesture is as yet unclear, but one concrete outcome is a pilot project that will map, monitor and identify roles and responsibilities during the full cycle of temporary labor mobility. Designed to create an efficient and humane system for circular migration, the pilot project targets 3,000 migrant workers in the hospitality and health care sectors (in the Philippines and India) and the construction sector (in India).

The UAE is funding the project, which will focus on recruitment practices (for instance, ensuring that potential migrants have full information on work conditions), the prevention of abusive practices (for instance, illegal fees), fair and consistent contracts, standards of accommodation, migrant health and job safety, and possibilities for contributory pension schemes.[22]

Conclusions

It is too soon to know whether the GFMD or the Abu Dhabi Dialogue will lead to concrete changes that significantly improve the rights, working conditions and living situation of migrant workers in the GCC. To date, the UAE has taken the principal leadership in the international and regional forums in which migrants' rights issues are discussed. While other GCC countries participate in both the GFMD and the Abu Dhabi Dialogue, they have not yet demonstrated that they see these processes as significant ones. Some are taking unilateral steps to improve migrants' rights while others appear to be less motivated to make serious changes in their policies or practices. The extent to

[21] Randall Hansen, *An Assessment of the Principal Regional Consultative Processes on Migration* (Geneva: International Organization for Migration, Migration Research Series, 38, 2010), p. 26.
[22] Ibid., p. 27.

which officials with on-the-ground knowledge of the issues debated are fully engaged in preparations for the discussions is also questionable. My own discussions with source country embassy staff in Doha revealed that they knew little about the Abu Dhabi Dialogue.

How sustainable the Abu Dhabi Dialogue will be is an open question. If its website is any indication, there appears to have been little follow-up since the January 2008 Declaration, except in terms of the UAE's activities outlined in reference to the GFMD. The planned 2010 meeting did not take place, though officials note that it will occur in 2011. By contrast, the Colombo Process brought together the eleven source countries of migration to the GCC in a senior officials' meeting in October 2010. While the GCC countries often attend the Colombo Process as observers, such participation will not substitute for the type of consultation that takes place when both source and destination countries meet as full partners.

The agenda set out in the Abu Dhabi Dialogue remains a useful one for consideration. In particular, there continues to be a need for the discussion of ways to prevent illegal recruitment practices and promote welfare and protection measures for contractual workers, supportive of their well-being and preventing their exploitation at origin and destination—the theme of the third partnership outlined in the declaration. The GFMD conclusions in Mexico, and the UAE's commitment to fund pilot programs and a workshop on recruitment practices, should be helpful in generating potential models for accomplishing this aim, but it is more likely that tangible progress in developing strategies that address the full lifecycle of migration—from pre-migration to return or settlement—will be reached more readily in direct consultations between source and destination countries of migrants coming to the GCC.

Index

of, 106, 119, 123; Congress Party, 151; *dalal* system in, 111, 126, 136; Delhi, 113, 143; domestic workers from, 38; Goa, 143, 145–8, 151; Government of, 139, 147, 151, 153; health care sector, 230; Hindu population of, 106; Indian Emigration Act (1983), 107, 141; Indian Passport Act (1967), 107; Karnataka, 138, 142; Kerala, 17, 50, 76, 81, 105–6, 113–16, 122–3, 125, 129–30, 132, 136, 138, 146, 148, 150, 153; migrant communities in, 45; migrants from, 17, 50, 105, 128, 138–9, 143, 148, 153; Ministry of External Affairs, 140; Ministry of Foreign Affairs, 27; Ministry of Overseas Indian Affairs (MOIA), 139–41, 143, 145, 147, 151, 153; Mumbai, 24, 143, 145–6; Muslim population of, 106, 123; participant in Abu Dhabi Dialogue, 229; Pune, 143, 145–6; Rajasthan, 146; recruitment agencies in, 141; Tamil Nadu, 139, 146; Uttar Pradesh, 148

Indian Council of Overseas Employment: findings of, 139

Indonesia: 33, 90, 222; human trafficking in, 96; Jakarta, 86; migrants from, 85; Ministry of Labor, 86; participant in Abu Dhabi Dialogue, 229

Informal economy: 15–16, 86–7, 95, 98, 101–2; abusive nature of, 90, 92, 100, 103; appeal of, 100–1; criminal activity in, 101; sex workers in, 85, 88–9, 97

International Labor Organization (ILO): 221, 226; Convention concerning Abolition of Forced Labor (No. 105), 219; Convention concerning Forced or Compulsory Labor (No. 29), 219; Convention concerning Migration for Employment, 219; Convention concerning Migrations in Abusive Conditions and the Promotion of Equality of Opportunity and Treatment of Migrant Workers (No. 143), 219;

Discrimination (Employment and Occupation) Convention (No. 100), 219; Equal Remuneration Convention (No. 100), 219

International Organization for Migration (IOM): role in Abu Dhabi Dialogue, 229

Iran: 1, 31, 34, 86; migrants from, 24, 90

Iraq: 1, 31; migrant population of, 180

Islam: 106, 117, 129, 173, 190, 195–6; conversion to, 33; *dhuhr*, 72; *jumma*, 124; *nikkah*, 125; Ramadan, 200; *shari'a*, 190; shehadeh, 33; social justice, 195

Islamism: 134; political presence of, 190

Israel: 226; migrant population of, 180

Japan: cultured pearl industry of, 64; migrant population of, 180

Jordan: 71

Kafala: 24, 26–7, 29, 31–2, 70, 90–1, 132–3, 206, 214; abuse of individuals in, 11; concept of, 11, 22; domestic workers and, 39; impact of, 68, 202; *kafeel*, 24, 26–7, 32, 97–8, 201, 208, 213; opposition to, 205; structure of, 97, 201; system of, 39, 42, 88, 101, 110, 203, 207, 210; use in GCC member states, 42, 110

Khaliji: 32; concept of, 25

Kristoff, Nicholas: writings of, 91

Kuwait: 14, 23–4, 27, 36, 147, 205, 207; coast of, 116, 121; *dawa* movement, 33; Iraqi Invasion of (1990), 8; Kuwait City, 31, 115; member of GCC, 155, 184; migrant population of, 158, 170; national constitution of, 25; non-citizen population of, 21; participant in Abu Dhabi Dialogue, 229

Lebanon: 71; cuisine of, 125; migrants from, 33